Green Generation

Protecting the Planet

ENVIRONMENTAL ACTIVISM

by Pamela Dell

Content Adviser: Roberta M. Johnson, Ph.D.,
Director, Education and Outreach,
University Corporation for Atmospheric Research, Boulder, Colorado

Science Adviser: Terrence E. Young Jr., M.Ed., M.L.S.,
Jefferson Parish (Louisiana) Public School System

Reading Adviser: Alexa L. Sandmann, Ed.D., Professor of Literacy,
College and Graduate School of Education, Health, and Human Services,
Kent State University

Compass Point Books
151 Good Counsel Drive
P.O. Box 669
Mankato, MN 56002-0669

Copyright © 2010 by Compass Point Books
All rights reserved. No part of this book may be reproduced
without written permission from the publisher. The publisher
takes no responsibility for the use of any of the materials or
methods described in this book, nor for the products thereof.
Printed in the United States of America.

This book was manufactured with paper containing
at least 10 percent post-consumer waste.

Photographs © Alamy: Mike Hill 8; AP Images: EyePress/File 15; Art Life Images: age fotostock/Sergio
Ferraris 16; Capstone Press: Karon Dubke 19 (all), 52; Corbis: Neil Rabinowitz 44, Peter Turnley 22,
Royalty-free/Tim Pannell 60; DigitalVision: 7, 47; Getty Images: Hulton Archive 13, Martin H. Simon-Pool
42, National Geographic/Michael Melford 39, Riser/David Woodfall 21, Visuals Unlimited/Wally Eberhart
33(b); iStockphoto: BirdImages 54, GlobalP 51, Jusant 11, MCCAIG 17, mikered 29, Thornberry 33(t);
Minden Pictures: Gerry Ellis 38; NASA: JPL 5; Shutterstock: Anna Kaminska 6(b), Arvydas Kniuksta
31, Avalon Imaging 32, Brian A. Jackson 58, Chris Burt 57, Chris Kruger 46, Evok20 28, forest badger 24,
Frontpage 53, gary yim 36–37, imageshunter 26, Joe Mercier 50, Mark William Richardson 10, maxstock-
photo 4, 14, 20, 30, 35, 45, 56, Sascha Burkard 6(t).

Editor: Jennifer VanVoorst
Designer: Heidi Thompson
Media Researcher: Wanda Winch
Art Director: LuAnn Ascheman-Adams
Creative Director: Joe Ewest
Editorial Director: Nick Healy
Managing Editor: Catherine Neitge

Library of Congress Cataloging-in-Publication Data
Dell, Pamela.
  Protecting the planet: environmental activism / by Pamela Dell.
    p. cm. — (Green generation)
  Includes index.
  ISBN 978-0-7565-4248-1 (library binding)
  ISBN 978-0-7565-4295-5 (paperback)
  1. Environmentalism—Juvenile literature.
  I. Title. II. Series.
  GE195.5.D45 2010
  333.72—dc22   2009008782

Visit Compass Point Books on the Internet at *www.compasspointbooks.com*
or e-mail your request to *custserv@compasspointbooks.com*

Contents

"You see that pale blue dot? That's us. Everything that has ever happened in all of human history has happened on that pixel. All the triumphs and all the tragedies, all the wars, all the famines, all the major advances. ... It's our only home. And that is what is at stake, our ability to live on planet Earth, to have a future as a civilization. I believe ... it is our time to rise again to secure our future."

—Al Gore, environmental activist, Nobel Prize winner, and former vice president of the United States

Our Beautiful Blue Planet

introduction

One of the most famous photographs in the world was shot in December 1972. This photo, taken at a distance of 28,000 miles (45,000 kilometers) out in space by the *Apollo 17* astronauts, was one of the first color images of planet Earth.

The dramatic photograph gave people who viewed it a sense of awe. From this cosmic perspective, Earth looks like a beautiful blue marble.

The National Aeronautics and Space Administration began capturing even more images of our planet. In 2002 NASA produced what it called a "photolike mosaic" using four months of data. The resulting image, named *Blue Marble*, was the most accurately colored and detailed image of Earth's surface that had ever been available. Looking at it gives the viewer a deeper appreciation of this living sphere we call home.

The blue of the ocean, the windswept swirls of white clouds, the vast stretches of red or tan desert, and the green forestlands tell the story of a planet that is extraordinarily alive.

The first "blue marble" photograph, taken by *Apollo 17* astronauts in 1972, prompted public interest in conservation.

This precious "blue marble" is a miracle of life in a solar system of otherwise lifeless orbs. Do we appreciate this life-nurturing place? How often do we take the astronaut's eye view and really think about what an amazing thing our planet is?

Earth provides everything we need, not just to live but also to thrive. We breathe its air and drink its water. We eat food that grows in its soil and use its natural resources to make homes to shelter us and clothes to keep us warm. What happens to Earth affects us in every way. But human beings are not alone on this planet, and all living things are directly affected by changes that occur throughout our world. For the sake of all of Earth's living things, it makes sense to value and protect these resources that keep us alive.

Today there is a global call to pay more attention to this vibrant life, because it is being threatened on all sides. The crises are many: Global warming, freshwater loss, and the destruction of plants and animals that make up the world's diverse ecosystems are just a few of the problems the planet faces.

Climate fever: Global warming is the most significant threat to Earth as we know it. Our planet is warming up, and this threatens the health of the planet and all things that live on it. Scientists believe that the way we use our planet's resources has given Earth a fever. We burn fossil fuels, such as coal, oil, and natural gas, to create electricity, power vehicles, and heat and cool our homes. Burning these fuels emits vast amounts of carbon dioxide into the atmosphere. Carbon dioxide is a greenhouse gas. It and other gases create a blanket that traps the sun's heat close to Earth, much like the glass walls of a greenhouse. When

Global warming is causing polar ice to melt, affecting ocean levels worldwide.

large amounts of these gases are released, the atmosphere warms up too much. The heat threatens life-forms that have adapted to earlier climate conditions. Earth's temperature has been rising for some time, and we are beginning to see the dire effects.

As the planet heats up, ice caps melt, causing sea levels to rise and leading to flooding in coastal areas.

Scientists predict that global warming will cause major shifts in weather patterns, creating stronger hurricanes, heavier snowfalls, and more severe droughts. Global warming also threatens the habitats of millions of living things besides humans. Many plants and animals will not be able to adapt to changes, and many species—and some entire ecosystems—could be lost.

Hurricanes and other extreme weather are increasing in intensity because of rising global temperatures.

This could mean irreversible changes in the way we exist on Earth.

Some shocking statistics:

Compared with other living things, human beings have always exploited Earth's resources on a grand scale. But until the last century or so, our use of these resources had little effect. The damage to Earth was happening gradually. In recent decades, however, the situation has taken a dramatic turn for the worse. How much worse? Consider this: In only the last 35 years, people have used up an astounding one-third of Earth's natural resources. If we keep up this tremendous rate of consumption, will there be anything left in another 70 years?

The United States consumes — and wastes — far more than any other nation. The United States has just 5 percent of the world's population, yet its citizens create 30 percent of the world's waste and use 30 percent of the world's resources. Today only 4 percent of this country's original forests still exist. Forty percent of U.S. waterways are too polluted to drink from. American industries release 4 billion pounds (1.8 billion kilograms) of poisonous chemicals into the air every year. At least that's how much businesses admit to. The actual amount may be even greater.

Becoming globally green:

These are only a few of the facts, but they add up to an urgent situation. Fortunately global awareness of these problems has been rising. The United Nations has developed eight goals that it has challenged the world to accomplish by 2015. Called the Millennium

Development Goals, they range from ending world hunger to creating a partnership of nations that will cooperate on every level. One of the goals is called Environmental Sustainability. It focuses on reducing greenhouse gas emissions, preserving freshwater, preventing deforestation, and protecting wildlife. With high-profile celebrities such as U2 rock star Bono promoting the U.N.'s program, the goals get a lot of attention.

National governments are enacting and enforcing important laws to protect resources as well. In fact, in 2009, the U.S. Environmental Protection Agency declared carbon dioxide and five other greenhouse gases to be pollutants. This allowed federal regulation of the heat-trapping gases

The burning of fossil fuels by power plants is one of the primary causes of global warming.

for the first time in history. Three important U.S. laws to protect the environment are already on the books: the Clean Air Act, the Clean Water Act, and the Endangered Species Act.

On a nongovernmental level, much is going on, too. Governments make the laws, of course, but individual people get the ball rolling. Countless environmental groups and individual citizens are working worldwide. They are tackling the pressing environmental problems of our time, trying to meet the challenges caused by human consumption. These people and organizations are trying, in a wide variety of ways, to reverse the damage already done. Their efforts range from improving the quality of air and water to saving endangered plants and animals. They include developing safe, environmentally friendly sources of energy and promoting green living in all ways. It has never been more important to take care of the planet, and people everywhere are pitching in to "green up" their lives and life on Earth in general.

Future generations will inherit a world that is still strikingly alive and rich with resources—or they will not. You can become an environmental activist and get involved in making our planet a better place. It's all up to us and the actions we take, starting right now.

Earth Day

On April 22, 1970, an event took place that, two decades later, *American Heritage* magazine called "one of the most remarkable happenings in the history of democracy." That event was the first-ever Earth Day. Since then, April 22 every year has been Earth Day.

Earth Day was the idea of U.S. Senator Gaylord Nelson of Wisconsin. He was upset about the negative effects of human activity on the air, land, and water. Although his concerns were shared by millions of people, Nelson noticed that two groups almost completely ignored the problems. These were America's political leaders and news media. Frustrated by this lack of attention, Nelson began trying to get some political and media focus on environmental problems. At a conference in the fall of 1969, Nelson announced that a nationwide public demonstration would protest the lack of governmental concern about the environment. Anyone who wanted to join the protest was welcome.

"The response was electric," Nelson later said. "It took off like gangbusters." This first "national day of observance of environmental problems," as *The New York Times* called it, was a big success. In cities and towns from coast to coast, about 20 million demonstrators showed up. People everywhere organized festivities of all kinds, including activities to clean up, beautify,

GO DEEP

Kids in New York City celebrated the first Earth Day by cleaning up their neighborhoods.

or otherwise honor the planet.

Nelson said that once he had announced the event, "it organized itself." That was because thousands of passionate volunteers, most of them of college age, made sure it did. The attention Earth Day brought to important issues led directly to vital environmental protection laws, such as the Clean Air Act and Clean Water Act.

By 1990 Earth Day had spread to 141 countries and had as many as 200 million participants worldwide. By 2000 Earth Day activists around the world were linked by the Internet. In 2009 Earth Day was celebrated by more than 1 billion people.

> " Oh beautiful for smoggy skies, insecticided grain. For strip-mined mountain's majesty above the asphalt plain. America, America, man sheds his waste on thee. And hides the pines with billboard signs, from sea to oily sea."
> —George Carlin (1937–2008), comedian

The Air We Breathe

chapter 1

In 1684 a well-known English diarist named John Evelyn wrote that London's smog problem was so great that "hardly could one see across the street." Evelyn was not the only one disturbed by the situation. The complainers, though, were few and far between. Now, more than 300 years later, those voices have risen to a global chorus that won't be ignored. Much more aware of the dangers of pollution, people everywhere are cleaning up their act. Still, in most places, the air, water, and soil could use a lot of improvement.

Have you ever had one of those days when you looked outside and couldn't see the usual distant panorama — say the mountains or the city skyline? You knew they were there, but a brownish layer of smog was hiding them entirely. If you've never experienced a "bad air day," you're lucky. The lack of a good scenic view is a downside of air pollution, but there are much more serious consequences. Since each of us takes in an average of about 3,000 gallons (11,370 liters) of air every day, it's important for the air to be clean. Breathing dirty air every day can cause many physical and mental problems. Some of the most serious are asthma, brain damage, birth defects, and cancer. But air pollution doesn't just hurt humans and other animals. It can

China is particularly affected by pollution, and its citizens sometimes wear masks for protection.

damage crops, trees, and even bodies of water, such as lakes. Acid rain is one effect of air pollution that can have a disastrous impact on the environment. Burning coal gives off chemical particles that turn to acids when they mix with moisture in the air. Eventually the chemicals fall back to Earth as acid rain or snow. Acid rain can make the water of a lake so acidic that it kills organisms in the lake. On land acid rain can damage or kill trees and other plants.

Another problem with air pollutants is that some of them rise high into Earth's upper atmosphere. Their presence there thins the protective ozone layer. Without the ozone layer, the sun's rays stream down to Earth much more power-fully. With the blanket of greenhouse gases holding

Acid rain and snow destroys forests, makes water too acidic for life, and even breaks down stone.

warm air close to Earth's surface, the increased intensity of the sun's rays can cause the planet to heat up even more quickly.

The Clean Air Act:

Fortunately elected officials in the United States acknowledge the problems caused by air pollution and have passed legislation to address it. First enacted in 1970, the federal Clean Air Act includes guidelines for reducing toxic pollutants in the air and stopping the most common types of air pollution. The law also sets emission standards for cars, trucks, and other motorized vehicles and has guidelines for enforcing those standards. It contains information on dealing with air pollution carried into the United States from elsewhere, as well as guidelines for protecting the ozone

Tough new rules for U.S. vehicle emissions and mileage standards will begin to take effect in 2012.

layer. In 1990 the Clean Air Act was dramatically updated. The new, revised law is much tougher on those who create air pollution. State and local governments, as well as the governments of tribal nations, are also doing a lot to enforce the law and go after violators.

You can help! Those whose work is enforcing the Clean Air Act and dealing with air polluters are on the job every day. For everyone else, pollution can be an easy problem to forget, especially when there isn't enough smog to actually make the air visible. But that air may still be unhealthy to breathe. Here are some ways you and your family can help reduce the problem—whether you can see the pollution in the air or not.

- If you think you've found a source of air pollution, report it to the U.S. Environmental Protection Agency. This organization enforces laws that protect the environment.
- Motor vehicles are among the planet's biggest polluters. Walk, bike, or use public transportation, such as buses or trains, as much as possible.
- Report motor vehicles that are emitting a lot of tailpipe smoke.
- Conserve energy by turning off all appliances and lights when you leave a room. Most electricity is made by burning fossil fuels. This process releases pollutants, including the greenhouse gas carbon dioxide, into the atmosphere.
- Don't wait in long drive-through lines, letting the car engine idle. Idling wastes energy and need-lessly pollutes the air.

Park and walk in!

- In cold weather, don't start your car long before you leave in order to warm up the inside. Just get in and drive off.
- Recycle glass, plastic, paper, aluminum cans, and cardboard. This reduces manufacturing emissions and saves energy, too.
- Plant a tree. Trees give off oxygen and take in carbon dioxide, helping remove one of the worst greenhouse gases from the environment.

Let your plastic bottle live again by recycling it. It might come back as a fleece jacket or a ballpoint pen.

"Water and air, the two essential fluids on which all life depends, have become global garbage cans. ... We forget that the water cycle and the life cycle are one."
–Jacques Cousteau (1910–1997), marine explorer and conservationist

The Water We Drink

chapter 2

Benjamin Franklin supposedly said, "When the well runs dry, we shall know the value of water." Around the world, people everywhere take their water supply for granted. It rains, so there will always be more, right? Wrong.

Water is considered a renewable resource because the natural cycle of evaporation and condensation constantly circulates water, so that it is always new. But the amount of freshwater that people can use is shrinking. That's because global warming is causing Earth's water to be redistributed. Furthermore,

Treated water dumped into lakes and streams may not be entirely rid of environmental poisons.

the waste and pollution of freshwater are using up our supply faster than natural processes can make more of it. Some water is permanently polluted, so it can never be used. Some scientists consider the loss of freshwater the world's greatest environmental crisis. Today about 2.8 billion people—about 40 percent of the world's population—live in areas with some degree of water scarcity.

Global warming is one thing that is reducing the freshwater supply. Rising temperatures are causing Earth's glaciers to shrink. This is decreasing the water supply that comes from glaciers. For thousands of years, glaciers in the southern Himalayas have helped feed major rivers in South Asia. The rivers provide freshwater for more than 1 billion people. That's nearly a sixth of the world's population. But now these life-giving masses of ice are in danger of disappearing. In addition to the glaciers, a lot of lakes will shrink and disappear as the world's air continues to warm up. For example, Lake Chad in central Africa was once the sixth largest lake in the world. Today it has shrunk to one-twentieth of its former size, and experts expect it to disappear completely in this century. The main reason is a lack of rainfall caused by a warming climate.

The false belief that water will always be readily available has led to many of the world's water problems. Scientists have documented some startling facts about this. For example, badly planned dams are causing reservoirs to lose millions

Lack of rainfall is threatening the water supply for many people in Africa.

Water Use

By the Numbers

According to the U.S. Environmental Protection Agency, global water consumption increased sixfold between 1900 and 1995. This is more than double the world's population growth rate. Farming is responsible for 70 percent of this usage, and much of the water used is wasted. Some experts say 50 percent of water used for crops and yards is wasted because of overwatering, evaporation, or being blown away by wind.

of gallons of water through evaporation. Meanwhile, the trickle of water passing through some of these dams is so small that the surrounding wetlands are going dry. For the past century, the world's water use has grown more than twice as fast as its population. This means that rivers, lakes, and the underground waters that supply wells and springs are being drained faster than rain can refill them.

Equally disturbing is the problem of water pollution, most of which is also caused by humans. Every time it rains, poisons from pesticides, fertilizers, and other chemical products flow into the water supply. Sewage and seawater are also finding their way into many freshwater systems, making them unusable. Oil spills frequently turn bodies of water into slick toxic dumps. Everywhere

Oil spills kill birds and marine animals and threaten the health of humans as well.

on Earth, people casually dump trash of all kinds into lakes, streams, and oceans every day.

Water pollution doesn't just ruin people's water activities and spoil the beauty of nature. It limits the supply of freshwater and hurts living things. It can lead to serious diseases in humans and, in some cases, even death.

The Clean Water Act:

The Clean Water Act is one of the U.S. government's most important tools for protecting the water within the nation's borders. When the law was passed, in 1972, its purpose was mainly tracking and reducing chemical water pollution. The law focused on common sources of pollution, such

Bringing Life to Lake Erie

Concerned about water pollution? Don't underestimate your ability to make a difference. Your government can help. Here's one example: In the 1960s, Lake Erie, one of the Great Lakes, was considered by environmentalists to be a "dead" lake. Fish and other animals died, and the lake's surface was covered by a smelly scum. Scientists discovered that chemicals called phosphates, which are found in laundry detergents, were making their way into the lake and causing a chain reaction that used up the oxygen in the lake. But in the 1970s, U.S. citizens worked through their government to ban phosphates in laundry detergents. Eventually Lake Erie came back to life.

as sewage systems and factories. But in the 1980s, other causes of pollution began to get attention. The Environmental Protection Agency started monitoring construction sites, urban storm sewer systems, and agricultural activities much more closely. Today those who enforce the law work to preserve healthy waters and to restore waters that have become polluted.

You can help! With so many threats to the planet's water supply, it's a good thing scientists and government watchdogs are on the job. But even if you don't work for the EPA, there are plenty of ways you can help keep our water fresh, clean, and plentiful. According to businessman and politician Ross Perot, "The activist is not the man who says the river is dirty. The activist is

Trash in rivers and lakes threatens the health of all living things.

Gross Violations

The Environmental Protection Agency has a fat file full of records of criminal violations of the environmental protection laws. One example is a case from 2008. The Eco Finishing Company, based in Fridley, Minnesota, was found guilty of criminally violating the Clean Water Act. The company's business of coating metal products was resulting in the dumping of illegal levels of metals and cyanide into the local sewer system. Cyanide is a strong poison that instantly kills people if it is swallowed.

During visits by EPA inspectors, the company reduced the amount of toxins it was discharging to make it look as if no violations were occurring. This was purposeful deception of the government. But an employee of the company reported the violation. The company's president and chief executive officer was found guilty of committing crimes, including two counts of felony violations of the Clean Water Act. He was sentenced to serve 15 months in prison and do 200 hours of community service after his release. He also had to pay a $250,000 fine. A special agent of the EPA's Criminal Investigative Division said, "This sentence should put companies ... on notice. We will continue to vigorously prosecute crimes committed against our environment."

GO DEEP

the man who cleans up the river." Here are some ways you can help:

- Turn off the faucet while brushing your teeth and save eight gallons (30 liters) of water every day.
- Don't use the toilet as a wastebasket. Because each flush can use as much as 4.5 gallons (17 liters) of water, don't waste water flushing items that can be simply thrown in the trash.
- Don't flush medicine. When drugs are flushed down the toilet, they can end up in the water

Turning off the water while you're brushing your teeth can save thousands of gallons a year.

people and animals drink. Make sure your family disposes of old pills properly. Many pharmacies recycle unused medicine. Find out whether your pharmacy has a recycling program.

- Take short showers rather than baths, which use much more water.
- Get leaky faucets and showerheads fixed immediately. One drip per second equals approximately 3,000 gallons (11,400 liters) wasted each year.
- Two gallons (7.6 liters) of water are used for each minute the tap is running. If you wash dishes by hand, clean them in a sink full of warm soapy water rather than holding them under a running tap. When all are washed, rinse them together — quickly.
- If you use a dishwasher, save water and energy by washing only full loads of dishes, and scrape them off rather than rinsing them before putting them in the dishwasher. Similarly, wash only full loads of clothing.
- Chill drinking water in the refrigerator rather than letting tap water run until cold.
- Don't throw any kind of trash, oil, or other non-biodegradable liquid or object into a body of water — or into the gutter. It can harm animals and, when rain comes, it may wash right into a sewer system.

"To forget how to dig the earth and tend the soil is to forget ourselves."
–Mohandas K. Gandhi (1869-1948), Indian political and spiritual leader

The Ground We Plant In

chapter 3

The world needs plentiful, healthy soil if living things are going to grow in it. Without good soil, we'd have a lot fewer delicious things to eat. So the lack of rich, clean soil is another issue to get active about. The biggest problems are erosion, compaction, nutrient loss, and chemical leaching.

The natural removal of soil by wind and water has been going on for eons. But these days human activity is accelerating erosion to an alarming degree. Deforestation plays a major role. When trees are cut down or burned, there are no longer any living roots to hold

the soil in place, nor any leafy canopies to protect the ground from the effects of rain and wind. Farming that uses heavy, powerful equipment is another cause of erosion. These machines not only erode soil, but they can cause soil compaction, too. The weight of these machines presses the ground down into a hard, solid mass. For a plant's root system to dig down into the ground and absorb nutrients, the soil must be loose. Compacted soil is as hard to penetrate as a clenched fist.

The nutrients that plants need for growth are most often used up by conventional farming. Land preparation and plant cultivation remove nutritious organic matter from the soil. So does burning vegetation to clear land for crops. When the soil nutrients are gone, little plant

Erosion happens when trees are cut down, allowing wind and rain to wash away the soil.

life will grow. This in turn increases erosion.

Many farmers use pesticides to kill insects and weeds that harm their crops. But pesticides sometimes damage more than unwanted pests. The chemicals in artificial pesticides can remain in the soil for many years. They can get into vegetables, fruits, or grains that people eat and make their way into the water supply.

Organic alternatives:

Conventional farms give us lots of wonderful things to eat, but their practices are hard on the soil. Organic farms are a gentler option. Organic farmers grow crops without using chemical pesticides and artificial fertilizers. Instead they use natural methods to improve the soil and discourage pests. They might practice crop rotation, in which a different crop is

Pesticides and chemical fertilizers stay in the soil for many years and can have negative effects on animals.

grown on a piece of land each season in order to keep the soil fertile and discourage pests that damage certain crops. The farmers might create habitats for animals, such as birds, that eat insects that threaten their crops.

Organic farmers also use compost to enrich the soil. Compost is rotting organic matter, such as grass clippings, leaves, and vegetable scraps, that can be used as a fertilizer. Mixed with soil, it releases its nutrients and helps plants grow naturally—and without causing pollution.

Composting yields rich organic material to enrich the soil.

You can help! There are many small things you can do to give back to the soil a little of what's been taken away. Here are a few ideas:

- Plant a tree. You'll help prevent erosion, clean the air, and create wildlife habitat all at the same time.
- Buy organic foods, or grow them yourself. You don't have to worry about being exposed to dangerous chemicals, and many people think organic fruits and vegetables just taste better.
- Compost your vegetable scraps and add the mixture to your garden. Besides helping your garden grow, compost keeps kitchen waste from adding to landfills.

- Instead of fertilizing your lawn with chemicals, leave grass clippings on the lawn when you mow. The clippings are full of nitrogen, which promotes lush, green growth.
- Dispose of hazardous materials properly. Don't put them in landfills, where toxic chemicals might get into the soil.

Check It

Recycle With Care
Here are just a few of the many household items that are considered hazardous. Check with your recycling center for the best ways to dispose of them. Don't ever just throw them away!
- motor oil
- leftover paint
- medications
- batteries
- electronic equipment

> "Is civilization progress? The ... final answer will be given not by our amassing of knowledge, or by the discoveries of our science, or by the speed of our aircraft, but by the effect our civilized activities as a whole have upon the quality of our planet's life—the life of plants and animals as well as that of men."
>
> —Charles A. Lindbergh (1902–1974), aviator, author, and environmentalist

Saving the Forests

chapter 4

Some people still use the term tree-hugger in a not-so-complimentary way when referring to those who care passionately about the living world, especially forests. But it's past time for a planetary push to protect trees and all other life on Earth. If we don't watch it, there soon won't be that much left to hug!

Our breathing forests:

The planet's forests—especially the vast tropical rain forests—have been referred to as Earth's lungs. But unlike human lungs, they take in carbon dioxide and emit oxygen. Trees

are one of the planet's best weapons in the fight against global warming. They clean the air, stabilize the soil, and provide habitat for animals. Trees are crucial to our planet in ways that are too numerous to count. But deforestation is putting our woodlands under increasing stress. Most of this deforestation is occurring in the world's rain forests, where more than 37 million acres

The world's rain forests contain more species than any other ecosystem on Earth.

(15 million hectares) are destroyed every year. Brazil's rain forests are being hit the hardest. There, between 2000 and 2005, 7.9 million acres (3.1 million hectares) of forest were destroyed each year. From 2005 through 2008, Brazil's Atlantic forest regions suffered a loss nine

Rain forests are being cleared for farming and lumber at an alarming rate.

times as great as in the previous three years. The area cleared during those years equaled the size of almost 1,000 soccer fields!

Unfortunately it's the forests made up of the oldest and largest trees that are mostly being cut down. With only about 20 percent of old-growth forests left in the world, the state of our planet's woodlands is critical. Our lives depend in part on the oxygen generated by these biologically complex forests. They give us plants that are invaluable in a multitude of ways. And of course they also support the lives of many kinds of animals.

Most deforestation occurs to make room for farms,

to get lumber for fuel, or to satisfy the world's huge appetite for wood products. Companies that log these forests point out that they often put tree farms in the bare areas. According to a United Nations study, 57 wealthy nations reported that their areas of forest cover actually grew between 2000 and 2005. The problem is that the replacement trees that are planted usually belong to a single species. This sacrifices biological diversity, which is important for making an environment healthy. In other words, tree farms don't make a forest.

The rich complexity of life contained in old-growth

Farming is one of the main causes of rain forest destruction.

The Amazing Rain Forest

20% The amount of Earth's oxygen that scientists estimate is produced in the Amazon rain forest

30% The percentage of Earth's forests that have been destroyed in the past 200 years

700 The number of tree species contained in a single 25-acre (10-hectare) plot of rain forest on the island of Borneo—a number equal to the total number of tree species in North America

Less than 1% The percentage of rain forest species studied by scientists for their active components or possible uses

70% The percentage of plants with anti-cancer properties that are found only in the rain forest

50,000 The number of plant and animal species believed to be lost each year because of rain forest destruction

forests doesn't spring up overnight. It takes countless decades for a forest full of giant trees and varied species to develop. When all this is wiped out, we lose plants and animals we know about, as well as untold numbers of species we haven't even discovered. One of the most critical losses is of plants that might hold cures for diseases. Tree farms will never adequately make up for old-growth deforestation. The bottom line is this: The world needs these forests, and everything must be done to protect what's left of them.

You can help!

Small efforts or changes you make to your lifestyle can help prevent deforestation and its effects. Here are some easy ways to help:

- Some companies destroy rain forests to grow orange trees, especially in Brazil. If you drink packaged orange juice, be sure the container label says it comes from U.S.-grown oranges.

Check It

Ten Foods First Found in the Rain Forest

- bananas
- oranges
- lemons
- peanuts
- cocoa
- eggplant
- avocados
- coconuts
- vanilla
- sugar

• Plant a tree. There may not be deforestation in your area, but it's definitely happening. Any tree—anywhere—can remove carbon dioxide from the air and slow global warming.

• Try to eat nuts and dried fruits whose package labels say they come from "sustainably harvested rain forests." This means they were grown in ways that don't damage the rain forests or any living thing in them.

President Barack Obama helped plant a tree at an event organized by the Student Conservation Association.

Save the Trees

When Hannah McHardy moved to Seattle, Washington, from Arkansas, she fell in love with the forests of the Pacific Northwest. When she discovered that logging was destroying the old-growth forests that had become so important to her, she began working hard to educate people about forestland destruction and how to take action against it. In 2004 her efforts won her the Brower Youth Award and $3,000 from the Earth Island Institute. This annual award honors young people who show outstanding leadership in projects that promote environmental conservation, preservation, or restoration.

"With the rapid rate our planet is being destroyed," Hannah says, "we are the last generation that will have the choice of wilderness, clean air, abundant wildlife, and ancient forests unless something is done. ... It is up to the youth to keep the movement innovative, effective, fresh, and most importantly FUN! Just go out and make yourself heard!"

- Cut down on beef in your diet. Every year thousands of acres of rain forest are destroyed to make grazing pastures for cattle. For every single quarter-pound fast-food hamburger you eat that comes from rain forest cattle (and most ground beef does), a forested area the size of a small kitchen (about 55 square feet, or nearly 5 square meters) is destroyed.

• Half of all felled trees end up as paper — so use less! Take a canvas bag to the store to carry home your purchases. Use both sides of printer paper, and recycle it when you're finished. Avoid using paper cups and plates.

• Ask your parents not to buy products made from endangered rain forest trees. These include teak, ebony, rosewood, and mahogany. The wood is beautiful, but logging companies are bringing these trees close to extinction because of consumer demand.

A logger seems small next to an old-growth tree he has felled.

> "If all the beasts were gone, men would die from a great loneliness of spirit, for whatever happens to the beasts also happens to the man. All things are connected. Whatever befalls the Earth befalls the sons of the Earth."
> —Chief Seattle (c. 1786-1866), Native American leader

Animals in Danger

chapter 5

All the threads that make up Earth's rich tapestry are interconnected. When air is polluted, it affects the water. When water becomes polluted, it affects the plants that depend on it for nourishment. So it's only natural that deforestation, global warming, and other environmental problems are putting animals at risk. According to the International Union for Conservation of Nature, 99 percent of all species are endangered by human activity. Another report predicts the extinction of a full 25 percent of all plant and vertebrate

Wildlife in Africa is becoming increasingly threatened by nearby human activity.

animal species by 2050. There are many success stories about bringing living things back from the edge of permanent disappearance. Yet many remain on the list of endangered or threatened species, and often new ones are added.

One of these is the polar bear, the world's largest carnivorous mammal. In May 2008, the U.S. Department of the Interior added the polar bear to the list as a threatened species. Since many politicians favor massive oil and gas development where polar bears live, this is a positive step.

It's also a seemingly necessary step. Scientists at the U.S. Geological Survey believe that by 2050 at least two-thirds of the world's polar bears could be wiped out because of global warming. This would include all of Alaska's big white bears.

Records show that, in general, global warming is causing Arctic sea ice to melt a little earlier each summer. This makes it more challenging for polar bears to hunt for prey, so it's difficult for them to gain the weight they need to get through the winter without food. The cubs born in the spring are lighter and less healthy. It's harder for smaller, thinner cubs to survive in their harsh habitat. The decrease in sea ice also makes polar bears have to swim much farther. Scientists have reported stranded or drowning polar bears, something they had not seen until recently.

Polar bears will be at risk of extinction because of habitat destruction if global warming continues.

The Encyclopedia of Life

One of the most interesting conservation projects today is the Encyclopedia of Life. The EOL is an online database that someday could include all forms of life known on Earth.

Leading this vast, visionary project of information-gathering is E.O. Wilson, a biologist at Harvard University. His aim is to collect every known bit of information about every living thing. This ranges from the largest mammals on Earth right down to organisms so small they're invisible to the naked eye. Each species will have its own Web site, which will be continually updated as new information is gathered.

The purpose of this project is to help save the planet. EOL's coordinators believe that having a source of "central intelligence" will aid in the effort to understand the planet's problems and decide how to fix them.

It makes sense. Humans have identified about 1.8 million organisms, but scientists estimate that

As animal habitats shrink or are destroyed by global warming or human development, more alarming reports are coming to light. Orangutans are being killed or pushed out of their homelands as palm oil plantations are created, destroying their habitat.

Coral reefs are dying because of global warming, destroying habitat for hundreds of thousands of marine species. Overfishing, pollution, and global warming threaten to deplete the world's fisheries by the middle of this century. And this is just some of the bad news.

this is only 10 percent of all living things on Earth. Discovering the other 90 percent, Wilson says, will be made much easier by having the collective knowledge about all known organisms in one database. And with the discovery of previously unknown living things, new possibilities appear. Perhaps some of the undiscovered species hold the key to curing diseases or solving other critical problems we deal with today.

The EOL isn't just for scientists. Anyone can access the database. In the same spirit of sharing, anyone will be able to add to this giant "map of biodiversity." Scientists and nonscientists alike can contribute information, which will be checked for accuracy by experts. The EOL encourages students and even whole classes to sign up and get involved. If you are looking for a class project, the EOL may be a great starting place.

Poaching for profit:

One of the greatest worldwide threats to wildlife is poaching, which means illegally capturing or killing endangered animals. The sale of wildlife around the world brings in billions of black-market dollars. People want animals for their skin, fur, tusks, and meat. Whatever the reason, the criminals profit while the world's wildlife population is rapidly being diminished.

In many poor, rural regions of the world, poaching is motivated by the need to survive. Often people in these areas find it difficult

The poaching of elephant tusks puts an already endangered species at greater risk.

to balance the need to preserve wildlife habitat with their own need to make a living. On the upside, many worldwide animal-protection organizations are educating people and helping them find other ways to sustain themselves. The movement to protect animals of every kind, from polar bears to the tiniest bugs on Earth, has become increasingly important all around the world.

The Endangered Species Act: One U.S. law helping to fight the decline of certain wildlife populations, no matter the reason, is the Endangered Species Act. The law, passed in 1973, is considered one

of the most successful laws on the books. It established the list of endangered and threatened species and prohibits the unauthorized taking, possession, sale, or transporting of these species. There are penalties for violations of the law and rewards for people who give information that helps catch and punish violators. One of its most important effects is protecting the ecosystems where America's threatened and endangered species live.

You can help! When most people hear "endangered species," they think of manatees, polar bears, whales, and other large, exciting animals. If these creatures don't live in your area, you might think there is nothing you can do to help. But the endangered species list contains nearly 1,300 plants, birds, fish, mammals, and other species. You're likely

Comeback Kids

Thanks to human efforts, 10 species that were once almost extinct are now no longer in danger:
- American alligator
- gray wolf
- blue poison frog
- grizzly bear
- koala
- black-footed ferret
- California condor
- bison
- bald eagle
- African white rhinoceros

Check It

to find some animal that lives in or migrates through your area. People play a critical role in protecting our country's wildlife and plants. Here are some ways you can be an activist:

- "Adopt" an endangered species native to your area. Find out how you can help protect it, and tell people in your community about your adopted plant or animal. You could make a Web page, write a newspaper article, give a speech, distribute brochures, or do whatever else you can think of.

Talk with your neighbors, and encourage them to get involved in environmental causes.

Cars are a hazard for many animals, so watch the road!

• When your family is driving in areas where animals may be present, slow down and look out for wildlife. Collisions with cars and trucks are a major problem in certain areas for many endangered species, such as Florida black bears, Florida panthers, desert tortoises, Key deer, indigo snakes, and Houston toads. About 65 percent of Florida panther and Florida black bear deaths are related to highway accidents.

Turn your backyard into a wildlife habitat. You can learn a lot about animals by watching them up close.

- If you see evidence that people have killed wildlife illegally, contact your state's fish and game department. State agencies handle violations of state wildlife laws and deal with most local wildlife management problems.
- Don't buy products that come from endangered or threatened plant and animal species.
- Make your backyard wildlife-friendly. Plant native trees and bushes with berries or nuts that provide birds and other creatures with food and a place to live.

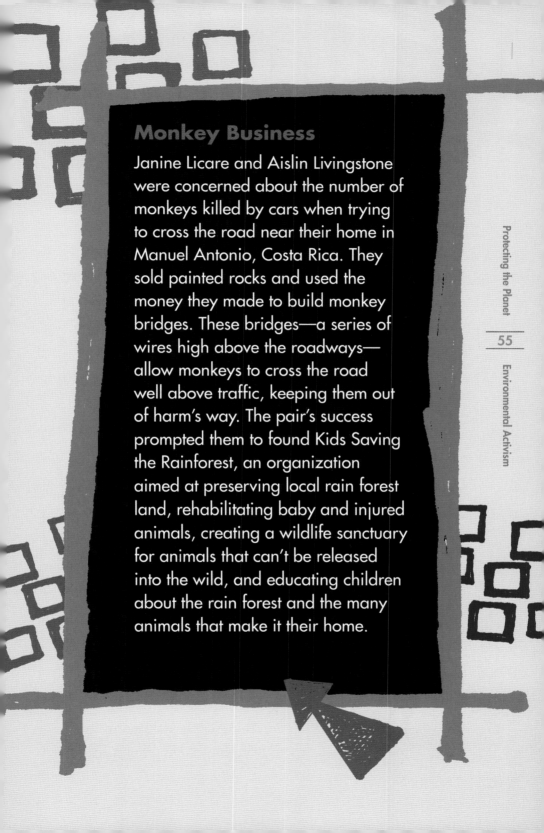

Monkey Business

Janine Licare and Aislin Livingstone were concerned about the number of monkeys killed by cars when trying to cross the road near their home in Manuel Antonio, Costa Rica. They sold painted rocks and used the money they made to build monkey bridges. These bridges—a series of wires high above the roadways— allow monkeys to cross the road well above traffic, keeping them out of harm's way. The pair's success prompted them to found Kids Saving the Rainforest, an organization aimed at preserving local rain forest land, rehabilitating baby and injured animals, creating a wildlife sanctuary for animals that can't be released into the wild, and educating children about the rain forest and the many animals that make it their home.

"You don't have to be a lawmaker, scientist, or in the White House to take action to protect the environment. Reduce your own impact on the environment in your daily lives. Most importantly, get educated."
—Leonardo DiCaprio, actor and environmental activist

Looking to the Future

chapter 6

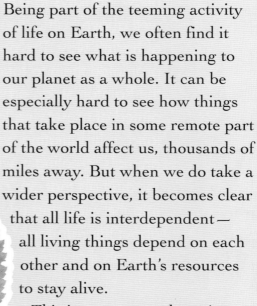

Being part of the teeming activity of life on Earth, we often find it hard to see what is happening to our planet as a whole. It can be especially hard to see how things that take place in some remote part of the world affect us, thousands of miles away. But when we do take a wider perspective, it becomes clear that all life is interdependent— all living things depend on each other and on Earth's resources to stay alive.

This interconnectedness is complex. It means that when something breaks down in the environment somewhere, the effect ripples outward around the globe. Eventually all living things feel the consequences, to a greater or lesser degree. With assaults against the environment occurring on nearly every front, the efforts to reverse things must be a global undertaking. And there's no time to waste—the clock is ticking.

Urgent matters: As it turns out, not every negative effect can be reversed. In January 2009, the National Academy of Sciences reported that some global warming is already irreversible. "This is really a wakeup call about the seriousness of this issue," said Princeton University geoscientist Jorge

Global warming is limiting many animals' access to water.

Sarmiento. Indeed it is.

On a positive note, though, millions have already responded to this wakeup call. Awareness of the world's urgent environmental problems has never been greater. And the technologies available to fix much of what's wrong have never been more advanced. Clean, renewable energy can be made using the sun, wind, water, plants, and Earth's internal heat. These types of energy are becoming increasingly available and affordable. Reducing or eliminating our need for fossil fuels is the most important thing we can do to stop global warming and preserve the abundant life on Earth.

Wind turbines convert the movement of air—a clean, renewable resource—into electrical power.

Ten Earth-Focused Groups

- Global Green
  http://globalgreen.org
- Greenbelt Movement
  www.greenbeltmovement.org
- Greenpeace International
  www.greenpeace.org
- National Wildlife Federation
  www.nwf.org
- Natural Resources Defense Council
  www.nrdc.org
- Rainforest Action Network
  http://ran.org
- Sierra Club
  www.sierraclub.org
- Windstar Foundation
  www.wstar.org
- World Environmental Organization
  www.world.org
- World Wildlife Fund
  www.worldwildlife.org

Saving the blue marble:

Renewable energy is vital in preserving our planet's future, but there's another renewable resource that has even broader promise. As Al Gore, the environmental activist, Nobel Prize winner, and former vice president, has said, "The will to act is a renewable resource." Humanity really can stop the destruction. If we all pitch in, much can be done to save planet Earth, our beautiful blue marble, so that

Working with others to protect the environment increases both your effectiveness and your enjoyment.

it remains a vibrant habitat for all living things. It is time for everyone to become an environmental activist. Simple steps you take today will help to preserve the air, water, soil, trees, and animals for generations to come. Together we can become a force for change. What will you do to help?

Glossary

biodiversity — variety of species of plants and animals in an environment

carbon dioxide — greenhouse gas most responsible for global warming

compost — mixture of decayed organic material that is used for fertilizing

deforestation — action or process of clearing forests

fertilizers — substances, such as manure or chemicals, used to make soil richer and better for growing crops

fossil fuels — fuels, including coal, oil, and natural gas, made from the remains of ancient organisms

global warming — rise in the average worldwide temperature of Earth's atmosphere

greenhouse gases — gases in a planet's atmosphere that trap energy from the sun

ozone layer — layer of the upper atmosphere that absorbs harmful ultraviolet light

natural resources — substances found in nature that people use, such as soil, air, trees, coal, and oil; some are renewable, while others have a fixed supply

non-biodegradable — unable to decay and be absorbed by the environment

organic — grown without the use of chemical fertilizers, pesticides, or other artificial substances

pesticides — substances, usually chemical, applied to crops to kill harmful insects and other pests

smog — haze caused by pollution

Investigate Further

MORE BOOKS TO READ

Amsel, Sheri. *The Everything Kids' Environment Book*. Avon, Mass.:
Adams Media, 2007.

Coley, Mary McIntyre. *Environmentalism: How You Can Make a
Difference*. Mankato, Minn.: Capstone Press, 2009.

Hall, Julie. *A Hot Planet Needs Cool Kids*. Bainbridge Island, Wash.:
Green Goat Books, 2007.

Thornhill, Jan. *This Is My Planet: The Kids' Guide to Global Warming*.
Toronto: Maple Tree Press, 2007.

INTERNET SITES

FactHound offers a safe, fun way to find Internet
sites related to this book. All of the sites on
FactHound have been researched by our staff.

Here's all you do:
    Visit *www.facthound.com*
FactHound will fetch the best sites for you!

Index

About the Author

Pamela Dell began her professional career writing for adults and started writing for young readers about 12 years ago. Since then she has written fiction and nonfiction books, written numerous magazine articles, and created award-winning interactive multimedia.

S0-AZO-700

To Bill,

Thankyou for the opportunities which gave me the knowledge and experience to write this book.

I am proud to have you as a contributor to this book. You are very special and a major influence in my life

With Love,
Linda

The Handbook of

EMERGENCY

NURSING

MANAGEMENT

EILEEN C. ALEXANDER, RN, MSN, CEN
Coordinator, Emergency/Trauma Nursing
West Virginia University Hospital
Morgantown, West Virginia

JOSEPH BLANSFIELD, RN, MS, CEN
Clinical Nurse Specialist, Emergency Department
Boston City Hospital
Boston, Massachusetts

SANDRA GREEN, RN
Risk Manager
Kennedy Hospital
Philadelphia, Pennsylvania

LYNNETTE HOLDER, RN, MSN, CCRN, CNAA
Director of Nursing Services
Albert Einstein Medical Center–Northern Division
Philadelphia, Pennsylvania

MARGARET DALY McKENNA, RN, MN, CEN
Acute Care Clinical Specialist for Emergency Services
Our Lady of Lourdes Regional Medical Center
Lafayette, Louisiana

CYNTHIA POSSANZA, RN, MSN, CCRN, CEN
Staff Development Instructor
Albert Einstein Medical Center–Northern Division
Philadelphia, Pennsylvania

WILLIAM M. WARFEL, RN, MSN, CNAA
Associate General Director
Albert Einstein Medical Center–Northern Division
Philadelphia, Pennsylvania

The Handbook of

EMERGENCY

NURSING

MANAGEMENT

Linda Buschiazzo, RN, BS, CEN, CNA

Albert Einstein Medical Center
Philadelphia, Pennsylvania
and
Emercon Associates
Cheltenham, Pennsylvania

AN ASPEN PUBLICATION®
Aspen Publishers, Inc.

1987

Rockville, Maryland
Royal Tunbridge Wells

Library of Congress Cataloging in Publication Data

Buschiazzo, Linda.
Handbook of emergency nursing management.

Includes index.
1. Emergency nursing — Administration. 2. Hospitals — Emergency service —
Administration. 3. Nursing service administration. I. Title.
RT120.E4B87   1987   362.1'8   86-23128
ISBN: 0-87189-612-5

Copyright © 1987 by Aspen Publishers, Inc.
All rights reserved.

Aspen Publishers, Inc. grants permission for photocopying for personal or internal use,
or for the personal or internal use of specific clients registered with the Copyright
Clearance Center (CCC). This consent is given on the condition that the copier pay a
$1.00 fee plus $.12 per page for each photocopy through the CCC for photocopying
beyond that permitted by the U.S. Copyright Law. The fee should be paid directly to the
CCC, 21 Congress St., Salem, Massachusetts 01970.
0-87189-612-5 $1.00 + .12.

This consent does not extend to other kinds of copying, such as copying for general
distribution, for advertising or promotional purposes, for creating new collective works,
or for resale. For information, address Aspen Publishers, Inc.,
1600 Research Boulevard, Rockville, Maryland 20850.

Editorial Services: Lisa J. McCullough

Library of Congress Catalog Card Number: 86-23128
ISBN: 0-87189-612-5

Printed in the United States of America

1 2 3 4 5

With love to Horacio
and our children
Michele, Alex, and Michael

In memory of my father
Morris Bush

Table of Contents

PART I   THE EMERGENCY NURSING
MANAGEMENT ENVIRONMENT

PART III   PLANNING AND
DEVELOPING NEW PROGRAMS

Preface

Changes in health care, largely due to stricter regulatory mechanisms governing reimbursement, the growth and recognition of emergency services, improved technology, and the increasingly competitive atmosphere of health care systems, have created new challenges for emergency nursing managers. The special nature of the emergency department's organization, function, and relationships requires that you, as a nurse manager, possess specific management knowledge, experience, and skills to be able to meet the goals of the hospital and emergency department (ED), while meeting the expectations and needs of the public.

I wrote this book to share specific, practical information that I learned, adapted, and found useful during 15 years as an ED nurse manager so that others can benefit from my experiences. The contributors to this book also have a good deal of experience in emergency nursing and management, which enhances their contributions.

Acknowledgments

I want to express my appreciation to the Corporate and Northern Division administrative staff of Albert Einstein Medical Center for their support and assistance during the preparation of this book. Special thoughts and thanks are extended to Bill Warfel and Lynn Holder, my role models and mentors. Their guidance, encouragement, and management knowledge and styles greatly influenced my development as a nurse manager. Their contributions to this book are appreciated.

Special thanks to Paul LoRusso for his assistance with the chapter on computer information systems.

I also want to thank Pat Epifanio and Peggy Trimble-Bullock from the Maryland Institute for Emergency Medical Services System for their help; Sandy Green, my friend and a former ED assistant nurse manager for helping me write the legal chapter; my brother Marty Bush for lending me his computer with a word processor, which made the task of writing easier; and Darlene Como, editorial director, Aspen Publishers, whose encouragement and guidance made this book possible.

Many thanks to the ED nursing staff and especially the ED assistant nurse managers, Maureen LeDent and Nancy Duffy Pokorny, for their support and assistance at Albert Einstein.

Lastly, but of most importance, I want to express my love and appreciation to my husband and three children for their understanding and encouragement during the preparation and writing of this book; for the time that was taken away from them so that I could achieve my goal of writing this book.

Introduction

In past years, the emergency department (ED) was viewed by hospital administrators as a nonprofit patient care area. As a result, hospitals were unwilling to invest money into the ED, which led to an unintentional or intentional neglect of updating or improving emergency services. With this lack of financial and personnel support, resources were at a minimum, thereby preventing or delaying growth in ED management, planning, and development. There was little understanding of the need for the patient's experience in the ED to be seen as a positive one, even though it formed the patient's first contact and image of the hospital.

In addition, the nursing administration often did not recognize emergency nursing as a specialty requiring special knowledge, training, and skills. EDs were (and in many cases, still are) understaffed, and nurses were provided little to no continuing education specific to emergency nursing. Down time, which is inevitable in all EDs, resulted in a misinterpretation of staffing needs. Although intensive care and cardiac care units received recognition for their special needs, emergency nursing did not. Yet, no other nursing care area provides nursing care for both inpatients and outpatients and for medical, surgical, pediatric, gynecologic, psychiatric, critical care, and multiple trauma patients all in the same unit by the same nursing staff.

In recent years, the ED has been viewed more as an integral part of the hospital. With proper management and sufficient resources, it can be a positive force in the marketing and financial activities of the hospital. Effective and efficient management of the ED, which includes emergency nursing management, is essential to foster the understanding and acceptance of the ED's contribution to the hospital and community. The ED is now gaining deserved recognition and organizational status.

The growth of Emergency Medical Services Systems (EMSS), the increased number of emergency trained physicians, the development of the Emergency Nurses Association (ENA), and certification for emergency nurses have resulted in an expanded awareness of emergency nursing as a specialty. Knowledge and skills required by the emergency nurse have been improved and standardized.

EDs have undergone accelerated organizational and operational changes during more recent years because of current health care trends. These include the rising incidence of chronic illness, an aging population, an increase in the birth rate, more sophisticated technology, stricter federal and state regulations, decreasing resources, third party reimbursement cost-containment measures, increasing competition, and growing consumerism.

Health maintenance organizations (HMOs) and preferred provider organizations (PPOs), which are organized by private companies and physician groups, require preadmission approval for hospital services. They offer financial incentives to physicians to keep their patients out of hospitals. When the patient finally requires admission, the acuity state is high, and emergency admission is usually required. If a patient seeks services in the ED without prior approval from the HMO or PPO, the hospital is not paid for services rendered. Emergency patients sometimes have to be transferred to another hospital that has a contract with their HMO or PPO.

Prospective payment systems and DRGs are resulting in the premature discharge of inpatients, causing "repeaters." Recently discharged patients return to the ED because their acuity level is unmanageable for them or their family in the home setting.

Patients also arrive in the ED because they do not have approved admission diagnoses and are afraid or too ill to remain at home. The ED staff often winds up in the middle between the third party payer who will not pay the hospital for unapproved diagnoses and the patient who wants to be admitted.

The ED is no longer the back door to the hospital; it is now the front door. Health care consumers are actively choosing and challenging health care services to meet their standards.

All these factors have led to increased competition and marketing efforts in the health care field. All hospital managers must accept and must adapt to the importance of these factors. As a manager in the ED, you must be aware of changes and trends in the health care field so that you can meet hospital and department goals through effective, efficient, and creative management. To perform effectively, the ED nurse manager of today must possess both general and specific management knowledge and skills and be responsible and accountable as well.

Although EDs vary in size, number of patient visits, acuity levels of patients, personnel and financial resources, and organizational structure, the purpose and goals of all emergency departments are similar. This book addresses both these differences and similarities so that the nurse manager from the rural hospital ED that may see 15,000 patients per year and the nurse manager from the urban teaching hospital ED that may see 150,000 patients per year may both benefit from reading this book.

Part I

The Emergency Nursing Management Environment

Chapter 1

Organization of the Emergency Department

TYPES AND CATEGORIZATION OF EMERGENCY SERVICES

Emergency services are the care rendered by qualified staff to the patient requiring emergent or urgent care. This care is given in a variety of places in addition to hospital EDs. Emergent care may be initiated in the community by prehospital care providers, in schools, in freestanding emergicenters, and in specialized facilities for burns, trauma, spinal cord injury, and the like.

The degree of hospital control and involvement with the ED varies, ranging from a high degree of control with corporate ownership and provision of finances and management to no control in which space is rented to an independent group of physicians who operate and manage the ED. Or, there may be a contract between the hospital and a private physician group under which expenses and revenues are shared.

The purpose of categorization of emergency services is to identify the readiness and capabilities of the hospital to receive and treat emergency patients. Several professional organizations have developed systems of categorization. The American Medical Association classifies hospitals according to their capability to provide care in specific critical care areas, which include:

- acute medical
- behavioral
- burns
- cardiac
- neonatal/perinatal
- poisoning and drug
- spinal cord
- trauma

3

Each of these special care areas is categorized by levels from 1 (highest capability) to 3 (least capability), with established standards for each level. Regionalization of centers for the provision of specialized care is gaining greater acceptance. These centers provide comprehensive care by trained and experienced staff, with wider distribution of facilities to render that care. Table 1–1 shows the American College of Surgeons standards for trauma categorization.

The Joint Commission on the Accreditation of Hospitals (JCAH) categorizes emergency services into four levels, with standards for each. In Emergency Services Standard 3.1 of the *Accreditation Manual for Hospitals:**

3.1.3 A hospital's emergency department/service is classified according to the levels of the services provided.

Regardless of the nomenclature assigned, the levels of emergency services range from a comprehensive to a first aid/referral level of care.

3.1.4 Specific and general requirements are established for four levels of emergency services. Other comparable classifications, such as state or regional, are acceptable, and the hospital is evaluated for compliance at the appropriate level.

A. Level I emergency department/service offers comprehensive emergency care 24 hours a day, with at least one physician experienced in emergency care on duty in the emergency care area. There is in-hospital physician coverage by members of the medical staff or by senior-level residents for at least medical, surgical, orthopedic, obstetrical/gynecological, pediatric, and anesthesiology services. When such coverage can be demonstrated to be met suitably through another mechanism, an equivalency is considered to exist for purposes of compliance with the requirement. Other specialty consultation is available within approximately 30 minutes; initial consultation through a two-way voice communication is acceptable.

The hospital's scope of services includes in-house capabilities for managing physical and related emotional problems on a definitive basis.

A. Level II emergency department/service offers emergency care 24 hours a day, with at least one physician experienced in emergency care on duty in the emergency care area, and with specialty consultation available within approximately 30 minutes by members of the medical staff or by senior-level residents. Initial consultation through two-way voice communication is acceptable. The hospital's scope of services includes in-house capabilities for managing physical and related emotional problems, with provision for patient transfer to another facility when needed.

*Reprinted from *Accreditation Manual for Hospitals,* pp. 23–25, with permission of the Joint Commission on Accreditation of Hospitals, © 1986.

Table 1–1 Standards for Trauma Categorization

	LEVELS		
	I	II	III
A. HOSPITAL ORGANIZATION			
1. Trauma service	E*	E	D*
2. Surgery departments/divisions/services/sections (each staffed by qualified specialists)			
Cardiothoracic surgery	E	D	
General surgery	E	E	E
Neurologic surgery	E	E	
Obstetric-gynecologic surgery	D	D	
Ophthalmic surgery	E	D	
Oral surgery—dental	D	D	
Orthopedic surgery	E	E	
Otorhinolaryngologic surgery	E	D	
Pediatric surgery	E	D	
Plastic and maxillofacial surgery	E	D	
Urologic surgery	E	D	
3. Emergency department/division/service/section (staffed by qualified specialists)	E	E	E
4. Surgical specialties availability			
In-house 24 hours a day:			
General surgery	E	E	
Neurologic surgery	E	E	
On-call and promptly available from inside hospital:			
Cardiac surgery	E	D	
General surgery			E
Neurologic surgery			D
Microsurgery capabilities	E	D	
Gynecologic surgery	E	D	
Hand surgery	E	D	
Ophthalmic surgery	E	E	D
Oral surgery—dental	E	D	
Orthopedic surgery	E	E	D
Otorhinolaryngologic surgery	E	E	D
Pediatric surgery	E	D	
Plastic and maxillofacial surgery	E	E	D
Thoracic surgery	E	E	D
Urologic surgery	E	E	D
5. Nonsurgical specialties availability			
In-hospital 24 hours a day:			
Emergency medicine	E	E	E
Anesthesiology	E	E	E
On-call and promptly available from inside or outside hospital:			
Cardiology	E	E	D
Gastroenterology	E	D	
Hematology	E	E	D

Table 1–1 continued

	LEVELS		
	I	II	III
Infectious diseases	E	D	
Internal medicine	E	E	E
Nephrology	E	E	D
Neuroradiology	D		
Pathology	E	E	E
Pediatrics	E	E	E
Psychiatry	E	D	
Radiology	E	E	E

B. SPECIAL FACILITIES/RESOURCES/CAPABILITIES
   1. Emergency Department (ED)

	I	II	III
a) Personnel			
1. Designated physician director	E	E	E
2. Physician with special competence in care of the critically injured who is a designated member of the trauma team and physically present in the ED 24 hours a day	E	E	E
3. RNs, LPNs, and nurses' aides in adequate numbers	E	E	E
b) Equipment for resuscitation and to provide life support for the critically or seriously injured shall include but not be limited to:			
1. Airway control and ventilation equipment, including laryngoscopes and endotracheal tubes of all sizes, bag-mask resuscitator, sources of oxygen, and mechanical ventilator	E	E	E
2. Suction devices	E	E	E
3. Electrocardiograph-oscilloscope defibrillator	E	E	E
4. Apparatus to establish central venous pressure monitoring	E	E	E
5. All standard intravenous fluids and administration devices, including intravenous catheters	E	E	E
6. Sterile surgical sets for procedures standard for ED, such as thoracostomy, cut-down, etc.	E	E	E
7. Gastric lavage equipment	E	E	E
8. Drugs and supplies necessary for emergency care	E	E	E
9. X-ray capability, 24-hour coverage by in-house technicians	E	E	E
10. Two-way radio linked with vehicles of emergency transport system	E	E	E
11. Pneumatic anti-shock garment (needed also as supply replacement item for EMS crews)	E	E	E
12. Skeletal tongs	E	E	E
2. Intensive Care Units (ICU) for trauma patients; ICUs may be separate specialty units			
a) Designated medical director	E	E	E

Table 1–1 continued

	LEVELS		
	I	*II*	*III*
b) Physician on duty in ICU 24 hours a day or immediately available from in-hospital	E	E	D
c) Nurse-patient minimum ratio of 1:2 on each shift	E	E	E
d) Immediate access to clinical laboratory services	E	E	E
e) Equipment			
1. Airway control and ventilation devices	E	E	E
2. Oxygen source with concentration controls	E	E	E
3. Cardiac emergency cart	E	E	E
4. Electrocardiograph-oscilloscope-defibrillator	E	E	E
5. Temporary transvenous pacemaker	E	E	E
6. Cardiac output monitoring	E	E	D
7. Electronic pressure monitoring	E	E	D
8. Mechanical ventilator-respirators	E	E	E
9. Patient weighing devices	E	E	D
10. Pulmonary function measuring devices	E	E	E
11. Temperature control devices	E	E	E
12. Drugs, intravenous fluids, and supplies	E	E	E
13. Intracranial pressure monitoring devices	E	E	D
3. Postanesthetic Recovery Room (PAR) (surgical intensive care unit is acceptable)			
a) Registered nurses and other essential personnel 24 hours a day	E	E	E
b) Appropriate monitoring and resuscitation equipment	E	E	E
4. Acute hemodialysis capability (or transfer agreement)	E	D	D
5. Organized burn care			
a) Physician-directed burn center/unit staffed by nursing personnel trained in burn care and equipped properly for care of the extensively burned patient			
OR			
b) Transfer agreement with nearby burn center or hospital with a burn unit			
6. Acute spinal cord injury management capability; in circumstances where a designated spinal cord injury rehabilitation center exists in the region, early transfer should be considered; transfer agreements should be in effect.			
7. Radiological special capabilities			
a) Angiography of all types	E	E	D
b) Sonography	E	D	
c) Nuclear scanning	E	D	
d) In-house computerized tomography with technician	E	E	
8. Rehabilitation medicine	E	D	
C. OPERATING SUITE SPECIAL REQUIREMENTS: EQUIPMENT/INSTRUMENTATION			
1. Operating room adequately staffed in-house and immediately available 24 hours a day	E	E	D

Table 1-1 continued

	LEVELS		
	I	II	III
2. Cardiopulmonary bypass capability	D	D	
3. Operating microscope	E	D	
4. Thermal control equipment for patient and for blood	E	E	E
5. X-ray capability	E	E	E
6. Endoscopes, all varieties	E	E	E
7. Craniotome	E	E	D
8. Monitoring equipment	E	E	E
D. CLINICAL LABORATORIES SERVICES AVAILABLE 24 HOURS A DAY			
1. Standard analysis of blood, urine, and other body fluids	E	E	E
2. Blood typing and cross-matching	E	E	E
3. Coagulation studies	E	E	E
4. Comprehensive blood bank or access to a community central blood bank and adequate hospital storage facilities	E	E	E
5. Blood gases and pH determination	E	E	E
6. Serum and urine osmolality	E	E	E
7. Microbiology	E	E	E
8. Drug and alcohol screening	E	E	D
E. PROGRAMS FOR QUALITY ASSURANCE			
1. Medical care evaluation involving:			
a) Special audit for trauma deaths	E	E	E
b) Morbidity and mortality review	E	E	E
c) Trauma conference, multidisciplinary	E	E	
d) Medical nursing audit, utilization review, tissue review	E	E	E
e) Medical records review	E	E	E
2. Outreach program: telephone and on-site consultations with physicians of the community and outlying areas	E	D	
3. Public education: injury prevention in the home and industry and on the highways and athletic fields: standard first-aid; problems confronting public, medical profession, and hospitals regarding optimal care for the injured	E	E	D
F. TRAUMA RESEARCH PROGRAM	E		
G. TRAINING PROGRAM			
1. Formal programs in continuing education for			
a) Staff physicians	E	E	
b) Nurses	E	E	
c) Allied health personnel	E	E	
d) Community physicians	E	E	

*E = essential; D = desirable.

Source: Reprinted from *American College of Surgeons Bulletin,* Vol. 68, No. 10, pp. 13–18, with permission of the Committee on Trauma of the American College of Surgeons.

A. Level III emergency department/service offers emergency care 24 hours a day, with at least one physician available to the emergency care area within approximately 30 minutes through a medical staff call roster. Initial consultation through two-way voice communication is acceptable. Specialty consultation is available by request of the attending medical staff member or by transfer to a designated hospital where definitive care can be provided.

A. Level IV emergency service offers reasonable care in determining whether an emergency exists, renders lifesaving first aid, and makes appropriate referral to the nearest facilities that are capable of providing needed services. The mechanism for providing physician coverage at all times is defined by the medical staff.

3.1.5 Hospitals that offer critical therapeutic services in such specialized clinical areas as spinal cord injury, burns, trauma, and so forth are considered as providing comprehensive (Level I) services for the specific clinical focus of care, while the emergency services otherwise provided are evaluated at the appropriate level.

ORGANIZATIONAL STRUCTURE

The complexity and comprehensiveness of emergency services create many demands on hospital management. Because of neglect or lack of understanding of emergency services, the ED is frequently misplaced on the organizational chart of the hospital. In many instances, the placement of emergency services on the organizational chart actually changes with each turnover of hospital administrators. The services may be placed under the department of surgery, department of medicine, or ambulatory care; as a subdivision of one of the major departments; or as a separate department reporting to the top level of hospital management.

Within a period of 8 years, the author had the experience as an emergency nursing head nurse of reporting first to the department of medicine, then to the department of surgery, then back to the department of medicine, to finally and currently having the ED function as a decentralized separate department. Nursing services had become decentralized before the ED was decentralized. Emergency nursing began to report to the Director of Critical Care Nursing. To complicate matters, the physicians reported to the department of medicine, the clerks reported to the department of unit management, and the receptionists reported to the admissions department. For those of us directly involved with the day-to-day operations of the emergency unit, these changes in organizational structure led to frustration and a drastic increase in the time required for decision making and program development. With each change in organization, new upper-level managers had to learn about emergency services. Projects were halted and started again from the beginning.

With decentralization, planning and decision making became the responsibility of a small team of managers directly involved with the ED. (The team concept of management in this structure is discussed in Chapter 2.) With decentralization, my growth, responsibility, and accountability as a nurse manager were enhanced. There was a positive effect on the overall operations and functions of the ED.

Recently, the trend nationally, has been to organize emergency services as a separate department. Several factors must be considered in determining the type of organizational structure, including the:

- goals and objectives of the hospital
- goals and objectives of the department
- number of patient visits
- types of patient visits
- patient acuity levels
- staffing of the department (physicians, nurses, clerks, administrators, etc.)
- type of community
- type and size of the hospital
- available personnel
- skills of current managers
- benefits and disadvantages of structural change

Figures 1–1 to 1–5 illustrate both centralized and decentralized ED line structures. There are obvious disadvantages of the centralized management shown in Figures 1–1 and 1–2. The large number of people involved is the most glaring problem. The time involved for planning, decision making, and implementation of decisions is drastically increased in comparison to a decentralized organization. As a result, the lower-level managers who have the responsibility for the day-to-day operations of the ED often experience frustration and decreased initiative. The authority for making decisions is in the hands of administrators far removed from the ED. These administrators may not have the understanding, available time, or priorities that reflect the actual needs of the ED. Decision making is therefore far removed from the area where the decision will be applied.

Decentralization places decision-making responsibility and accountability at the level of managers directly involved with the ED (Figures 1–3, 1–4, and 1–5). This form of organization has become increasingly common. Benefits of decentralization include:

- Decision making authority is close to the point where the decision is to be applied.
- Managers at lower levels are responsible and accountable for making decisions that directly affect them.

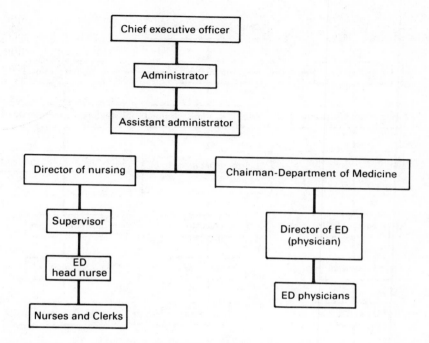

Figure 1–1 A Centralized Line Matrix in a Small Nonteaching Hospital

- There is timeliness in decision making.
- It promotes growth and motivation of lower-level managers.

In a decentralized organization, managers must be both generally and specifically skilled for decision making, as well as for other management functions, many of which are discussed in later chapters.

EMERGENCY MEDICAL SERVICES SYSTEM AND THE COMMUNITY

Ambulance services began in the late 1800s as hospital-based programs. In the 1940s, small communities began to operate volunteer ambulance services. The initial intent of ambulance service was to bring patients to a medical facility quickly where they could receive emergent care. The ambulances had no equipment and carried untrained personnel. There was little first aid or stabilization at the scene, but this volunteer service was the beginning of the emergency medical services system (EMSS).

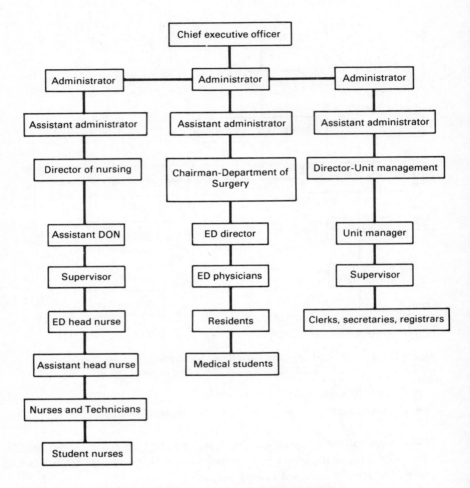

Figure 1–2 A Centralized Line Matrix in a Large Teaching Hospital

The Highway Safety Act of 1966 provided federal funding for the purchase of basic medical equipment for ambulances and training for ambulance personnel. In 1969, basic training courses for emergency medical technicians (EMT) were developed. An advanced training course for EMTs was piloted between 1971 and 1973, which created several levels of training for EMTs and the development of the paramedic role in the EMSS.

Currently, there are three levels of EMTs, with the EMT paramedic being the most highly trained and qualified for advanced emergency care. As a result of advanced training for EMTs, the quality of prehospital care has improved with

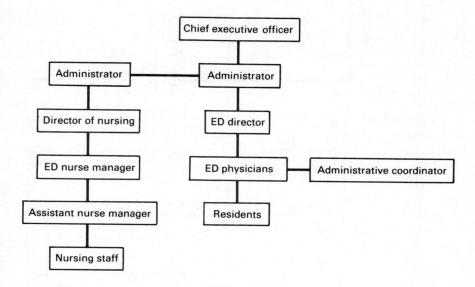

Figure 1–3 Decentralization in which Nurses Report to a Director of Nursing in a Decentralized Nursing Department

---

higher success rates for cardiopulmonary resuscitation and other emergent situations.

The Emergency Medical Services Systems Act of 1973 (Public Law 93-154) defines EMSS as

> a system which provides for the arrangement of personnel, facilities and equipment for the effective and coordinated delivery, in an appropriate geographical area, of health care services under emergency conditions (occurring either as a result of the patient's condition or of natural disasters or similar situations), and which are administered by a public or not-for-profit, private entity that has the authority and the resources to provide effective administration of the system.

The hospital ED plays a major role in the EMSS due to its location in the community, capabilities, hours of operation, and staffing. Coordination of hospitals with area independent prehospital programs is essential to ensure effective care of emergent patients.

The EMSS has also benefited from the availability of advanced transportation vehicles, ranging from a basic ground ambulance to the medical intensive care unit

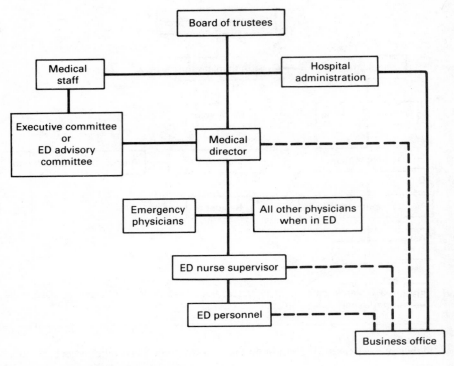

Figure 1-4 A Decentralized Line Matrix

Source: Reprinted from *Emergency Medicine: A Comprehensive Study Guide* by American College of Emergency Physicians, p. 985, with permission of McGraw-Hill Book Company, © 1985.

ambulance to helicopter and fixed-wing critical care transport vehicles. The number of airborne vehicles has been steadily increasing since 1980.

There are several types of prehospital care programs, including those sponsored by community agencies, such as the police and fire departments and county government, and hospital-based programs. These programs can be funded publicly or privately with staff who are volunteers or salaried. The extent of the hospital's role with the prehospital care programs also varies (Exhibit 1-1).

The EMT Paramedic in the Hospital Emergency Department

As EMT paramedics have become more highly educated and trained, their use in hospital EDs has become more common. The initial rationale for hiring EMTs in the ED was to supplement the short supply of nurses and to contain costs. The role of EMTs in the ED has been supported by JCAH, which requires that the duties and responsibilities of EMTs in the hospital setting, under the supervision

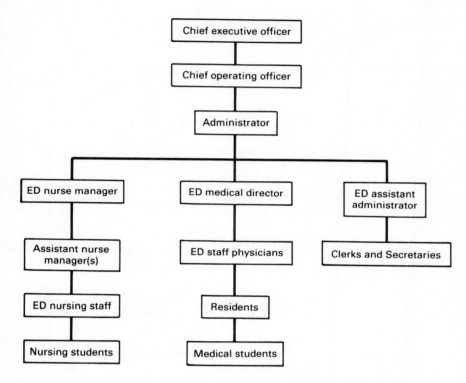

Figure 1–5 A Decentralized Organization with a Team Concept of Management

and direction of a nurse or physician, shall be defined in writing. However, there have been reported instances in various states of EMTs performing inappropriately and not under supervision in the hospital ED. Not every state has defined the scope of practice and function of the EMT outside of prehospital setting.

However, at its 1984 Scientific Assembly, the Emergency Nurses Association (ENA) took the position that the use of EMTs in the ED is not an acceptable replacement for RNs, who have a wider educational background and can ensure unfragmented, quality care to emergency patients, and that EMTs should therefore not be hired in the ED. There is continued debate nationally over the use of EMT paramedics in the ED to perform nursing functions. If EMT paramedics are used in the ED, their tasks must be defined within their scope of practice, and they must work under the supervision of a nurse or physician.

JCAH's Standard 3.1 for Emergency Services requires that each hospital develop a well-defined plan for emergency care, including both internal and

Exhibit 1–1 Maryland Institute for Emergency Medical Services System
(MIEMSS)

OBJECTIVE

The MIEMSS, as mandated by state law, serves as the lead emergency medical services agency for the state of Maryland. In so doing, the MIEMSS provides for all institutions, groups, physicians, nurses, prehospital care providers, and others involved in the provision of emergency medical care throughout Maryland and surrounding states, a facility wherein all can work to solve problems related to new concepts in emergency patient care, teaching, research, and EMS management. This includes the development of innovative techniques in the treatment of patients with life-threatening injuries and illnesses. To develop new modes of therapy, the MIEMSS' research programs focus on a fundamental understanding of severe injury at the organ and cellular levels. Viable education programs, stressing the various specialties of medicine, involve the physician, the nurse, and the paraprofessional. The general public must also be integrated into the system through public education and prevention programs.

An important aspect of the integration of a statewide system of emergency medical care is the MIEMSS' coordination of a prehospital care system of patient management and transportation to the appropriate care facility.

To meet these goals, the MIEMSS has marshalled together the diverse disciplines of medicine, science, and engineering, including clinical medicine, surgery, radiology, nursing, psychology, social work, physiology, pathology, biochemistry, biophysics, mathematics, computer science, transportation, communications, engineering, and administration to study the benefits of a comprehensive EMS system.

Through a cooperative, collective effort of the various institutions, agencies and disciplines, the MIEMSS strives to achieve the following objectives:

1. To continue to function as the catalyst for the further development of the statewide emergency medical services system.
2. To function as an adult trauma, neurotrauma, and critical care facility for the state of Maryland and neighboring states.
3. To coordinate a system of specialty referral centers and trauma centers for the state of Maryland and neighboring states, including a designation and evaluation process.
4. To extend and disseminate the acquired knowledge on the severely injured and ill.
5. To define innovative systems of care of the emergency critically ill.
6. To extend and disseminate knowledge on the injured cell.
7. To standardize resuscitation measures by:
   a. making results more predictable since knowledgeable people are not always available to give treatment.
   b. formulating rules for the care of the acutely ill by restructuring the recently acquired knowledge and making it available to institutions throughout the country for immediate results in the care of the critically ill and injured patients.
   c. demonstrating the usefulness of specialized facilities to care for the critically ill and injured patients.
   d. establishing comprehensive paraprofessional training programs and prehospital treatment protocols that can be implemented through multidisciplinary levels of prehospital education.

Exhibit 1–1 continued

8. To develop new modes of therapy.
9. To provide clinical trials of therapy under standard conditions.
10. To continue to expand on the concept that rehabilitation begins at the time of injury and to further improve rehabilitation since EMS should be considered the medium for propagating a total patient care program.
11. To develop a statewide rehabilitation program in conjunction with the University and areawide Trauma Centers. Rehabilitation is recognized as a component of the Echelons of Trauma Care and the MIEMSS will be working toward a statewide network integrating Trauma Centers with rehabilitation centers.
12. To provide educational programs in critical care medicine, critical care nursing, and prehospital emergency care.
13. To identify and develop new specialists within the statewide EMS program to augment the implementation of new programs and to provide technical assistance necessary to the academic and clinical growth within the EMS system.
14. To coordinate with all health care resource agencies statewide, as well as organizations that impact on the levels of EMS services provided within individual health care facilities in the ongoing development of the EMS programs.
15. To provide stimulation and incentives for improved trauma patient care at the Areawide Centers consistent with state and national standards constituting a more comprehensive delivery of emergency medical services regardless of where the injury or illness occurs.
16. To continue to expand on the concept that medical emergencies know no boundaries, therefore, emphasizing the necessity of maintaining and coordinating policies, establishing agreements, and exchanging data with other states, and to assist in the development of a more effective, comprehensive, statewide, and interstate Emergency Medical Services System that will provide for the more consistent levels of patient care.
17. To utilize state-of-the-art techniques in data processing and analysis to continually evaluate the effectiveness of the EMS system.

Source: Reprinted with permission from "Echelons of Trauma Care," Maryland Institute for Emergency Medical Services System, pp. 3–5, May 1983.

external disasters, based on community need and the capability of the hospital. A communication system, such as radio-telephone or other means that permit instant contact with law enforcement agencies, rescue squads, and other emergency services within the community, is required to provide advance information concerning critically ill or injured patients.

The Departments of Health in most states have provisions in their regulations for emergency services that specify that every hospital, regardless of the scope of services offered, must initiate lifesaving measures and emergency care before transfer of the patient if so required. Examination and/or treatment should be prompt to all patients who come or are brought to the hospital in need of emergency care, regardless of their ability to pay.

The original purpose and function of hospital emergency rooms was to treat life- or limb-threatening illness or injury. However, during the past 25 years, increasing numbers of patients have utilized the ED for nonemergent care. They do so because they lack a primary care physician and because of their definition of an emergency, which is what they consider as the need or desire for immediate physician attention. The convenience of the ED's location in the community and its hours of operation are additional reasons for the increasing nonemergent use of the emergency facility (Tables 1–2 and 1–3).

The ED also serves a secondary health care role, treating patients who require more extensive examination or treatment than was able to be provided by the primary physician or in a clinic setting. For example, a patient goes to the family doctor for abdominal pain and is referred to the ED for further evaluation and possible surgery for acute appendicitis.

EDs also render tertiary care when it is required by the critically ill or injured patients.

Because of the different roles played by the ED, conflict with the patients or their family sometimes occurs. The patients are not always aware or concerned with the different roles and priorities of the hospital and ED and may expect immediate attention no matter what their illness or injury may be. Often, a patient with a cold or sore throat for several days complains because a patient with chest pain is treated first. It is our responsibility as health care providers to educate the public about ED usage, while dealing with them in these situations appropriately and courteously. A patient information sheet can be given to all patients and visitors in the ED to explain its system (Exhibit 1–2). In the competitive times of the 1980s, it is even more essential that the patients who come to the hospital are treated as valued consumers. This concept is discussed later in the book.

Health Education Programs for the Community

Education of the public by the ED staff benefits the community and can be a rewarding experience for the nurses. Programs can be developed to teach first aid, cardiopulmonary resuscitation (CPR), practical information relating to prevention and immediate care for medical emergencies, and the role of the ED. Topics can be discussed in a single session or can be combined in a workshop. These programs can be held at the hospital or at community organization meetings.

Table 1–2 Emergency Department Visits in the United States

Year	Number of Visits	Number of Reporting Hospitals
1984	78,492,455	6,872
1983	77,522,259	6,888
1982	81,147,512	6,975

Source: Hospital Statistics, American Hospital Association, © 1983, 1984, 1985.

Table 1–3 Reasons for Utilization of the Emergency Department*

Characteristics of Patients	Number of Visits (millions)	Patients with Life-Threatening Conditions	Patients without Life-Threatening Conditions	Other Care Not Available	Reasons for Utilizing ED Best Place for that Condition	Reasons for Utilizing ED Used for Most Medical Care	Other
Total	31.9	13.5	85.5	37.0	27.6	4.3	16.6
Age							
Under 17	9.9	10.0	88.8	44.3	26.4	3.7	14.4
17–44	14.2	10.3	89.1	37.3	28.3	5.1	18.3
45 and older	7.9	23.6	74.6	27.2	28.1	3.3	16.0
Sex							
Male	16.0	12.6	86.1	35.4	30.0	3.7	17.0
Female	16.0	14.4	84.7	38.6	25.2	4.8	16.1
Race							
White	25.9	12.9	86.4	37.9	28.4	3.6	16.5
Black	6.0	16.3	81.2	33.1	24.4	7.0	16.7
All other	4.8	16.5	80.8	33.5	33.7	6.5	17.1
Family income							
Less than $10,000	9.1	17.3	81.5	32.4	26.9	6.9	15.3
$10,000–24,999	13.6	12.5	86.1	37.9	29.0	2.9	16.3
$25,000 or more	5.4	10.2	89.1	41.3	27.0	3.1	17.6
Unknown	3.8	12.6	87.0	38.5	25.3	4.4	18.8

*One-time study conducted January–June, 1980. Numbers are percentages unless otherwise noted.

Source: National Center for Health Statistics, preliminary report No. 2, DHHS Pub. No. (PHS) 83-20000 Public Health Service, Washington, D.C., U.S. Government Printing Office, Feb. 1983.

Exhibit 1-2 Emergency Department Patient Information

Welcome to the Emergency Department of _____Hospital. We are located on the first floor of the main building. The Emergency Department is open and staffed 24 hours a day, 7 days a week for the immediate treatment of illnesses and injuries that threaten a person's health or life. Our staff includes physicians qualified in emergency medicine, general medicine, and surgery. Specialists in all fields are available for consultation when needed. The staff also includes nurses experienced and certified in emergency nursing and advanced life support.

TRIAGE

When you arrive at the Emergency Department, a professional nurse will check your temperature, pulse, and blood pressure. You will be interviewed about your present illness or injury, allergies, and current medications. If necessary, the nurse may ask you for urine or blood samples to send to the laboratory, which will speed up your care. Minor treatments, such as ice packs, splints or bandages, may be applied at this time. The triage nurse will evaluate the severity of your condition. If your condition is more severe than that of others waiting, the triage nurse will bring you directly into a treatment room.

REGISTRATION

You will then be seen by a registration clerk, who will ask for additional information, such as your address and medical insurance. Once you have been a patient at this hospital, most of your registration information is already in our computer. Minimal information will be needed if you have been a patient here in the past. The registration clerk will then ask you to sign your name to the Emergency Department record, giving permission for emergency care. If surgery or other special procedures are needed to treat you, you will be asked to sign an additional permission slip later on.

You will then be asked to have a seat in the waiting room if your condition is not of a life-threatening nature. Those patients with serious illnesses and/or injuries will be taken into the treatment area immediately.

Patients are treated according to how ill or injured they are in comparison to other patients waiting to be treated. We do not treat patients in the order in which they came to the emergency department. Please be patient with us. Waiting time is difficult for everyone, but if your problem is less severe, a nurse will call you in for treatment as soon as a treatment room becomes available. You will be seen by a physician as quickly as possible. The triage nurse is available to answer any questions that you may have.

TREATMENT AREA

When you are called in to a treatment room, friends and relatives will be asked to wait in the waiting room. The nurse assigned to your care will keep them informed of your progress.

Once inside the treatment area, you will receive a wrist identification bracelet and be asked to change into a hospital gown. The nurse will retake your pulse and blood pressure. The physician will be with you as soon as one is available. After your examination, additional tests may be needed.

We have 18 treatment rooms; some of them are very specialized for applying casts, suturing, or doing gynecologic exams. We have separate treatment areas for cardiac and for shock/trauma

Exhibit 1–2 continued

patients. This allows for immediate care of life-threatening emergencies. X-ray facilities are located in the Emergency Department.

We ask all patients to wait for results of tests so that you can receive appropriate treatment before you leave the Emergency Department. It generally takes about 1 hour to receive all of the test results. We cannot give test results by phone to patients.

ADMISSION/DISCHARGE

If the physician determines that you need to be admitted into the hospital, you will receive emergency care and then you will be transferred to an inpatient unit. Please send all valuables home with your family.

If you are discharged, you will receive written discharge instructions and possibly prescriptions for medicine. You will be referred to your private doctor or to one of our clinics for follow-up care. If you require the services of Social Services or Home Care, we will refer you to those departments.

Thank you for coming to _____Hospital for your care.

One of my most rewarding experiences was teaching accident prevention and first aid to students at an elementary school. Two weeks after my presentation, I invited the children to tour the ED. The tour was both exciting and educational for the students. It also helped reduce their fears about coming to the ED in the future as a patient. The children were given first aid handouts that they shared with their parents, which indirectly educated the parents.

Educational programs for the community also help improve relationships between the community and the hospital, as well as giving program participants practical and needed health care information. The nurses receive satisfaction both from the teaching role and the recognition and compliments that they receive from those who attend the programs. The hospital should also recognize the staff who develop and present the educational programs for the community.

RELATIONSHIP TO OTHER DEPARTMENTS

Standard 3 of the *JCAH Accreditation Manual* requires integration of the Emergency Department/services with other hospital departments and units. EDs must rely on the services of various other departments for the comprehensive care of the ED patient. These departments may include:

- laboratory services for performing analyses of blood, urine, and other body fluids; arterial blood gas determination; microbiologic and toxicologic studies; and blood storage facilities
- radiology for routine diagnostic studies, angiography, sonography, and nuclear studies

- operating room with prompt access for emergency surgery
- anesthesiology
- pathology
- medical staff and residents
- nuclear medicine
- medical records
- pharmacy
- housekeeping
- admissions
- social services
- nursing services
- security

Whether emergency nursing reports to nursing services or directly to administration, open lines of communication must exist between emergency nurses and other hospital nursing staff. There is constant contact with nurses of the other nursing units because many ED patients are admitted and transferred to in-house beds. Both written and verbal communications between the ED staff and nurses of other units are necessary for continuity of patient care.

The ED is the only nursing care area other than the outpatient department that has a ''one-way door'' within the hospital. Patients are transferred from the ED to other units, but it does not receive patients from in-house areas. Consequently, nurses from the inpatient units frequently view the ED and ED nurses as causing them extra work or stress by transferring additional patients when they are already short staffed or busy with existing patients on a particular unit. It is essential that the ED nursing staff members communicate appropriately with the nurses of receiving units while understanding their needs and current situation. Good communication can be achieved by using a friendly tone of voice and giving all information that is necessary for continuation of nursing care. Though the ED is an area of high stress, the nurses on the inpatient units also experience stress for different reasons, and this fact must be recognized by the ED staff.

You and the staff should be actively involved with hospital committees and special projects in order to maintain an awareness of the overall activity of nursing and other hospital departments. The input and recognition of your staff members are as important as that of any other hospital employee. Collaboration with staff members from other units helps improve interpersonal relationships. Frequently, you set the tone for the rest of the ED staff. When you take an interest and relate well with nurse managers of other areas, the staff will generally follow your example.

A few years ago, the ED staff and the ICU staff at the hospital where I work had poor interpersonal relationships. Actually they hated each other! If they found themselves at the same party, they would stay in their respective corners. In addition to hating the ICU staff, the CCU and the ED staff only tolerated each other. On rare occasions, staff was "pulled" from one of the three units to the other. The nurse who had to work on the new unit was angry and upset, knowing she would receive little to no assistance or communication from the other staff. In addition, when the ED needed to transfer patients to the ICU or CCU, the unit nurses never rushed to accept the patient. In fact, transfers were delayed. In the end, the patients suffered from the poor relationships among the nursing staff. It became obvious that interpersonal relationships among the three areas had to improve for the patients' sake.

The two nurse managers of the ICU and CCU and I grew to know each other better by meeting for lunch, discussing problems, and asking each other for advice and ideas. We visited each others' units in view of the staff, and on occasion, helped out on the others' units during extremely busy times. The ED staff became more comfortable with the other nurse managers and soon began to be more comfortable with the staff members of the other two units. Our assistant nurse managers worked on special projects together and became a peer support group. Soon, the staff was actually offering to help the staff of the other units in special situations, without having to be pulled by nursing management. Such special situations occurred when the ED received multiple trauma victims, when there were extreme shortages in staffing, and when staff members of one of the units wanted to attend a special educational program, which would later be reciprocated by the other units. Patient transfers became more timely, with an effort to relieve extremely busy activity in the ED.

The most rewarding result from the effort to improve relationships unfortunately occurred during a tragic situation. An ICU nurse was admitted through the ED, transferred to ICU with a terminal illness, and died while a patient in ICU. The personnel of the ED and CCU pulled together and staffed the ICU so that the ICU staff could grieve, attend the funeral, and participate in a hospital memorial service. This was done on the initiative of the staff nurses, with no direction from the nurse managers.

Additionally, we initiated nursing grand rounds between the ICU, CCU, post-anesthesia recovery (PAR), stepdown unit, and the ED. The nursing staff of each unit participated and attended. The patient chosen for discussion was one who was admitted through the ED and spent time in ICU, recovery room, CCU, and the step-down unit. Each unit shared in the care of the selected patient. Staff nurses presented their part of the patient's care while the patient was in their particular unit. Sharing knowledge and participating and working together further improved interpersonal relationships between the ED staff and the staff of the other critical care units.

Collaboration with physicians of all services is also important for appropriate and quality care of patients. The goal of all departments and health care professionals is the same: restoration of health and quality of life for patients. No person is an island. Neither is the ED. Communication, coordination, and collaboration are needed to meet the complex needs of patients.

TEAMWORK IN THE EMERGENCY DEPARTMENT

To provide effective and appropriate care to the patient population that the ED serves, all members of the ED staff must work together as a team to facilitate the smooth running of a high-stress and crisis area. Several disciplines comprise the team, with each being important in the overall functioning of the ED. The team may consist of physicians, RNs, LPNs, EMTs, aides, medical clerks, secretaries, registrars, and technicians.

At least 8 hours of each day, the ED staff members "live" with their ED family. They may spend more waking hours at the ED than with their families at home. The essentials of working together are the same as living together. For effective relationships, work output, and quality, the basic essentials of respect, caring, trust, sharing, support, and communication must be present.

The members of the team need to be sensitive and understanding of each other. They must recognize each individual's contribution and value. In an area of high stress, poor interactions between the staff magnify the level of stress and reflect negatively on the delivery of patient care.

Education of the staff may be necessary to achieve and maintain effective teamwork. Multidisciplinary group sessions may be helpful to instill a feeling of togetherness. Showing appreciation and recognizing each other's contributions, along with group effort on problem solving and decision making, can help build the team. Sharing of knowledge and learning together also have positive effects.

To increase awareness of each other's responsibilities and level of stress, it can be helpful to have the members of the nursing staff perform the job functions of other team members. A nurse who has to perform as clerk or registrar in a busy ED may find that he or she is not able to deal with the constant telephone calls, requests from staff and patients, and repetitive tasks. Similarly the LPN may learn and better understand the stress level of the charge nurse if placed in that role for a short period (under supervision).

The responsibility for making the department work effectively should be shared by each member of the staff. Each individual has something to offer that can enhance and ensure good patient care. Once the team concept has developed among the staff, it is easier to have positive interactions with personnel of other departments and ultimately with patients and their families.

REFERENCES

Allerman, Geraldine; McCay, Joanne; Novotny-Dinsdale, Valerie. "Use of Prehospital Care Providers in Emergency Departments—A National Survey." *Journal of Emergency Nursing (JEN)* 11(1):35–39, 1985.

American College of Emergency Physicians. "Emergency Care Guidelines" (Position paper). *Ann Emerg Med* 11:202–226, 1982.

Andreoli, Kathleen, and Musser, Leigh Anne. "Challenges Confronting the Future of Emergency Nursing." *JEN* 11(1):16–20, 1985.

Bernstein, Theodore, et al. "Patient Flow and Resource Consumption in a Hospital Emergency Department." Baltimore, MD: Department of Health and Human Services, 1984.

Brown, Cynthia. "Toward a Healthier Emergency Care Family." *JEN* 11(4):174–176, 1985.

Cross, Ralph E. "Emergency Departments: Putting the Stress on Structure." *Health Services Manager* 15(4):1–3, 1982.

Joint Commission on Accreditation of Hospitals. *Accreditation Manual for Hospitals.* Chicago, 1986.

"Echelons of Trauma Care." Maryland Institute for Emergency Medical Services System. Baltimore, May 1983.

McCay, Joanne. "Historical Review of Emergency Medical Services, EMT Roles and EMT Utilization in Emergency Departments." *JEN* 11(1):27–31, 1985.

Myerburg, Robert, et al. "Survivors of Prehospital Cardiac Arrest." *JAMA* 247(10):1485–1490, 1982.

Peisert, Margaret. "The Hospital's Role in Emergency Medical Services System. Chicago: American Hospital Publishing Company, pp. 1–36.

Pennsylvania Department of Health. "Pennsylvania Bulletin" 15:4. Harrisburg, 1984.

Westra, Bonnie. "Prehospital Care Providers in the Emergency Department." *JEN* 9(5):241–243, 1983.

U.S. Congress. Highway Safety Act (Public Law 89–564), 1966.

U.S. Congress. Emergency Medical Services Act (Public Law 93–154), 1973.

Appendix 1–A

Emergency Care Guidelines (Revised)*

Although these guidelines are a statement of suggested capability, they are advisory and are not designed to be interpreted as mandatory by legislative, judicial, or regulatory bodies. Revision approved by the Board of Directors of the American College of Emergency Physicians on December 10, 1985, and by the Board of Directors of the Emergency Nurses Association on December 15, 1985. The original Guidelines appeared in the *Journal of Emergency Nursing*, July/August 1982, vol. 8, No. 4.

Emergency health care exists for the individual benefit of the patient or family who perceives a need for emergency care, and for society's benefit in mass casualty incidents. The American public justifiably expects an emergency facility to be staffed by medical, nursing, and ancillary personnel who are trained and experienced in the treatment of emergencies. Each year, approximately 80 million visits are made to emergency facilities by patients who depend on emergency care providers to see them promptly, apply appropriate triage methodologies, provide appropriate medical treatment and nursing care, and link prehospital and emergency facility care with secondary and tertiary care when needed.

The American College of Emergency Physicians and the Emergency Nurses Association have developed the following guidelines to detail the resources necessary to evaluate and treat any patient who presents to an emergency facility with a life- or limb-threatening condition.† The guidelines, which are presented in

*Reprinted from *Journal of Emergency Nursing*, Vol. 12, No. 3, pp. 25A–28A, 30A–31A, with permission of The C.V. Mosby Company, St. Louis, © May/June 1986.

†The guidelines are statements of suggested capabilities necessary for treatment of life- or limb-threatening conditions and do not describe the scope of emergency medicine, which is more completely presented in the "Emergency Medicine Core Content"[1] and in the "Definition of Emergency Medicine."[2]

three sections, are intended to guide emergency physicians, emergency nurses, and facility administrators in planning and measuring their ability to meet objective criteria in preparation for the treatment of critically ill or injured patients.

The first section outlines the responsibilities of emergency care providers and acknowledges the public's expectation that emergency care providers be able to evaluate and stabilize all life- or limb-threatening conditions. Emergency care must be available to all such patients without regard to their ability to pay. Evaluation, management, and treatment of the patient with a life- or limb-threatening condition must be appropriate and timely. The unscheduled, episodic nature of patient emergencies mandates the constant availability of emergency care.

The second section designates components that should exist within the physical bounds of the emergency facility, specifically those elements required to help the patient from the time he enters the care of the emergency physician until care is transferred to another physician or the patient is discharged. The section outlines current guidelines for administration, staffing, facility design, equipment, and drugs.

The third section describes the relationships between the emergency care facility and those entities with which it must interact. Emergency care often begins in the prehospital setting with the provision of care by emergency medical technicians, continues in the emergency facility, and concludes with appropriate follow-up care by other health professionals. The emergency physician and emergency nurse are central figures in this continuum of patient care, for they are responsible for facilitating relationships that ensure continuity of care.

In summary, these guidelines have been developed to assist a facility's planners in offering emergency care that meets the public's right to receive prompt and appropriate health care for life- or limb-threatening conditions. The American College of Emergency Physicians and the Emergency Nurses Association believe the patient has the right to have these guidelines met or exceeded.

I. PROFESSIONAL RESPONSIBILITIES AND PUBLIC EXPECTATIONS

Emergency care, by definition, includes the immediate evaluation of and intervention in illnesses or injuries that are life- or limb-threatening. The critical nature of these services creates both public expectations and professional responsibilities on the part of emergency care providers. This section outlines conditions necessary to meet responsibilities accruing from public and professional expectations.

A. Facilities using the term "emergency," "emergent," or "emergi-" or terms with similar connotations should have the physical design, equipment, and personnel to evaluate and stabilize patients with life- or limb-threatening conditions.

B. Physicians and nurses providing emergency care should have, at a minimum, the knowledge and skills necessary to provide appropriate initial evaluation, management, and treatment to patients who present to the facility with life- or limb-threatening conditions.

C. Timely emergency care should be available continuously, 24 hours a day, seven days a week. This does not require that every emergency facility operate continuously but, rather, that 24-hour access to emergency care be available in each community.

D. Emergency care should be provided to all patients without regard to their ability to pay, but with the understanding that they are financially responsible for the charges incurred in the course of their care.

E. Emergency care facilities should have an active public education program that details the capabilities of the facility, its appropriate use, and hours of operation, including a list of facilities open 24 hours a day if the facility is not open on such a basis.

II. PRINCIPLES OF EMERGENCY CARE

This section of the guidelines outlines those elements of emergency care, including facility administration, staffing, design, and materials, that are essential to the treatment of life- or limb-threatening conditions.

A. Administration

1. The emergency facility should be organized and directed to meet the health care needs of its patient population.

2. The medical director of an emergency facility, in collaboration with the director of emergency nursing with appropriate integration of ancillary services, should assure that quality, safety, and appropriateness of emergency care are continually evaluated.

3. All emergency care personnel should maintain their skills and knowledge in treating life- or limb-threatening illnesses and injuries.

4. The duties and responsibilities of medical and nursing personnel within the emergency service area should be defined in writing by the medical director and director of emergency nursing.

5. Triage of those seeking care should be determined by specially trained personnel using guidelines established by the medical director of emergency services, in collaboration with the director of emergency nursing.

6. A physician is ultimately responsible for the evaluation, diagnosis, and recommended treatment of the emergency patient.

7. The medical and nursing care response must be timely for all patients with life- or limb-threatening conditions.

8. A formal facility orientation program should be required for all new staff members who provide patient care.

9. Emergency facility operations should be guided by written policies and procedures.

10. The emergency facility should maintain a control register identifying all those seeking emergency care.

11. A medical record on every patient receiving care in an emergency facility should be established and permanently maintained.

B. Staffing

1. The emergency facility should be staffed by appropriately educated and experienced emergency care professionals, including a physician, during all hours of operation.

2. The patient care provided in the emergency facility shall be directed by a physician. The medical director of emergency services should:

a. Possess training or experience in emergency medicine sufficient to meet the qualifications for taking the American Board of Emergency Medicine certification examination or its equivalent††; and

b. Possess competence in management and administration of the clinical services in an emergency facility; and

c. Ensure that the staff is adequately qualified and educated.

3. All staff physicians who practice in an emergency facility should possess training and experience in emergency medicine sufficient to evaluate and initially manage and treat all patients with life- or limb-threatening conditions.

4. The nursing care provided in the emergency facility should be directed by a registered nurse. The director of emergency nursing or nursing supervisor should:

a. Possess education or experience in emergency nursing sufficient to meet the qualifications for taking the Certified Emergency Nursing examination; and

b. Possess competence in management and administration of the clinical services in an emergency facility, and

c. Ensure that the nursing and ancillary staff are adequately qualified and educated.

---

†† "The American College of Emergency Physicians believes that certification of knowledge and skill in emergency medicine can result only from successful completion of examinations administered by a recognized board in emergency medicine. The successful completion of any course or series of courses may serve as evidence of knowledge and skill of a certain sub-area within emergency medicine. The completion of such, however, does not serve as an acceptable substitute for certification of knowledge and skills required to practice the specialty of emergency medicine."[3]

5. All staff nurses should:

    a. Possess adequate previous emergency department or critical care experience, or have completed an emergency care education program; and

    b. Possess competence in advanced life support; and

    c. Possess the knowledge and skills necessary to evaluate, manage, and educate patients in accordance with the *Standards of Emergency Nursing Practice*.[4]

C. Equipment and Supplies

1. Equipment and supplies should be of high quality and should be suitable for all patients anticipated by an emergency facility.

2. All reusable direct patient care medical equipment should have documentation of a preventive maintenance schedule specifically designed to ensure patient safety.

3. Necessary equipment and supplies should be immediately available in the facility during the hours of operation (Table 1).

D. Pharmacologic/Therapeutic Drugs and Agents

Necessary drugs and agents should be readily available in the facility during the hours of operation (Table 2).

E. Facility

1. The emergency facility should be designed to enable the provision of safe and effective care with adequate and convenient access to treatment areas for both ambulatory and nonambulatory patients.

2. The emergency facility should be designed to protect, to the maximum extent possible consonant with medical necessity, the right of the patient to visual and auditory privacy.

3. Radiological services should be immediately available during the hours of operation to provide diagnostic imaging of patients with life- or limb-threatening conditions.

4. Laboratory services should be immediately available during the hours of operation to provide appropriate diagnostic tests for patients with life- or limb-threatening conditions.

5. Appropriate signs that are consistent with the applicable laws should indicate the direction of the emergency facility from major thoroughfares and whether or not the facility is designated as a specialized emergency care center.

Table 1 1985 Suggested List of Equipment for Emergency Facilities

---

The specific equipment to be available in an emergency facility should be determined jointly by the medical director and the director of emergency nursing, in consultation with ancillary services.

General examination room
Oxygen and administration tubing and devices
Suction device with catheters and tubing
Airways in infant, pediatric, and adult sizes
Adequate patient lighting

Resuscitation room
Oxygen with administration tubing and devices
Suction device with catheters and tubing
Adequate patient lighting
Monitor defibrillator with electrode patches,
  patient cable, defibrillation pads or gel, and
  adult and pediatric paddles
Two-way communication with nursing station
12-lead EKG machine
Portable x-ray equipment available within the
  emergency facility
Pharmacological agents (Table 2)
Cardiac board
Blood pump
Blood warmer
Blood tubing
Pediatric and adult ventilation devices
IV administration sets
IV catheters, scalp veins in infant, pediatric,
  and adult sizes
Central line IV devices for fluid administration
  and pressure monitoring in infant, pediatric,
  and adult sizes
Airways in infants, pediatric, and adult sizes
Closed chest tube drainage system
Endotracheal tubes—assorted cuffed and
  uncuffed sizes
Laryngoscopes—blades in infant, pediatric,
  and adult sizes
Nasogastric suction devices in infant,
  pediatric, and adult sizes
Bladder catheterization and collection
  equipment
Restraints
Pneumatic antishock trousers, pediatric and
  adult
Cervical spine stabilizing equipment
Spine boards

**Special treatment and examination
trays**
Eye examination tray
ENT/epistaxis tray
Suture tray
Cutdown tray/CVP tray
Gastric lavage tray
Slit lamp
Burn tray
Precipitous delivery tray
Gynecological examination tray
Trays (immediately available to
  resuscitation room) containing
  supplies and equipment for:
  Peritoneal lavage
  Cricothyreotomy
  Pericardiocentesis
  Tube thoracostomy
  Thoracotomy
  Pacemaker insertion
Evidence collection equipment

Miscellaneous equipment
Toxicology information
Medical reference library

Table 1 continued
Extremity splinting devices
Intravenous solutions
Transthoracic and transvenous pacemaker
   setups

Note: This list catalogs suggested equipment for the diagnosis and management of patients with potentially life- or limb-threatening illness or injury. Support equipment, such as clipboards, pencils, and bandaging equipment, is not mentioned on this list. Common general examination equipment, such as stethoscopes and blood pressure cuffs, has not been itemized.

ENT = Ear, nose, and throat; CVP = central venous pressure.

III. RESPONSIBILITIES FOR THE CONTINUITY OF PATIENT CARE

Emergency care begins in the prehospital setting, continues in the emergency facility, and concludes when responsibility for the patient is transferred to another physician or the patient is discharged. To ensure effective treatment of emergency patients, this transfer of responsibility must be accomplished in an effective and predictable manner. This section describes the relationships that should exist among facilities and providers for proper continuity of care.

A. Prehospital

1. Prehospital emergency care should be provided consistent with the American College of Emergency Physicians' position paper entitled "Medical Control of Prehospital Emergency Medical Services."[5]

2. Emergency facilities should be a designated part of the emergency medical services (EMS) plan and community disaster plans. The local EMS/disaster coordinating body should determine each emergency facility's role in the local EMS/disaster plans.

3. Patients should be transported to the nearest appropriate emergency facility in accordance with local, regional, or state planning.[6,7]

4. When ambulance services are used to transport patients to an emergency facility, a communication system, such as a two-way radio or other appropriate means, should be available to allow for notice of arrival or advance information concerning critically ill or injured patients.

5. Transport personnel should provide complete written clinical documentation of all prehospital care provided for the patient. A copy of the document should be immediately available upon transfer of care and should be included in the patient's emergency facility permanent record.

Table 2 1985 Suggested List of Pharmacologic Therapeutic Drugs and Agents for Emergency Facilities

---

The specific pharmacologic/therapeutic drugs and agents available in an emergency facility shall be determined by the medical director in collaboration with other appropriate individuals.

Antibiotics, systemic
Cephalosporins
Erythromycin
Gentamicin sulfate
Oxacillin sodium
Penicillins
 Ampicillin
 Benzathine penicillin
 Penicillin G potassium
 Penicillin G procaine
Trimethoprim/
 sulfamethoxazole

Antihistamine drugs
Diphenhydramine
Meclizine

Autonomic drugs
Parasympatholytic
 (cholinergic blocking)
 agents
 Atropine sulfate
Parasympathomimetic
 (cholinergic) agents
 Endrophonium
 chloride
 Neostigmine
 methylsulfate
 Physostigmine
Sympathomimetic
 (adrenergic) agents
 Dobutamine
 Dopamine
 Epinephrine HCl
 Isoproterenol HCl
 Norepinephrine
 bitartrate

**Blood formation and
 coagulation**
Anticoagulants
 Heparin sodium

**Central nervous system
 drugs**
Analgesics and
 antipyretics
 Acetaminophen
 Aspirin
 Codeine
 Meperidine-HCl
 Morphine sulfate
 Nonsteroid anti-
 inflammatory drug
Anticonvulsants
 Diazepam
 Phenobarbital
 Phenytoin
Narcotic antagonists
 Naloxone
Psychotherapeutic
 agents
 Diazepam
 Haloperidol

Diagnostic agents
Blood contents
 Reagents for
 estimating blood
 glucose
Myasthenia gravis
 Edrophonium chloride
 Neostigmine
 methylsulfate
Stool contents
 Stool tests for occult
 blood
Urine contents
 Test tapes for urine
 bilirubin, blood,
 sugar, ketones, pH,
 urobilinogen,
 protein

Gastrointestinal drugs
Adsorbents
 Charcoal, activated
Emetics and anti-emetics
 Ipecac syrup
 Prochlorperazine
Cathartics
 Magnesium salt

**Hormones and synthetic
 substitutes**
Adrenals
 Dexamethasone
 Hydrocortisone
 Methylprednisolone
Insulins and antidiabetic
 agents
 Glucagon HCl
 Insulin, regular
Thyroid
 Levothyroxine sodium

Local anesthetics
Bupivacaine
Lidocaine HCl
Procaine

**Serums, toxoids, and
 vaccines**
Serums
 Antivenin, black widow
 spider bite, equine
 origin (geographic-
 area-specific)
 Antivenin, snake-bite,
 polyvalent, equine
 origin (geographic-
 area-specific)
 Rabies immune
 globulin, human
 Tetanus immune
 globulin

Table 2 continued

Anticoagulant reversing
  agents
  Aqueous vitamin K
  Protamine sulfate

Cardiovascular drugs
  Cardiac drugs
    Bretylium HCl
    Calcium chloride
    Digoxin
    Lidocaine
    Procainamide HCl
    Propranolol
    Sodium bicarbonate
    Verapamil HCl
  Hypotensive agents
    Diazoxide
    Sodium nitroprusside
    Trimethaphan
  Vasodilating agents
    Amyl nitrite
    Nitroglycerin

**Electrolytic, carloric, and
  water balance**
  Diuretics
    Furosemide
    Mannitol
  Hypoglycemic agents
    Dextrose 50% in
      water
  Replacement solutions
    Dextrose 5% in water
    Potassium chloride
    Ringer's injections,
      lactated
    Sodium chloride

**Eye, ear, nose, and
  throat preparations**
  Topical anesthetics
    Cocaine solution
    *Proparacaine
    *Tetracaine
  Topical antibiotics
    Gentamicin
    Polymyxin
      B/neomycin/
      hydrocortisone otic
      solution
    Sulfacetamide

Tetanus immune
  globulin
Toxoids
  Diphtheria and tetanus
    toxoids and pertussis
    vaccine adsorbed
  Tetanus and diphtheria
    toxoids adsorbed,
    adult and pediatric
  Tetanus toxoid
    adsorbed

Spasmolytics
  Parenteral
    Aminophylline
    Terbutaline sulfate
  Inhalation
    Metaproterenol sulfate

Unclassified agents
  Cyanide antidote kit

Vitamins
  Vitamin B complex
  Thiamine HCl

*Either proparacaine or tetracaine.

B. Emergency Facility

  1. Emergency facility personnel should be familiar with medical care protocols used by the prehospital providers in their community.

  2. A physician, registered nurse, or other appropriately trained person should promptly conduct initial patient assessments of all patients with life- or limb-threatening illnesses or injuries who are brought to the facility.

C. Referral

  1. Appropriately qualified physicians who are willing to accept inpatient responsibility for patients should be identified in advance for referral.

2. Appropriately qualified physicians or other health care professionals who are willing to accept outpatient responsibility for all patients referred to their care should be identified in advance.

D. Transfer

1. Emergency facilities should have a written plan for transferring patients, when necessary, by a vehicle that has appropriate life-support capabilities.

2. A patient with a life- or limb-threatening condition should not be transferred from an emergency facility until appropriate evaluation and stabilization procedures are instituted.

3. Arrangements for transfer should include physician-to-physician communication to exchange clinical information and to ascertain that the receiving physician will accept the patient, that the receiving institution has anticipated services, and that the space is available for the transferee.

4. Patients should be transferred from the care of one physician to the care of another physician.

5. Appropriate patient care documents, including laboratory and radiology test results, should be transferred along with the patient.

6. Medical responsibility for the patient during transfer must be established before the transfer commences.

7. Transfer agreements should be entered into with institutions that provide definitive care not available at the transferring facility.[8]

REFERENCES

1. American College of Emergency Physicians: Emergency medicine core content (revised). *Ann Emerg Med* (publication pending).

2. American College of Emergency Physicians: Definition of emergency medicine. *Ann Emerg Med* 10:385–388, 1981.

3. American College of Emergency Physicians: Section on certification, in ACEP Position Summaries 1986, p 9.

4. Emergency Department Nurses Association: *Standards of Emergency Nursing Practice*. St. Louis, 1983, The C.V. Mosby Co.

5. American College of Emergency Physicians: Medical control of prehospital emergency medical services. *Ann Emerg Med* 11:387, 1982.

6. American College of Emergency Physicians: Emergency ambulance transport to medical facilities. *Ann Emerg Med* 12:187, 1983.

7. Committee on Trauma, American College of Surgeons: Hospital and pre-hospital resources for optimal care of the injured patient. *ACS Bulletin* 68:11–18, 1983.

8. American College of Emergency Physicians: Patient transfer guidelines. *Ann Emerg Med* 14:1221–1222, 1985.

The Emergency Department
Nurse Manager

ROLE AND RESPONSIBILITIES

In recent years, the ED nurse manager's role has evolved from serving as a head nurse in a white uniform and being counted as part of nursing care hours for patient care in the ED to the nurse manager of today who has operational, personnel, and financial responsibilities and accountability. The nurse manager may be titled head nurse, supervisor, clinical or nursing coordinator, director, or nurse manager. Whatever the title, the role is that of a manager, and we must view ourselves as a vital part of the hospital management team.

This role is similar to the role of other managers in any business organization and requires similar functions and skills. Yet, we sometimes have difficulty separating our managerial role from the responsibilities of direct patient care. This may result from lack of confidence in the management role, inexperience in the role, or a feeling of guilt about relinquishing the responsibility of hands-on patient care. Yet, if we do not separate the worker and management functions and responsibilities, the staff and patient care will ultimately suffer. Trying to fulfill two roles simultaneously leads to frustration as neither role can be carried out effectively. If we try to perform the role of nursing staff and then catch up with management responsibilities, the result will be extended hours of work on a daily basis, which will quickly lead to burnout.

The ED can be most challenging and exciting for a nurse manager because of its diverse activities and interactions. However, we need to remain aware of the current and changing health care environment that is influenced by prospective payment systems (PPSs), PPOs and HMOs. Greater emphasis is now being placed on home care, ambulatory care, emergency care, competition, and marketing. Cost containment reimbursement regulations for inpatient services are resulting in an increase in census and acuity of patients in the ED and increased hospital admissions through the ED. As the ED assumes increased importance for the future of the hospital, our role becomes even more vital.

To understand the role of a manager, you must understand management, which can be defined as the process of getting things done effectively and efficiently through people and other resources. It is planning what should be done to accomplish the mission and goals of the hospital and department. Management effectiveness depends upon having basic management skills and competence in management functions. Clinical expertise and leadership ability do not ensure that a nurse can function as a manager. Management skills are learned and developed. Many believe that a manager can manage in any setting. However, because of the special nature of the organization, function, and relationships of ED, ED clinical knowledge and experience will enhance your performance as nurse managers.

The role of the ED nurse manager is very complex; we must wear many hats for each distinct aspect of our role. We must serve as a:

- authority figure
- planner: goal setting, decision making, problem solving, evaluating systems and outcomes
- supervisor: directing and guiding staff work, scheduling, disciplining and rewarding
- leader: directing others toward productivity and achievement, influencing the thoughts and actions of others
- counselor: listening, advising, assisting the staff with identification of problems and decision making processes; following up and reinforcing positive behavior; referring to appropriate resources
- coordinator: interacting with physicians, other nurses, other hospital departments, and EMSS; coordinating patient care activities and flow
- entrepreneur: creating and developing new ideas for increasing census and revenues
- liaison: interacting with administration, the ED medical director, EMSS, other hospital departments, and the community for the purpose of planning and problem solving for the ED
- mentor: developing the assistant nurse manager's and staff's ability to assume a management role
- educator: determining the learning needs of staff and patients; teaching staff, patients, paraprofessionals, students, and members of the community
- resource: sharing and teaching specific knowledge and skills in which we have expertise

- consultant: solving problems, determining and suggesting alternatives for decision making, sharing special information or knowledge that we possess and is needed or wanted by others
- controller: ensuring delivery of quality care, safety, and cost efficiency
- advocate: supporting, speaking for, or acting on behalf of the administration, staff, and patients
- researcher: searching for and evaluating new ideas and means to improve function, effectiveness, and efficiency
- student: continuing to learn and develop knowledge and skills through educational programs and colleagues' knowledge and experience

How to fulfill these roles is discussed throughout the remainder of this book. Although some EDs have available personnel resources to share part of the role responsibilities, it is we as ED nurse managers who have the ultimate responsibility and accountability for nursing care. Exhibit 2–1 provides a sample job description for the ED nurse manager.

MANAGEMENT FUNCTIONS

Peter Drucker describes the functions of management as "planning, organizing, integrating, and measuring."[1] These functions require the skills of organization and priority setting, which are learned through the educational process and through experience. They form the core of our role. Sophisticated and specialized skills are required to adapt to the problems, needs, and changes in the fast-paced emergency services atmosphere. Figure 2–1 illustrates the management functions and required skills of the nurse manager.

Planning

Planning is an ongoing activity that is the most vital function of the ED nurse manager. You have the knowledge and expertise that are needed for planning and for determining the best course of action for emergency nursing and, in collaboration with the medical director, for the overall functioning of the ED. If the planning is left to others, decisions will be made by those who do not have the same level of knowledge or background that you possess. In addition, there is little to compel upper-level managers to respond to issues relating to emergency nursing. Day-to-day crisis management, rather than effective planning, then results. If major issues are not raised by the people closest to the ED, the issues may be avoided or unrecognized. Planning for major issues related to the ED

Exhibit 2–1 Emergency Department Nurse Manager Job Description

---

Primary Function

Assesses, plans, organizes, directs, and evaluates ED activities, including patient care, human resource, and operational management

Examples of Work

A. *Patient Care Management*
   1. Defines and establishes standards, policies, and procedures for ED patient care; collaborates with the medical director to integrate medical and nursing management of the emergency care patient
   2. Provides direction to educational programs and efforts for patients, their families, and the community
   3. Defines and maintains emergency nursing standards of care
   4. Interprets, communicates, and enforces hospital and ED policies and procedures
   5. Investigates methods of patient care and ED systems and organization; evaluates and revises current practices as indicated
   6. Monitors and evaluates patient care; performs ongoing quality assurance activities with written documentation; collaborates with the ED medical director for overall ED quality assurance
   7. Assumes the role of patient advocate according to the guidelines in the Patient Bill of Rights
   8. Provides for and promotes humanistic patient care
   9. Ensures appropriateness of patient care assignments based on the nursing needs of the patient and scope of practice of different levels of staff
   10. Serves as a resource person
   11. Utilizes hospital and community resources and agencies effectively
   12. Maintains an open line of communication with patients and their significant others

B. *Human Resource Management*
   1. Defines and communicates job descriptions for emergency nursing personnel
   2. Communicates expectations of each employee
   3. Interviews and selects prospective employees
   4. Provides direction for the development of all ED nursing personnel
   5. Monitors and evaluates performance of staff; regularly provides feedback to all ED nursing personnel and conducts performance appraisals
   6. Recommends and implements employee counseling and discipline
   7. Plans for, evaluates, and maintains 24-hour nurse staffing for the ED with staffing patterns that meet usual requirements of patient activity
   8. Fosters professional growth and development of the nursing staff and provides for educational efforts specific to emergency nursing and emergency patient care
   9. Ensures certification in basic and advanced life support for emergency nurses; promotes certification for emergency nurses through the ENA
   10. Encourages staff participation and membership in the ENA and other professional organizations
   11. Collaborates with and develops the skills of the assistant nurse manager in all aspects of ED nursing and departmental activities
   12. Encourages and provides for ED staff participation on nursing service committees

Exhibit 1–2 continued

13. Collaborates with the staff development instructor/clinical specialist to provide direction and support for the education of staff
14. Actively and continually stimulates and motivates staff to perform at optimal and cost-effective levels
15. Serves as a resource for clinical instructors of nursing students
16. Plans and leads regular staff meetings
17. Promotes open communication between all ED personnel, and other units and departments

C. *Operational Management*
1. Maintains a safe, clean, comfortable, healthy environment for patients, visitors, and staff
2. Defines and communicates goals and objectives
3. Develops and controls a fiscal budget; monitors operating expenses, including patient care, personnel, and capital expenses; justifies variances
4. Evaluates and sets standards for the quality and cost of equipment and supplies and monitors their utilization
5. Ensures programs for orientation and procedures for fire drills, evacuation procedures, internal/external disaster plan and procedures, and transfers
6. Maintains awareness of evolving trends in emergency services and plans for changes accordingly
7. Integrates with other department managers; maintains ongoing relationships and lines of communication with other managers, police, fire-rescue, prehospital care providers, and community agencies
8. Acts as a liaison between other departments, physicians, and staff

D. *Professional Growth and Development*
1. Participates actively in nursing and hospital committees
2. Attends educational and professional meetings and workshops to continue own education and enhance personal knowledge, skills, and growth
3. Serves as an educational resource to others
4. Initiates, supports, and/or participates in research programs relating to emergency care, prevention of illness and injury, and health maintenance
5. Participates in and supports professional organizations, such as the ENA national and local chapters
6. Shares information relating to emergency nursing through lectures, publications, and informal and formal communication with other emergency nurses

should be a collaborative process with the ED medical director. However, still many EDs do not have a physician with administrative responsibilities. It is vital, then, that you initiate planning for the ED and participate in the planning process.

Basic management skills are necessary for effective planning. "These skills include goal setting, decision making, and interpersonal relationships."[2]

The first step in planning—goal setting—is achieved by identifying problems and alternative solutions of them. First, make a list of issues that directly relate to the mission and goals of the hospital, department, staff, and patients. Table 2–1 provides an example of such a list. Once issues are identified, then consider

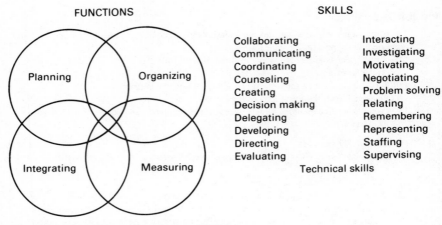

FUNCTIONS

SKILLS

Collaborating   Interacting
Communicating   Investigating
Coordinating   Motivating
Counseling   Negotiating
Creating   Problem solving
Decision making   Relating
Delegating   Remembering
Developing   Representing
Directing   Staffing
Evaluating   Supervising
Technical skills

Figure 2–1 Management Functions and Skills

alternative solutions. Before a plan is selected and implemented, carefully evaluate each alternative for its strengths, weaknesses, adaptability, and potential effect.

Planning may be either tactical or strategic. Tactical planning is short term and concerned with such details as determining assignments and meal breaks for the day. Strategic planning involves longer-term issues and broader goals. Examples of the different types of planning are presented in Table 2–2.

Tactical Planning

An example of tactical planning would be determining ways to increase staff productivity. There are several alternative ways of accomplishing that goal. At certain times of the day productivity is low due to low patient census. In most EDs this down time occurs early in the morning. It is obvious that the entire day shift staff is not needed then if the activity level does not increase until later in the morning. A plan could be developed to increase productivity of the staff during the down time by decreasing the number of day shift staff who arrive at 7:00 or 8:00 A.M. and/or by staggering the shift hours to a later starting time. Another possibility would be to assign the day shift staff to indirect patient care responsibilities during low activity time. These responsibilities could include the checking of equipment, stocking of treatment rooms, quality assurance activities, and the like.

In planning ways to increase staff productivity, the first alternative that I chose and implemented was the use of staggered shifts. Activity did not increase until approximately 9:00 A.M., reached and maintained a peak from 12:00 noon to 8:00 P.M., and slowly decreased until after 3:00 A.M., at which time it greatly

Table 2–1 Planning Issues in the Emergency Department

Issue	Cause	Plan
Insufficient staffing of ED nurses	Increased census Increased patient acuity Increase in nurse transports Delays in transfer of admitted patients at change of shift and mealtimes Need to improve quality of care Deficient meal coverage Delays in bed assignment by admission office for admitted patients	ED statistics Critical care patient statistics, patient classification system Statistics Meeting with nursing administration Staff utilization, productivity, assignments, staffing patterns, standards of care Staffing patterns Meeting with admissions director
Delay in patient disposition	*Labs* Delay in delivery of specimens to labs Delay of lab reporting Inability of lab to do certain studies at night Low priority for ED stats	Utilization of nursing aide, messenger service, volunteers Meet with director and administrator of labs, pregnancy testing in the ED
	Radiology Unavailability of technicians Delays in interpretation Delays in reporting Unavailability of radiologist after 7 P.M. Inaccuracy of reports, calling patients back	Meet with director and administrator of radiology
	Admissions office Lack of awareness of available beds Elective admissions priority over ED patients Direct admissions through the ED Bed allocation system	Meet with admissions
	Residents Workups in ED State orders for resident convenience Inappropriate use of ED due to inadequate support services on inpatient units	Meet with ED medical director

Table 2–1 continued

Issue	Cause	Plan
	Delays in decision making Lack of experience, junior residents	
	Private physicians Usage of the ED as a quick way into the hospital for patients requiring admission Convenience	Meet with ED medical director
Need to improve human relation skills between staff and patients/relatives	Decreased staff sensitivity Staff stress Patient stress Environment Burnout of senior staff Staff needs Patient/family needs and expectations	Sensitivity groups Utilization of professional resources Educational programs for staff Improvement of system problems Measures to decrease stress levels Changes/improvement of environment to meet patient/ consumer needs Expectations Patient questionnaire
Inadequate ED nursing documen- tation	Insufficient space on ED record Lack of standards Educational needs	Development of separate nursing form specific to the ED; development of new ED record Development of standards and guidelines Inservice programs on documentation
Lack of effective prioritization of patients to be seen	Lack of or inadequate initial assessment by a professional	Development and implementation of a triage program

diminished. On paper, the plan seemed to be perfect, with overlapping shifts, decreased number of staff arriving early in the morning, and additional staff arriving in the evening hours. It provided for less staff on duty during hours of lower activity, which in turn, increased the number of staff during the busier hours. The plan was discussed with the staff members so that they all would understand its purpose.

Table 2–2 Tactical and Strategic Planning

Tactical Planning	*Strategic Planning*
Scheduling	Development of a triage program
Standards of care	Marketing
Productivity	Changes in FTEs
Utilization of staff	Trauma program
Cost containment	Renovation or design of a new ED facility
Ordering of supplies	Computerized registration
Assignments	Budget

However, after evaluating the effect upon the staff and upon patient care, we realized that this change created stress and confusion. The staff was unhappy about the constantly changing working hours, and because none of them volunteered to work the unconventional shifts permanently, confusion was created by staff members reporting on and off duty at all hours of the day, evening and night. A total of eight different shifts had actually been created, with overlapping of each shift.

The disadvantages of this plan clearly outweighed its advantages. It increased the stress level of an already hectic and stressful environment. The continuity of patient care was adversely affected and patient-oriented quality primary care was replaced by task-oriented functional care. (This took place in a geographic primary nursing setting.)

The alternative plan that replaced the staggered shifts was a return to three shifts. However, each shift began one hour later than the traditional shift hours, with the addition of a fourth shift from 12:00 noon to 8:30 A.M. This plan provided for fewer staff members on duty early in the morning, coverage for meal breaks, and more staff members in the afternoon and evening hours that had the most activity. The evening shift remained longer into the night, which helped relieve the workload of the reduced number of nurses on the night shift. Because the noon shift became a permanent shift, nurses eventually volunteered to work it on a permanent basis. The goal of increasing staff productivity was met, and there was a positive effect upon the staff and care of patients.

Strategic Planning

"Strategic planning has a longer effect and is more difficult to reverse. In order to attempt strategic planning, the future needs to be anticipated."[3] Expertise, knowledge, investigation, and reliable information are necessary for strategic planning. Resolving interdepartmental issues that affect the ED is a form of strategic planning that requires a multidisciplinary planning group. To engage in strategic planning effectively, you must keep knowledgeable of health care and emergency services changes and trends.

The strategic planning process includes the following nine steps:

1. Determine the issue and objectives.
2. Determine who will participate in the planning process.
3. Select research methods and collect and analyze data and alternatives in a set time frame.
4. Develop strategies and write a plan of action that is clear, practical, and flexible.
5. Determine costs.
6. Evaluate advantages and disadvantages.
7. Communicate the plan.
8. Implement the plan.
9. Review, evaluate, update, or revise the plan.

Strategic planning initiation and participation by middle managers are becoming more common and necessary due to increasing decentralization. However, strategic plans that involve major change or costs require planning and decision making involvement by upper level management. Yet, even in these situations, nurse managers should have a participatory role in the planning process.

Participatory Planning

It is advantageous and advisable to include staff members in planning about issues that directly affect them or their work. Their knowledge, experience, ideas, and needs can be valuable resources in the planning process. When staff offer input, their acceptance and compliance will be greater when the plan is implemented. Their ideas and concerns are valuable when evaluating the results of the plan as well because they are the ones carrying it out.

ED Nursing Council. To facilitate staff involvement with planning, four years ago I formed a planning group made up of senior staff members, which was called the ED Nursing Council. The group chose a staff member as the leader. The group's purpose was to identify problems and determine alternative solutions. An example of the Council's work in deciding on a plan of action is presented below.

In 1984, we moved to a new ED facility in a new building of the hospital. The new ED was 2½ times larger than the original facility, with two entrances instead of one. The Council was very involved with planning for operational system changes we were obviously going to encounter in the new ED. One of their projects was to plan the setup of a new Shock/Trauma area. The area was stocked and equipped with all new state-of-the-art equipment, capable of handling three major trauma victims at a time.

Shortly after the new department was opened and the trauma area was used, the Council realized that its planning did not facilitate easy functioning or easy access to supplies and equipment. Alternate plans were implemented and re-evaluated until the most functional setup was achieved. The Council helped communicate and implement all changes in nursing systems and met with me on a weekly basis after the move to evaluate and plan for improvement.

Other issues for which the Council continues to help plan solutions include improvement of intradepartmental communications, development of nursing documentation forms and patient teaching materials, and determining how to meet staff, patient, and security needs of the ED.

Because planning must occur within a set time frame if goals and objectives are to be accomplished, the Council is divided into smaller groups that each have specific tasks and dates by which they are expected to complete their planning.

Because the physicians and nurses of the ED work toward many of the same goals, the ED staff physicians joined the Council planning process for consideration of issues that affected the overall functioning of the ED.

Planning for major strategic issues that affect the ED must be done by a multidisciplinary group led by upper management, but including the ED nurse manager and medical director. However, such a group often has to be initiated by the ED nurse manager and/or the ED medical director. As noted previously, the functioning of other departments can cause delays in patient care and disposition of patients in the ED, which lead to patient complaints and a backup in the ED. Increased stress for patients and staff results.

Issues, their causes, and alternative solutions should be identified before a proposal for this type of upper-level management planning group is made. The planning group should consist of top-level administrators and directors or managers of other departments that affect ED function, such as nursing, admissions, unit management, radiology, and laboratories. Its purpose should be to set goals and objectives and implement changes to improve the ED's functioning and image, which affect the overall image of the hospital. When problems are raised that are caused by departments not routinely included in this planning group, the directors of those departments should be invited to specific planning meetings. Because many of the issues affect the function of other departments, it is of upmost importance that top-level management with the authority to implement these changes, be involved in the planning process.

Implementation of Plans

If all of one's effort is placed on a complex planning process, the purpose of the planning may not be achieved. Priorities must be determined and plans must be implemented and evaluated, or everyone involved in the process has wasted his or her time. Too often, management by objectives (MBO) becomes the primary concern. However, one can look back to the previous year, review the objectives, and realize that little change had actually occurred because the planning process took too long or was not communicated, understood, or carried out. By setting priorities and resolving short-term issues before long-term issues, planning can achieve its goals.

The distinction that marks a plan capable of producing results is the commitment of key people to work on specific tasks. The test of a plan is whether management actually commits resources to action which will bring results in the future. Unless such a commitment is made, there are only promises and hopes, but no plan.[4]

Organizing

Organizing means arranging human and/or material resources into the best possible relationships or structure to attain goals. It involves analyzing activities, decisions, and resources; classifying and dividing the activities into specific jobs; and grouping these jobs into a structure. Individuals have to be selected to complete these jobs, with the tasks fitting the needs of the situation and the ability of the individual selected.

In the ED, nursing tasks must be organized with an equitable division of the work. Determining staffing patterns, assignments, and nursing activities requires good organizational skills. In an active ED that is not well organized, patients can actually get lost in the system.

For example, after an ED patient is examined by a physician, diagnostic studies are often ordered. A series of tasks, such as doing venipuncture for blood studies, filling out the laboratory slips, taking the specimens to the labs, receiving the lab report, documenting the report on the chart, and notifying the physician so that a patient disposition can be made must be done to follow through on the studies. Each of these tasks may be completed by different individuals, but there must be an organized means to ensure promptness and completion of the overall process. If one of the steps is delayed or incomplete, delays in patient care or disposition result. A patient may just sit and wait, with no one even realizing what the patient is waiting for while other patients are being given care.

The task of organizing assignments must be done on a daily basis; often these assignments must be revised during the shift to ensure patient care by the most qualified staff in relation to each patient's condition. Assignments also have to be organized in relation to patient activity. Triage may have one RN assigned to it, but if activity becomes extremely heavy or backed up, a second RN may have to be reassigned to triage for a short period of time. Another example of the need to revise nursing assignments occurs when an RN and an LPN are assigned together in a specific geographical area. If two critically ill patients arrive at the same time and are assigned to that area, it may be necessary to reassign the LPN to less acute patients in another area in exchange for an RN who is more qualified to provide the nursing care required for a critically ill patient.

Effective organization of ED staff and patient activities should ensure prompt, quality, cost-effective service to the ED patient population. To an "outsider," the ED often appears chaotic, with unexpected patients arriving continuously and simultaneously. There may be a child crying, a psychiatric patient screaming, a major trauma patient arriving, and a code situation all occurring at once. Little does the outsider know how organized the chaos actually is. Each staff member has his or her assigned work that is delegated and coordinated with the work of others to accomplish patient care in the hectic, acute, and often overcrowded ED setting. However, lack of organization in this environment could truly cause chaos.

You must be able to organize your own time and work, as well as that of the staff, and must know how to analyze, set priorities, make decisions, communicate, delegate, and direct others to accomplish work that is organized and effective. Whether organizing your own work or staff or patient activities, organizing is a primary part of your daily work.

Integrating

Integration encompasses communication, relationships, and representation—upward, downward, and sideways. The ED nurse manager is the link between administration, other hospital departments, the ED medical director, EMSS, the community and the nursing staff.

Downward integration to the staff is necessary to ensure that the staff members know and understand what is expected of them, to assist them to improve and develop their skills by giving them advice and information and to set standards that are understood.

Upward integration keeps administration informed and aware of ED staff and patient needs and concerns. Administrators also expect the ED nurse manager to inform them of the results of monitoring and measurement of nursing and patient activities and of budget justifications.

Sideways integration provides for problem solving and receipt of information from the ED medical director, other department managers, EMSS, peers and colleagues.

As a nurse manager, you are expected to support and to contribute to the goals and needs of the hospital while supporting and meeting the needs of the staff. To perform competently and effectively as the person in the middle, experience and special skills are required.

Communicating

Communicating is the most important skill needed to perform the integration function of management. Communication is a means of sending and receiving information to or from the nurse manager. Communications must be focused and clear and conveyed in a manner that the listener will understand. They involve what is said, how it is said, body language, and what is heard.

Verbal messages are the most frequently used form of communication. Yet, these messages can be misinterpreted by the listener, as what is said "travels through the grapevine." The message becomes inaccurate or gains a different focus as each individual hears and passes it on. For instance, I have often heard staff members tell their co-workers, "Linda said . . .," even though what they repeated was not what I actually said, but what was heard or interpreted. Content of a message can be changed by the listener's attitude, perception, attention, or concept of the message. The speaker's tone of voice, grammar, body language, and choice of words all have an effect on the interpretation of the message.

Written communications are usually more accurate because more thought goes into the process of writing, which allows the writer to reread and rewrite the message before sending it. The written form also allows the reader to reread the message for better understanding.

Upward communication can go to your superiors or can come upward from the staff. Usually, these communications are in the form of requests, reports, questions, or provision of information necessary for decision making. Upward communication from the nurse manager is more often written, whereas communication upward from the staff is more likely to be verbal, unless written communication is specifically requested.

Downard communication goes from superiors to you or from you to the staff. The purpose of this type of information is generally to give information and to establish goals, standards, and expectation. It may also be used to request a subordinate to complete a task. Too often, this type of communication is written without personal interaction. Therefore, balance written and verbal communication so that memos from superiors to subordinates are not excessively used and eventually ignored. Communicate verbally when possible, with follow-up written communication. Figure 2–2 illustrates the ED nurse manager's lines of communication.

Communicating with Patients

When communicating with patients or their family members, pay close attention to nonverbal communication. Body language and actions must support spoken words so that the interpretation of what is being said conforms to what the speaker means. In the ED setting, with patients under stressful conditions, actions speak louder than words.

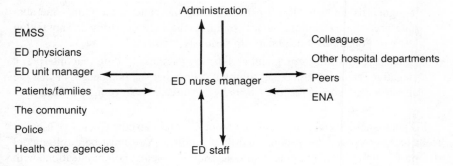

Figure 2–2 Lines of Communication

It is also important to understand the actions of a patient, which may convey quite a different meaning from what the patient is actually saying. For example, a male elderly patient becomes an ED frequent visitor, with the same or various complaints, and is evaluated and discharged home after each visit. Effective communication with the patient can yield a better understanding of the reason for the patient's frequent visits, which may be that he is lonely and comes to the ED for attention, personal interaction, and a change of environment. Once he is discharged, returning home may mean returning to an empty house with no one to talk to. Sometimes this type of patient visits increases in frequency during holiday seasons. The patient is communicating, "I am lonely," not "I am sick," even though that is what is verbally said.

A poor command of the English language and use of slang by patients may cause their statements to be misinterpreted by the nurse, such as when the patient tells you that he has been "vomiking clogs," instead of vomiting clots, or that he "fell out," meaning that he fainted.

Patients communicate fear in various ways. This type of communication also must be interpreted and understood by the staff.

In addition, patients may misinterpret the meaning of staff communications. The following examples of misunderstandings can occur in the emergency department:

- A patient is brought to the ED by the EMTs. The ED is already overcrowded with insufficient staff. The patient hears a staff member's comment to the EMT, "Not another one! Why didn't you take him to _____ Hospital?" The patient interprets the message as, "They don't want to take care of me. These people don't care."

- A family member of a critically ill patient sees physicians and nurses in the nurses' station, talking and some of them laughing. Even though the nurse assigned to the critically ill patient is with the patient, the family member interprets the scene in the nurses' station as the staff not caring and not taking their responsibility for human life seriously.

- A teenage girl who is pregnant and having vaginal bleeding may interpret a negative facial expression as communicating that she is indecent or that the nurse doesn't care if she loses the baby because she is so young or unmarried.

ED personnel's facial expressions and tone of voice can create negative impressions and perceptions by patients and their families. You must be a role model demonstrating and encouraging courteous, nonjudgmental communications with patients (Table 2–3).

ED Nurse Manager/Staff Communications

Communication with the staff should be ongoing. However, to promote communication with the staff, good interpersonal relations, trust, and respect must first exist between the individual staff members and you. Communications can be both formal and informal, but they should be timed appropriately if the mesages are to be heard, understood, and accepted. Communicating a change or complex message to the staff on an extremely hectic or stressful day, may cause it to be

---

Table 2–3 Factors Affecting Communication From the ED Nurse Manager

ED Nurse Manager	Staff	Patients
Clarity	Reception	Stress
Mode	Perception	Culture
Ability to set priorities	Stress	Education
Knowledge	Priorities	Language barriers
Respect and trust by staff	Conflict	Needs and desires
Credibility	Understanding	Preoccupation
Personality	Interest	Knowledge
Choice of words	Concern	Fear
Tone of voice	Personality	Perception
Nonverbal communications	Emotions	Listening skills
Concern	Bias	Interpretation
Understanding of behaviors	Preoccupation	Personality
Enthusiasm	Listening skills	Behavior
Stress	Reading skills	Mental state
Time constraints		
Personal feelings		
Listening and reading skills		
Feedback		
Relationships		

misinterpreted, forgotten, or rejected. Feedback from the staff indicates whether a message was clear and understood.

The ED nurse manager must participate in the development of ED policies and procedures. You must communicate hospital and ED policies and procedures to the staff in order to integrate and enforce those that affect nursing practice.

Clear communications help you direct the work of others and delegate responsibility. Direction and delegation are skills that we must be experienced and comfortable with because they enable nursing activities and systems to be carried out effectively with equitable sharing and division of tasks. An equitable division of labor can enhance job satisfaction and motivation of the staff. Delegation of responsibilities also facilitates the management of your time.

To communicate effectively with the staff, the nurse manager must also be able to communicate priorities clearly.

Often in the ED it is difficult to gather the staff together to tell them what you want them to know or do. The following methods are effective means of communicating to the staff so that the message is received by everyone as desired.

Unit Meetings. Schedule regular staff meetings for the purpose of giving and receiving information. However, in the ED, it is not uncommon that a patient code or multiple trauma victims arrive just as you are ready to sit down with the staff for a meeting. Flexibility on your part is needed either to postpone the meeting for another time, meet with small groups several times on each shift to share the same information, or hold impromptu meetings when activity is low. However the goal of the staff meeting is accomplished, it is necessary that you meet regularly with the staff to ensure effective management. You will usually be the leader of these group meetings, but you should also perform the role of facilitator or the communications will only go one way—to the staff. Staff members should have the opportunity and be encouraged to express their ideas and concerns.

Development of a Communication Book. Entries into this book should include information to be shared with all the staff, that cannot wait for a staff meeting, is of interest to others, is necessary information for the staff to have as soon as possible, or is written feedback of verbal communication. To ensure that everyone reads the book regularly and receives information that is timely, tell staff members that they are responsible for reading new entries on a daily or every other day basis. The book should include communications from the staff, in addition to those from you. However, strongly discourage its use as a means to complain. I also found it helpful to have the staff members sign their initials after reading each entry, so I could determine who was not receiving the information that they needed to have.

Meetings with Individual Staff Members. These foster better relationships and offer the individual the time to communicate his or her own needs and concerns. They also give you time to communicate the staff member's progress and overall performance, rather than only at the time that the employee performance evaluation is due. One of the most annoying and upsetting situations for an employee is to be told at the performance evaluation that his or her performance is not what it should be. Because employee performance reviews generally determine if the individual will receive a salary increase, the employee has the right to know his or her level of performance and weaknesses throughout the year. Individual meetings also are an opportunity to praise employees for good performance, which the employee also needs to hear.

In EDs with a large number of staff, it can be difficult to hold individual meetings with every staff member on a routine basis. Preplanning these meetings aids in management of your time, enabling time to be set aside for this purpose. The atmosphere should be informal so that the staff member is relaxed and you do not appear rushed. This will foster better and more open communications. It is essential that these meetings take place on the employee's time, which means that they need to be held on all shifts.

Bulletin Boards. These can be a very useful way to communicate written information. Unfortunately, most bulletin boards become overcrowded and disorganized. Each new item posted tends to blend with all the other items on the board. To promote staff reading of posted notices and information, the bulletin board must be organized and outdated items removed. The board can be divided into categories of information, such as:

- continuing education notices
- quality assurance
- ENA information
- for your information (FYI)

It may also be helpful to post information on colored paper to attract attention.

Where the bulletin boards are hung determines if and how often the staff will read what is posted on them. More than one board is usually necessary. Placing them in locker rooms, the staff bathroom, or the areas where every member of the staff visits at least once during the shift may encourage reading of posted information. Hanging a bulletin board in the nurses station is usually needed to display schedules, assignments, and information that all ED personnel needs to know. However, this particular board usually becomes overcrowded with information from physicians, clerks, and other personnel. There should therefore be separate bulletin boards for the nursing staff.

Communication Sheet. This sheet from the charge nurses to the nurse manager helps inform you of important information during hours that you are not in the ED. With 24-hour responsibility and accountability, you need to know what has occurred and how problems were resolved throughout the day. Depending always on verbal communication does not ensure that all the information is communicated in a timely fashion. Exhibit 2–2 illustrates a communication sheet of this type.

Other Important Lines of Communication

Open lines of communication with the nursing service, whether ED nursing reports to it or not, promotes cooperation and coordination of emergency patient care and transfer of admitted patients. Nursing services can also be a means of support, resource, and guidance for you, especially if you are new in the role. The staff members must communicate with other nurses as well. The more positive and courteous these communications are, the more accepting of information and transfers of ED patients will be the inpatient and clinic nurses. Good communications result in better interpersonal relationships with other hospital nurses.

Other nurse managers can be an important peer group for you. The peer group can offer advice, experience, and brainstorming for specific problem situations. In turn, you can serve as a resource and consultant for other nursing managers and staff. The peer group can be maintained by good communication with other nurse managers.

Communication with the ED assistant nurse managers (assistant head nurses/charge nurses), the medical director, and unit manager/administrative coordinator should be ongoing so that all the ED managers are working toward the same goals and not duplicating efforts. This subject is discussed in more detail later in this chapter.

Communication with other hospital departments, the police and fire departments, other facilities in EMSS, and the media is also required. The manner of these communications affects the nature of relationships, cooperation, and, in the end, the care of the ED patients. The more communication lines you are able to establish, the greater will be your authority, power, and ability to get things done.

Formal and Informal Communications

Communications can be formal or informal and directed at either individuals or groups. Formal communication is generally required to pass on information concerning standards, expectations, policies, procedures, implementation of change, counseling, and requests. It is also useful for control and measurement of activities and is appropriate when following the established chain of command in the organization. However, informal communications can be as important as the formal type. Informal communication promotes good relationships and the learning of knowledge that would not be obtained through formal channels; it is also a

Exhibit 2–2 Emergency Department Charge Nurse Shift Communication Sheet

			Date _____ SHIFT Day _____ Evening _____
Number of admissions _____	Number of critical care patients _____		Night _____
Unusual occurrences (public relations, VIPs, staff or patient injuries)			
Major trauma	*Name*	*(Injury)* *Diagnosis*	*Disposition*
Patients held over 8 hours	*Name*	*Reason*	*Disposition*
Transfers to other hospitals	*Name*	*Reason*	*Transferred to:*
Problems			

quicker way of disseminating information that the staff or others want or need to know. It is often a more accurate means of determining staff and patient needs and desires. At a staff meeting, a staff nurse may not feel comfortable stating an idea or desire in front of the group. Yet in a different setting and informally, the nurse may feel comfortable telling the idea to a peer or to you.

As mentioned previously, the disadvantage of informal communication is that the intended message can be misinterpreted. Informal communication in small groups can also lead to rumors. You should investigate rumors and validate or try to abort them. If rumors containing incorrect information are allowed to spread, they can be detrimental to the teamwork and morale of the staff members, which will adversely influence their overall effectiveness.

ENA Standards

The Emergency Department Nurses Association (currently the ENA) developed *Standards of Emergency Nursing Practice,* two of which concern communication:

*EMERGENCY NURSES SHALL ENSURE OPEN AND TIMELY COMMUNICATION WITH EMERGENCY PATIENTS, THEIR SIGNIFICANT OTHERS, AND TEAM MEMBERS

Rationale: The role of the emergency nurse as a patient advocate facilitates communication between the patient, significant others, and the emergency care system.

Outcome: Emergency nurses promote open communication to ensure the occurrence of effective therapeutic interventions.

Component Standards	*Outcome Criteria*
A. Patient and family liaison: Emergency nurses shall provide sufficient information to allow patients and significant others to participate in patients' care.	**A.** Emergency nurses involve patients and families in educative and decision-making processes of their care.
B. Community liaison: Emergency nurses shall participate in formal and informal education endeavors related to the emergency care setting and the community.	**B.** Emergency nurses actively participate in current emergency systems education at the community level.
C. Documentation: Emergency nurses shall accurately document pertinent data, nursing interventions, and patient responses.	**C.** Evidence of thorough, accurate documentation is provided by a nursing audit.

†EMERGENCY NURSES SHALL ACTIVELY COMMUNICATE WITH TEAM MEMBERS IN THE EMERGENCY CARE SYSTEM.

Rationale: Communication is an essential process for the transmission of data and information that contribute to comprehensive emergency health care.

---

*Reproduced by permission from *Standards of Emergency Nursing Practice* by Emergency Nurses Association, p. 37, The C.V. Mosby Company, St. Louis, © 1983.

†Reproduced by permission from *Standards of Emergency Nursing Practice* by Emergency Nurses Association, p. 65, The C.V. Mosby Company, St. Louis, © 1983.

Outcome: Emergency nurses function as liaisons between and among various health care professionals, health agencies, and community agencies.

Component Standards

A. Interactions: Emergency nurses shall interact as team members of the emergency care team, respecting the limits, capabilities, and responsibilities of team members.

Outcome Criteria

A. 1. Frequent interdisciplinary conferences are held related to patient care.

2. Emergency nurses actively collaborate in team decision and in each patient's care.

3. Emergency nurses serve on committees with agencies and communities, contributing nursing expertise to the decision-making process involving emergency care.

Developing and Maintaining Good Relationships

"Relationships define the place of the manager within the managerial structure. They largely define what the manager's job is, for these relationships are a crucial and essential part of the job content."[5]

To identify relationships that are necessary to the performance of your role, you must identify from whom you require information—upward, downward, or sideways—as well as who needs information from you.

Relationships to superiors and subordinates are two-way relationships, both dependent on the other. These relationships can be both formal and informal for the purposes of giving, receiving, and sharing information and defining and attaining common goals.

The purpose of your relationship to staff members is to assist them to attain both their own professional goals and objectives and those of the hospital. You have the responsibility to facilitate the performance of productive and efficient work by the staff.

This relationship to the staff is a downward relationship. A manager is responsible for the work that others do. The span of control is determined by how many people report to the manager. For example, you may be responsible not only for the staff members that work in the acute emergency care area but also for those working in a nonacute walk-in, acute pediatric, acute psychiatric, or subspecialty emergency care area, such as a trauma unit. Each area may be staffed by different groups of nurses who are consistently assigned to the same area. Or, different levels of workers may report to the ED nurse manager, such as staff RNs, LPNs, EMTs, clinical specialists, and unit clerks. The span of control is more difficult to manage as the number of relationships increases.

Your upward relationship may be to one or to a few people. This relationship should be an open one, with you making an effort to ease the work of the superior by helping meet his or her needs and objectives. The superior's relationship to you should be guiding, supporting, and mentoring.

Sideways relationships are not as crucial as upward and downward relationships. But, if you do not develop good relationships sideways, management becomes more difficult. The ED is dependent on the services of various hospital services, such as laboratories, social work, housekeeping, maintenance, and transport. Good relationships are necessary with others whose services improve and support the functioning of the ED.

Relationships with physicians should be colleagial and collaborative. To improve operations and ensure quality emergency care, there must be an effective working relationship with the ED director.

Nurse/patient relationships should be informative and supportive. Their objectives are to learn about the total patient, to understand the patient's needs, to implement nursing care, and to teach the patient and family information needed for discharge planning and patient wellness.

Consider the situation of a male chronically ill renal patient who frequents the ED during acute phases of his illness. The patient himself may be difficult to manage because of the physiologic and psychological effects of the disease. The demands of his wife may be constant and unrealistic, preventing staff members from wanting to develop any type of relationship with him or his wife. However, instead of avoiding the development of a relationship, an extra effort should be made to establish one with this patient. Doing so will promote better understanding that may actually result in a change in behavior of the wife, once she realizes that the nurses are empathetic and understanding.

My staff was involved in a situation similar to that one. One of the RNs, Sharon, developed an excellent relationship with a chronically ill renal patient and her demanding husband who were barely tolerated by the rest of the staff. Sharon maintained this special relationship with them for several years and was "their nurse" until the patient's death. There was a positive change in the behavior and cooperation of the husband. Sharon carried the relationship even further, by visiting the patient on the inpatient units during times of admission and checking on her at home after she was discharged from the ED. The intolerance of the rest of the staff changed to a tolerant, even *caring* attitude. When the patient finally died, her husband was so grateful for Sharon's care and support that he offered his time as a volunteer worker in the hospital. Sharon's relationship with the family aided them during illness and death.

We have a duty and obligation to ensure that all emergency patients are assessed, evaluated, and receive appropriate nursing interventions and medical care. ED nurses must communicate patient conditions clearly and in a timely fashion to an emergency physician. Patient advocacy should be a priority for you.

Maintaining good community relationships encourages the community residents to view the hospital as their hospital for all their medical needs; it also fosters support or approval from the community when it is necessary for specific hospital activities or improvements, such as the building of a multilevel garage or new buildings, development of a helicopter program, or changes in hospital traffic patterns.

Relationships with police and prehospital care providers should be developed and maintained to ensure mutual respect and continuity of patient care from the prehospital setting. During unusual situations in the ED, such as fights between patients or the threatening of a staff member by a patient or visitor, the police are more supportive and quicker to respond when needed if relationships with the ED are good.

The ED is a frequent source of information for the media. Poor relationships with the media can negatively affect the hospital, particularly in these competitive times. Information about the ED can improve the image of the hospital, or destroy it. In general the public believes what it hears through the media, which is free to report what it wants to report. Too, once a positive relationship is developed, the media can assist in the hospital's promotion and marketing efforts.

All relationships depend on the trust and respect that you must earn by the demonstration of your knowledge, ability, skills, communication, and good interpersonal relations. You must seek out and promote good relationships as part of the role and responsibility of the job and must encourage the nursing staff to do the same. Good relationships are crucial to your effectiveness.

ENA Standards

EDNA's (currently ENA) ''Professionalism—Comprehensive Standard III—Administration'' reads as follows:*

EMERGENCY NURSES IN MANAGEMENT SHALL FUNCTION IN COLLEGIAL RELATIONSHIPS WITH OTHER ADMINISTRATORS HAVING RESPONSIBILITIES IN THE EMERGENCY CARE SETTING.

Rationale: Inherent in the delivery of emergency care is the phenomenon of collegial and collaborative participation by varied health care professionals. Hence it is essential that policy decisions and communications at the management level are both collegial and reciprocal.

Outcome: Emergency nurses in management:

1. Are the ultimate decision makers on issues regarding emergency nursing.

2. Are recognized as peers by other managers with responsibilities in the emergency care setting.

---

*Reproduced by permission from *Standards of Emergency Nursing Practice* by Emergency Nurses Association, pp. 61–62, The C.V. Mosby Company, St. Louis, © 1983.

3. Direct, develop, and implement policies, procedures, and standards governing emergency nursing practice.

Component Standards	*Outcome Criteria*
A. Job description: Emergency nurses shall have a job description that reflects current standards of professional practice and lists specific responsibilities.	**A.** 1. Job descriptions are available at the time of interview. 2. Job descriptions are utilized in performance review. 3. Emergency nurses have input into periodic revision of job descriptions.
B. Performance review: Emergency nurses' performance shall be reviewed by emergency nurses in management, based on identified roles and responsibilities.	**B.** 1. The review contains input from the individual being reviewed and other appropriate health professionals. 2. Emergency nurses are evaluated on a periodic basis. 3. Emergency nurses' modification of practice in accordance with performance appraisal is reviewed.
C. Staffing: Emergency nurses in management shall take measures to ensure provision of qualified professional nurses to provide for safe care.	**C.** 1. The level of staffing reflects recognition of variables that affect the delivery of safe, effective emergency nursing care. 2. Staffing patterns provide adequate time for: • Triage, assessment, intervention, and evaluation of intervention • Crisis intervention • Patient and significant others referral and aftercare instructions • Breaks and mealtimes

Representing

As ED nurse managers, we have the responsibility of representing subordinates and patients. We must bring matters that affect or concern them to the attention of upper management. Your staff members, in particular, rely on you to represent their issues, ideas for improvements, needs, and contributions. If you fail to do so, they may lose trust and respect for you. Frustration and dissatisfaction on the part of the staff then result.

As a patient representative, you act as their agent to upper management. You must determine operational and functional requirements to provide safe, quality, humanistic care and then communicate them to superiors.

In order to represent patients and staff appropriately at hospital committee meetings where decisions are made that affect emergency care and the ED nursing staff, consistently maintain open communication with staff and patients. To perform the function of representation, keep informed, be assertive and objective, and have insight into the function and problems of other departments or nursing units. Attend and participate in problem-solving, planning, and decision-making activities of the following hospital committees:

- CPR or life-support committee
- disaster planning committee
- ED advisory or planning committee
- critical care committee
- emergency care committee
- trauma committee
- committees designed to plan physical or operational changes for the ED/service
- nursing committees—to maintain autonomy and as a resource contributing and sharing ideas
- professional organization committees, i.e., ENA at the local, state, or national levels
- community and state committees relevant to emergency medical services

Some of the above committees may be medical staff committees, however, in most hospitals, the ED nurse manager can participate as an invitee, so that there is input from emergency nursing into decision making that affects emergency nurses and emergency patient care.

Decisions made by committees that satisfy the needs of a particular department may negatively affect the function of the ED. An example of such a decision is revision of medical resident responsibility and procedures regarding emergency admissions in the ED. If the procedure affects ED function by prolonging patient length of stay and increasing nursing tasks, you must present these problems and work to solve them in committee meetings where these decisions are made. If you have no input into the planning and decision-making process, control will be lost.

In addition, you also have the responsibility and expectation to represent hospital management. You must interpret and convey administrative goals, policies, and decisions to the staff. You are expected to support management decisions and follow through with enforcement of those decisions. However, occasions may arise when you disagree with a policy or decision that you are expected to enforce. As a manager, concerns and opinions should be appropriately voiced to superiors; however, upper management must be supported once a final decision is made. Presenting management decisions to staff with a positive approach is essential. If the staff members sense disagreement, conflict, or lack of commitment on your part, their attitudes will be similar. They may also be confused about what is actually expected of them.

Representing management exemplifies your appropriate role and responsibility of being a manager, which differentiates your role from that of your staff. If philosophies and decisions of upper management are unacceptable or conflict with your beliefs to the point that you cannot be committed to enforcing them, you may have to make the choice of relinquishing your role and position or moving to another institution. If, however, conflict or difference of opinion is infrequent, and you have a strong commitment to the emergency staff and patients, you have an obligation and responsibility to try to influence decisions and make changes for improvement in a professional and objective manner.

You also act as a hospital representative to patients and visitors by serving as a patient advocate and demonstrating warmth, empathy, and a feeling of trust and confidence. By communicating, teaching, and serving as a resource to others through presentation of educational programs, participation in professional organizations, and preparation of publications, you also represent the hospital in the larger health care community.

Controlling and Measuring

Controls are necessary for consistency and for evaluation and measurement of activities and systems. Controls consist of rules, standards, policies, procedures, protocols, job descriptions, and expectations that must first be developed and communicated and then implemented, enforced, and measured to be effective. You must control both activities relating to emergency nursing and the "ED turf" so that others who have their own interests and needs do not control it.

Controlling may be as simple as setting staffing levels or determining how many nurses can take a meal break at once. Or, it may be more complex as in the development of nursing protocols and standards for the nursing care of the multiple trauma patient.

Necessary controls in the emergency department include:

- federal, state and JCAH requirements
- hospital objectives, policies, and procedures
- ED objectives, policies, and procedures
- emergency nurse qualifications and job description
- emergency nurse expectations
- personnel policies; hiring and firing procedures
- disciplinary procedures

- staffing levels and patterns
- emergency nursing standards and protocols
- ED systems and nursing processes
- triage procedure
- equipment and supply usage, par levels, and costs
- environmental and safety standards
- operational budget
- capital budget

Quality and costs must be controlled by human resource, patient care, and materials management. You are responsible for measuring the effectiveness and efficiency of all areas of management through the following mechanisms: performance evaluations, assessment of patient satisfaction, budget variance reviews and justifications, and other quality assurance activities that are discussed later.

You must also control ED activities by exercising authority to protect the nursing domain and power. Developing this control requires knowledge, skills, credibility, assertiveness, negotiation, innovation, political savvy, trust, and respect by staff, physicians, and other hospital managers.

You should have a collaborative, supportive, and collegial relationship with the physician director; however, you should be in control of nursing activities while the ED physician controls physician activities and medical care of patients. The physician director and you should work together as peers but with separate areas of responsibility and accountability. This type of relationship allows for checks and balances and promotes a team concept of management. In the ED there are also several areas or systems that require collaborative decisions, standards, and monitoring of activities by the physician director and nurse manager together.

TEAM CONCEPT OF MANAGEMENT

Management of the ED by the combined efforts of the ED physician director and nurse manager promotes coordinated goal setting, problem solving, and decision making for the department. Some EDs have the position of unit manager or administrative coordinator who has responsibility for the nonmedical, nonnursing activities of the ED. However, when each manager has input and is involved in the overall operational management of the ED, it is more likely that cooperation, good working relationships, creativity, and innovation will be enhanced. In addition, the team concept fosters appropriate decision making and planning for the ED that affects all levels of the ED staff and patients. This concept of management also helps increase the motivation and accountability of each ED manager, who gains more insight into and support of each other's needs and decisions.

Communication upward to hospital administration about major issues should be through a combined team mechanism.

Some functions and systems that improve with combined management efforts include:

- discharge planning and written patient instruction sheets
- general ED policies, procedures, and protocols
- patient and paper flow
- statistical record keeping
- budget planning
- standard orders
- development and revision of the ED treatment record and other ED forms
- triage procedure
- strategic planning for new programs
- quality assurance
- equipment evaluation and selection
- patient charge system
- goal setting for the ED
- educational programs for the community and prehospital care providers
- design and planning for a new facility
- marketing efforts

When you and the physician director work together as a team toward the same purpose and goals, it is more likely that the ED nursing and physician staff will also perform as a team, which is needed for optimal patient services and staff morale. Team management also increases the credibility and power of decisions that are made by the managers.

ED Nursing Management Team

This chapter has presented the numerous functions, skills, and tasks for which you have responsibility. For one person to perform all these activities independently would be frustrating, time consuming, and close to impossible, especially in EDs with high patient census and staffing levels. In addition, you cannot be present in the ED 24 hours a day, 7 days a week, so other nursing leaders must be relied upon for follow through of required activities. For these reasons, you must delegate management responsibilities to others. The position of assistant nurse manager (or three assistant nurse managers, one per shift) is most beneficial. In many organizations, however, the assistant role does not exist. Management responsibilities are delegated to charge nurses or to a level IV nurse in a career ladder system, who does not have the needed management knowledge or skill. The person in this role has increased responsibility and therefore should have additional education for management skills and an appropriate title that increases his or her authority as viewed by the staff. It is often difficult for a peer who may be in a charge role to aid in the discipline or evaluation of peers.

Some management responsibilities, however, can be handled by the staff. Delegating responsibility to staff members increases their feeling of worth and input into management decisions and planning.

Delegating

You must recognize the need and reasons for delegating responsibilities to others:

- better time management for the ED nurse manager by allowing others to do activities of which they are capable
- decreased management costs
- development and mentoring of staff
- increased staff input and creativity

The ED nurse manager who believes that everything can be done by one person is unrealistic, especially in the ED, which is so complex and demanding of organization and patient services.

To delegate effectively, determine what tasks to delegate and to whom. Also know why delegation is beneficial. Take the following steps:

- define what needs to be done
- describe the task and the reason why it needs to be done in writing
- select the person to complete the task
- explain the reason, purpose, and exactly what needs to be done and in what time frame
- explain how to do the task
- establish controls and checks with appropriate direction and guidance to ensure completion of the task

Specific responsibilities in the ED can be carried out by an individual nurse or a group of nurses. Whoever is chosen for the task should be capable, interested, knowledgeable, and willing to do it and follow it through to completion. Some of the tasks may be ongoing. These responsibilities may include:

- maintenance of statistical reports
- quality assurance activities

- educational program development and teaching
- evaluation of equipment and supplies
- orientation of new staff
- development of guidelines
- development or revision of ED nursing forms

Staff Development Instructor/Clinical Specialists

Some EDs have the additional resource of a staff development instructor or clinical specialist. Although the ED nurse manager maintains responsibility and accountability for the education and nursing care practices, these tasks can be delegated to an individual with the proper educational background who is hired for that specific purpose. The instructor/clinical specialist and you should plan collaborately for the learning needs of staff and patients. Allowing others to carry out these responsibilities frees time for you to fullfill other important management responsibilities. The clinical specialist can assist in the development of nursing care standards and protocols, provide clinical guidance, and monitor continually the clinical performance of the staff.

In EDs that lack the financial resources to hire someone specifically for this role, experienced staff members can be delegated some of the responsibilities of education and training. The ED cannot rely on a general hospital nursing orientation or educational program to meet the needs of emergency nursing. The differences in responsibilities, activities, and nursing forms are so great that it takes an experienced ED nurse to orient or teach another ED nurse. Experienced, capable staff can be assigned specific responsibilities as a preceptor, ED nursing class instructor, or planner to meet determined needs. A staff nurse can be given the responsibility of coordinating educational programs. All the responsibilities delegated to staff assist the nurse manager, but require your careful selection of these staff members and continual direction and guidance from you.

NOTES

1. Peter Drucker, *Management Tasks, Responsibilities, and Practices* (New York: Harper and Row, 1974), p. 393.
2. Carl Anderson, *Management Skills, Functions, and Organization Performance* (Dubuque: Wm. C. Browne Publishers, 1984), p. 19.
3. Janet Kraegel, *Planning Strategies for Nurse Managers* (Rockville, MD: Aspen Publishers).
4. Peter Drucker, *op. cit.,* p. 128.
5. Peter Drucker, *op. cit.,* p. 413.

REFERENCES

American College of Emergency Physicians. "Emergency Care Guidelines." *Ann Emerg Med* 11:222–226, April, 1982.

Anderson, Carl. *Management Skills, Functions, and Organization Performance*. Dubuque: Wm. C. Browne Publishers, 1984.

Cornett-Cooke, Pat, and Dias, Kathie. "Teambuilding: getting it all together." *Nursing Management* 15(5):16–17, 1984.

Curtin, Leah. "Keynote Address." ENA Scientific Assembly. New York, September, 1985.

Curtin, Leah. "Nurses—Manage your Future—A New Generation of Leaders." *Nursing Management* 16:11, 1985.

Drucker, Peter. *Management, Tasks, Responsibilities and Practices*. New York: Harper and Row Publishers, 1974.

Emergency Department Nurses Association. *Standards of Emergency Nursing Practice*. St. Louis: C.V. Mosby Co., 1983.

Frank, Iris. "Managers Ask and Answer." *Journal of Emergency Nursing (JEN)* 11(2):112–113, 1985.

George, James E. "Communication Problems in the Emergency Department." *JEN* 9(5):288–289, 1983.

Griffin, Jane. "Managers Ask and Answer." *JEN* 11(4):217–218, 1985.

Joint Commission on Accreditation of Hospitals. *Emergency Services, Accreditation Manual for Hospitals*. Chicago: American Hospital Association, 1986.

Keller, Coleen. "CBE for First-Line Managers." *Nursing Management*, November, 1984, pp. 63–67.

Kraegel, Janet. *Planning Strategies for Nurse Managers*. Rockville, MD: Aspen Publishers, 1983.

Miller, Margaret. *The Nurse Manager in the Emergency Department*. St. Louis: C.V. Mosby Co., 1984.

Mills, D. Quinn. "Planning with People in Mind." *Harvard Business Rev.* 63(4):97–105, 1985.

Myer, Barbara. "Managers Ask and Answer." *JEN* 11(5):272–273, 1985.

Nursing Department, Albert Einstein Medical Center. "Nurse Manager Job Description." Philadelphia: Albert Einstein Medical Center, Northern Division, 1985.

O'Sullivan, Patricia. "Analyzing Communication Patterns between an E.D. Manager and Staff Members." *JEN* 10(4):229, 1984.

O'Sullivan, Patricia. "Detecting Communication Problems." *Nursing Management* 16:11, 1985.

Sheehy, Susan Budassi, and Barber, Janet. *Emergency Nursing Principles and Practice*, 2nd edition. St. Louis: C.V. Mosby Co., 1985.

Sheridan, Donna; Bronstein, Jean; Walker, Duane. *The New Nurse Manager*. Rockville, MD: Aspen Publishers, 1984.

Sorgen, Carol. "Managers Ask and Answer." *JEN* 11(5):273, 1985.

Stevens, Barbara. *The Nurse as Executive*. Wakefield, Mass.: Nursing Resources Inc., 1980.

Stone, Sandra; Firsich, Sharon; Jordan, Shelley; Berger, Marie; Elhart, Dorothy. *Management for Nurses*. St. Louis: C.V. Mosby Co., 1984.

Vestal, Katherine W. "Promoting Excellence in the Emergency Department." *JEN* 9(5):290, 1983.

Chapter 3

Legal Issues

Sandra Green and Linda Buschiazzo

As high-risk areas, EDs are subject to various types of liability claims. These claims frequently account for a large percentage of total hospital losses. The high volume of patients, the brief duration of the visit, inadequate documentation, lack of discharge follow-up, ineffective communications, and poor ED staff attitudes are frequent causes for lawsuits. Less than adequate documentation in the ED hinders the hospital's defense against these claims.

The ever more sophisticated technology and the higher levels of knowledge and skills required by the ED nurse increase risks of liability. The ED nurse must continually update his or her knowledge and skills to care for all types of patients in the ED. The increasing availability of training programs, such as Advanced Cardiac Life Support, and the recognition of Certification for Emergency Nurses (CEN), have increased national standards for emergency nurses. Although critical care courses are mandated for nurses working in intensive or coronary care units, the same type of training has not been mandated in most EDs.

Lack of such education and training increases the liability of the hospital and ED nursing management if untrained ED nurses do care for critically ill and injured patients. You as the ED nurse manager are responsible for the nursing care and safety of ED patients. You can be held liable for inadequate educational preparation and training of nurses permitted to work in the ED and for lack of supervision of ED staff. With the increased use of EMTs and physician's assistants, there is even more potential for risk. It is essential that you set standards of ED nursing care based on specific requirements for education and training in emergency nursing to ensure that appropriate and safe care is rendered to all patients.

Attitudes play a part in increasing the risk of liability. Positive attitudes and effective communication by all ED personnel are imperative to decrease the risk.

Potential risks for claims include:

- patients signing out against medical advice
- refusal of treatment

- patients recently discharged from the hospital or ED
- unexpected abnormal diagnostic test results received after the patient was discharged from the ED
- x-ray reports that differ from the ED physician's interpretation
- medication and treatment errors
- discharge of patients who were not seen by a physician
- delays in treatment
- lack of prior physician/patient relationship
- insufficient staffing for patient volume and acuity
- lack of follow-up when test results and x-ray interpretation are received after patient discharge

SCOPE OF PRACTICE

Emergency nursing is gaining recognition as a specialty. The scope of practice of the ED nurse encompasses activities that involve various health problems and levels of complexity. ED nurses are looking for additional responsibilities; however, increased accountability and liability come with these new responsibilities. The standard used to determine nursing malpractice is whether the nurse deviated from what other members of the profession would do in a similar situation. Nurses who are certified in emergency nursing (CEN) can be held accountable for CEN standards of care. The Emergency Nurses Association (ENA)—formerly the Emergency Department Nurses Association (EDNA)—has published standards of emergency nursing practice.

Most states have nurse practice acts, but unfortunately, many do not clearly define the limits of nursing function. Some states are revising their nurse practice acts to broaden current definitions, which may assist ED nurses in determining which functions are legally within their scope of practice. ED nurses must adhere to their professional standards.

LEGALITIES OF NURSING

Nurses are personally liable for their acts of negligence. Negligence can be simply defined as a deviation from accepted standards of care. An employer is liable for the wrongful acts of employees (respondeat superior). Therefore, a hospital may be liable for a negligent act by an individual nurse. You can also be held liable for the actions of those under your supervision, as would the registered nurse who is supervising a practical nurse or EMT.

Acts of negligence by the ED nurse include, but are not limited to:

- *Failure to use adequate precautions to protect a patient against injury.* Falls constitute a large percentage of lawsuits against hospitals and nurses. Because most EDs utilize stretchers, rather than beds, it is imperative that siderails are always up and/or safety straps are secured when patients are left unattended. Another example of a needed precaution is protecting the seizure patient during seizure activity.
- *Failure to observe or interpret.* The ED nurse must be able to assess and interpret patient conditions, changes in patient status, and laboratory results. The triage nurse must accurately observe and interpret patient problems to ensure timely treatment of serious conditions. When an abnormal blood test is reported, the ED nurse must be able to interpret it as abnormal so that the ED physician, who may be with other patients, is notified and appropriate treatment is rendered.
- *Failure to communicate.* The ED nurse must inform the physician about situations that require immediate attention and changes in patient conditions. Nurses must communicate with each other to ensure continuity of patient care.
- *Failure to recognize the possible dangers of a physician's order.* The ED nurse must question and refuse to carry out orders that he or she believes is harmful to patients. In order to be aware of possible dangers, the ED nurse must have an appropriate level of education and skills.
- *Failure to judge properly.* Judgments have to be made constantly in the ED. Decisions have to be well thought through, utilizing common sense, knowledge, and skill gained through education and experience in emergency nursing.
- *Medication/treatment/procedure errors.* ED nurses must be expected to comply with established standards for dispensing of medications and doing procedures. In the chaos of a busy ED, errors are often caused by lack of patient identification and the great frequency of verbal orders. Many orders are carried out in a hurry because the ED nurse is very busy. All patients should be identified with an identification bracelet. The ED nurse must verify the order and the name of the patient who is to receive medication or treatment. Patient allergies must be clearly documented on the ED record.
- *Equipment-related problems.* All equipment must be safe and in working order. Preventive maintenance should be done on all equipment and electrical safety checks made on electrical equipment. If the ED nurse is aware that equipment is faulty or there are frayed wires or loose wheels, the equipment must not be used for patients. The faulty equipment must be immediately removed and repaired.
- *Elopements/AMA.* Patients who come to the ED seeking treatment become the responsibility of the hospital. Patients with altered mental status must be

continually observed so that they cannot leave the ED without staff awareness. Attempts must be made to prevent patients from leaving against medical advice, and these attempts must be clearly documented. Delays in patient treatment must be avoided as much as possible to prevent patients who require care from walking out without treatment because the wait was too long. The hospital can be liable if a patient who walked out due to extensive delays in treatment returns later with a worsened condition or dead on arrival.

- *Missing or damaged property*. ED nurses must appropriately handle, label, and list personal belongings of patients to prevent their damage or loss. The ED nurse must take care to list valuables and have them placed in a safe place, such as a safe in the hospital, or with the security department. The patient must sign the itemized list of valuables. If patients insist on keeping valuables with them, they should be asked to sign a form assuming full responsibility for the valuables and releasing the hospital of any liability. Clothing must not be left hanging on hooks behind doors or quickly thrown into a bag without checking for valuables. The patient's full name should be written on bags in which clothing and belongings are placed.

MEDICAL RECORDS AND DOCUMENTATION

Documentation on the ED treatment record must substantiate care that is provided. Assessments, treatment, diagnoses, changes in patient condition, discharge instructions, and follow-up care must be supported by documentation. A medical record must be maintained on every patient who comes to the ED for care. This ED record must be included as part of the patient's permanent hospital record.

The ED medical record should include the following information:

- patient information—name, address, telephone number, age, next of kin
- time and method of arrival
- care given to the patient before arrival
- allergies, current medications, and tetanus status
- complete vital signs and repeated when indicated
- chief complaint/presenting problem
- history and physical exam pertinent to the presenting problem
- other medical problems
- treatments and responses to treatments
- diagnostic and therapeutic orders that should be timed
- results of procedures and diagnostic tests
- final disposition and patient condition upon transfer or discharge

- discharge instructions that are written with a copy retained with the ED record; the patient should sign that instructions were explained, understood, and received.
- consent for treatment
- signature for leaving against medical advice

Nurses notes should be written on every patient. The ED record should be a replay of what transpired in the ED, and should include patient statements, assessment, nursing interventions, medications with time given, and patient problems. All documentation must be accurate and complete. Writing must be legible and in ink. All documentation should be timely, and all entries should be consistent. Contradictions and time gaps must be avoided. When changes of documentation are necessary, alterations should be made by drawing a line through the inaccurate entry, making sure that it can still be read. No entry should be completely obliterated. The entry should be dated and initialed, and the word "error" written next to it. The new entry can then be written in chronological order.

Some problems with ED records are:

- lack of sufficient writing space, which can impede documentation of all pertinent information
- blank spaces, if a space on the form is left blank because it is not applicable for a particular patient, indicate "not applicable"
- lack of continuity, time gaps, or incompleteness
- illegibility of documentation
- conflicting documentation
- lack of a discharge summary

CONSENT FOR TREATMENT

There must be documented proof of the patient's consent for treatment. Informed consent is required to avoid risk of liability for assault and battery. Assault is defined as an act placing an individual in a state of fear and apprehension of harm. Battery is the touching of one person by another without permission. Consent is implied in life-threatening situations when a patient is unable to provide written consent.

Consent for treatment of a minor must be obtained from the parent or legal guardian before treatment is rendered. A minor is defined as a person below the age of majority, which varies from state to state. However, as with the adult, consent is implied in life-threatening situations. Emancipated minors may give consent for themselves. Consent statutes for emancipated minors also vary by states. Generally, emancipated minors are those below the age of majority but who are independent from their parents, are self-supporting, married, or have been pregnant. In some states a minor may give consent for the determination and treatment of pregnancy, venereal disease, alcoholism, and drug abuse.

If a minor is brought to the ED for treatment by anyone other than a parent, all attempts must be made to contact the parents before treatment is rendered. Consent may be obtained over the telephone and should be witnessed by a second person listening in on a phone extension. There must be documentation on the ED record that consent was obtained from a parent via telephone, with signatures of the physician or nurse obtaining consent and of the witness. If a minor is brought to the ED by a teacher, school administrator, camp counselor, or other person who has temporary care of the minor, attempts must still be made to contact the parents. If however the parents cannot be contacted, it is acceptable to accept signed authorization by the parents for treatment of their child in their absence. Most schools and camps require parents to sign an emergency treatment authorization for just these situations. When a minor is with an adult relative and all attempts made to contact the parents have failed, signed consent can be obtained from the relative accompanying the minor, if emergency treatment is necessary. When a parent refuses consent for necessary treatment for a minor, the courts can be petitioned for an order to treat.

For patients who are physically or mentally incapable of consenting to treatment, implied consent or consent of an authorized person is acceptable. Sometimes it is necessary for the courts to appoint a guardian of the patient for purposes of consent.

Consent for treatment must be specific and informed. If a patient does not speak English, an interpreter may be necessary to inform the patient adequately. Special consent forms should be signed by patients before specific procedures are performed. The procedure and its risks and consequences must be explained in simple language. The consent form must include the name of the physician obtaining the consent, the name of the patient, the patient's signature, and the signature of a witness. The signature of the witness is to attest that the patient's signature is geniune. Consent forms should note the date and time that consent is obtained.

An adult who is conscious and mentally competent has the right to refuse treatment, even when the treatment is necessary to save life or limb. Giving treatment in the face of refusal may not be supported by law.

TRIAGE

Nurses who perform triage should be experienced emergency nurses, who have had supervised practice in the triage role. The triage nurse can be held liable for actions and/or inactions. The ED nurse manager can be held liable if an inexperienced nurse is assigned to triage, which results in poor judgment, inappropriate action, or lack of action. The triage nurse must maintain contact with the physician and the rest of the ED staff to keep them informed of patients requiring immediate treatment, changes in patient conditions, and special patient needs. The triage nurse must be a patient advocate to prevent unacceptable delays in treatment.

TELEPHONE ADVICE

As a general rule, diagnoses or treatment should not be given over the telephone to patients calling for advice. The person calling should be told that the problem cannot be diagnosed over the telephone and that they should either come to the ED for examination and treatment or see their private physician. The person giving medical advice over the telephone can be held liable for that advice.

AGAINST MEDICAL ADVICE

When a competent adult refuses treatment or admission, he or she must be informed of the potential risks of that action. The facts surrounding refusal and an explanation of the risks should be documented. A form releasing the hospital and ED staff from all responsibility for any ill effects resulting from the patient's decision to leave should be utilized. The patient's signature, as well as the signature of a witness, should be obtained on this form. If the patient refuses to sign the form, the refusal to sign should be documented and signed by a witness. It is important to document the competency of the patient who leaves against medical advice.

Proper documentation is the best defense against charges of abandonment or negligence on the part of the ED staff.

REFUSAL TO TREAT

Hospitals that receive funds under the Hill-Burton Survey and Construction Act must give a reasonable amount of services to those persons unable to pay or must provide care at a reduced rate to eligible persons who cannot afford to pay fully for their care. Patients cannot be turned away or discriminated against on the basis of race, creed, color, or national origin. Denying emergency care or failing to render necessary treatment can constitute negligence.

INCIDENT REPORTING

Incidents are defined as any untoward event that occurs in direct relation to patient care, any act or omission that gives rise to any injury, or a situation that may cause injury.

Incident reporting identifies the types of incidents that occur, so that action may be taken to prevent or reduce future occurrences. It also provides the ED nurse manager and hospital administration with the information to evaluate risk and/or liability. The reports may refresh nurses' memories if the incident becomes the subject of litigation several years after it occurred. Serious errors and accidents must be fully investigated. The following are examples of situations that require reporting:

- slips and falls in the ED, even if the patient has not been injured
- medication/procedure/treatment errors
- reactions to medications and other substances
- patients who refuse treatment or admission; leaving against medical advice
- unexpected abnormal diagnostic test results returned after the patient has been discharged
- a final x-ray report that differs from the ED diagnoses and/or the ED x-ray interpretation
- a patient who arrives dead on arrival who had been recently discharged from the hospital or the ED
- faulty equipment or any injury caused by equipment

Information contained in incident reports must be specific and objective. Assumptions must not be made, nor should co-workers be mentioned or blamed on the incident report form.

REPORTING LAWS

Each state has specific requirements concerning diseases that must be reported and for reporting of criminal acts, such as injuries inflicted by lethal weapons and unlawful acts. Other types of incidents that are reportable include suicide, rape, assault, dispensing or taking of narcotics, animal bites, suspected criminal abortions, and food poisoning.

The ED staff also plays an important role in the detection and reporting of child abuse. Some states require reporting of abuse or neglect of children and impose a penalty of fines, imprisonment, or both for a failure to report. Other states have more permissive laws that permit the reporter to decide whether to report or not.

States also differ as to the defined age of a child. Whatever the state law, health care professionals have an obligation to report any information to the proper authority when child abuse or neglect is suspected. The ED staff can easily observe and gather information about parental neglect and abuse of a child. Generally, the person reporting suspected child abuse is protected because the report was made ''in good faith.''

Some states have enacted laws dealing with protective services for adults. Abuse of the elderly is becoming more common. The ED staff should recognize that the elderly can be as dependent as children and may be incapable of self-care. The social service department should be notified of all suspected abuse cases.

SEXUAL ASSAULT

The requirement for reporting sexual assault, including rape, varies from state to state. However, if a child is a victim of alleged sexual assault, it should be reported under the child abuse or neglect laws. If the adult patient alleges rape and consents to it being reported, the police should be notified immediately.

All alleged rapes are potential court cases. It is essential that documentation on the ED medical record be complete, detailed, and accurate as there is a strong possibility that the ED medical record will be subpoenaed. The patient should be asked to sign all necessary consent forms for treatment, photographs, and release of information. Examination of the patient should be completed as soon as possible. A complete history of the alleged rape should be documented. Clothing and other evidence must be saved, listed, and given to the police. All specimens must be handled carefully and properly labeled. In many states, there are rape centers with staff members who have experience handling the medical and legal aspects of alleged rape.

BLOOD ALCOHOL

When a police officer brings a person who is suspected of drunken driving to the ED and requests a blood alcohol level, the ED staff may not know how to respond. A nurse may be liable if a sample of blood is taken without the person's consent. Each state has its own statutes and different legal conclusions regarding blood alcohol levels. Therefore, it is imperative that the ED staff know their state's position before drawing alcohol levels without consent of the patient. Consent may be implied in unconscious patients when a blood alcohol level is drawn to assist the physician in the diagnosis and treatment of a patient. Use of consent form authorizing taking of a blood alcohol level would be a wise step to protect the hospital and the ED staff from liability.

VERBAL/TELEPHONE ORDERS

In the ED many orders are given verbally because of the need for timeliness of emergency treatment. The ED nurse should always repeat a verbal order back to the physician to be sure that it was heard correctly. When the emergent situation is over, the order must be documented on the medical record by the physician. If a nurse has reason to believe that an order would injure a patient, the nurse should not carry out the physician's order. If a physician insists that a medication be given that the nurse believes will harm a patient, the nurse can prepare the medication and suggest that the ordering physician administer it.

PRIVATE PATIENTS IN THE EMERGENCY DEPARTMENT

Private physicians frequently tell their patients to meet them in the ED; however, when the patient arrives, the private physician may not be waiting in the ED or may not even be in the hospital yet. Hospitals should have specific policies pertaining to the private patient in the ED. While the patient is waiting for the private physician, the patient is the responsibility of the ED staff. An assessment should be made to determine if the patient requires immediate treatment or if the patient's condition changes while waiting. Any emergent situation should be reported to the ED physician. Vital signs and assessment should be documented, as well as any other pertinent information.

TRANSFERS

Any patient being transferred to another health care facility should be in a condition to survive the transfer. Whether a nurse or physician accompanies the patient depends on the condition of the patient; however, a general rule should exist that a professional who can assess and render life-saving measures should accompany all critically ill or injured patients during transfers. Patient transfers should be documented on the ED medical record. The ED physician should make arrangements with the receiving facility to ensure the patient's safe transport. Copies of the ED medical record should be sent with the patient to the receiving hospital. When the patient is transported without a nurse, a nursing report should be called in to the receiving nurse.

To decrease the risk of liability before patient transfer,

> "the transferring hospital must assume the responsibility of stablilizing the patient's condition, examining the patient to determine whether the patient can tolerate transferral, arranging for the receiving hospital to approve the transfer, arranging with the patient to approve the transfer,

and giving the patient supportive treatment until she or he is accepted as a patient by the receiving hospital."[1]

NOTES

1. Marguerite R. Mancini and Alice T. Gale, *Emergency Care and the Law* (Rockville, Md: Aspen Publishers, 1981), p. 113.

REFERENCES

Creighton, Helen. *Law Every Nurse Should Know*, 5th edition. Philadelphia: W.B. Saunders Company, 1986.

"Five Cardinal Rules Decrease ER Risks, Lawsuits." *Hospital Risk Management*, June, 1985, pp. 972–973.

George, James E. *Law and Emergency Care*. St. Louis: The C.V. Mosby Company, 1980.

George, James E. "The Right to Refuse Medical Treatment." *JEN* 9(4):234, 1983.

George, James E. "Emergency Nursing: Standards of Care." *JEN* 10(1):52–53, 1984.

George, James E. "The ED Record: Legal Implications." *Emergency Physician Legal Bulletin*, Spring, 1984, pp. 2–10.

Help News. *Health Care and Effective Loss Prevention*. Chicago: Alexis, 1984.

"IL Hospital Reduces ER Liability Risks." *Hospitals*, September 16, 1985, p. 66.

Mancini, Marguerite R., and Gale, Alice T. *Emergency Care and the Law*. Rockville, MD: Aspen Publishers, 1981.

Peisert, Margaret. *The Hospital's Role in Emergency Medical Services Systems*. Chicago: American Hospitals Publishing, Inc., 1984.

"Ways to Take High Risk Tag off Emergency Department." *Hospital Risk Management*, January, 1984, pp. 1–4, 12–13.

Part II

Managing Emergency Nursing Services

Chapter 4

The Employment Process: Emphasis on Interviewing

William M. Warfel

EMPLOYMENT PROCESS

One of the best ways to distinguish yourself as a nurse manager is to boost the esteem of your department through the selection of a competent professional staff. Surrounding yourself with qualified individuals reflects positively on you as a manager. It will make you and your department stronger, and positive perceptions of the ED will follow.

It is helpful to view the employment process as a succession of hurdles that the prospective employee has to leap. This is a useful analogy from the employers' standpoint because it can help them analyze whether there are hurdles in the process that filter out minority or protected classes. It is the employer's responsibility to ensure that the hurdles do not discriminate against selected groups. It is equally useful as a framework for understanding how the individuals who are applying for positions feel and respond as they attempt to jump the hurdles. At each hurdle they run the risk of being rejected. The realization that they must successfully compete at various levels in this process can be discouraging to some individuals. Prudent use of the process can help select the most qualified individuals from among the group of applicants.

You may advertise an open position in a variety of ways. In-house posting and newspaper advertising are the usual means, but word-of-mouth advertising may prove very beneficial in attracting candidates who are well qualified. Using your contacts gained through your participation in your local ENA or other special interest groups may prove to be a better investment than the usual advertising approaches.

Interested applicants then begin to jump each of these four hurdles in the employment process:

1. *Gross Prescreen:* An initial step is to select qualified candidates from among those who apply. This may be done by you, but frequently the prescreening

is done by a member of the personnel department or by the nurse recruiter. It is usually accomplished by reviewing the application form or through a brief telephone or personal interview.

2. *Testing:* Although hospitals usually do not administer elaborate psycho-metric tests as is sometimes done in determining suitability of applicants in the industrial/business sector, sometimes medication tests are administered or certification is required before the applicant can proceed further in the employment process.

3. *Interview:* For those who have reached this stage, the interview presents the most stressful aspect in this process. Your approach to the interview is discussed later in some depth.

4. *Security checks, reference checks, physical examinations:* All of these represent yet more hurdles to leap for the interviewee. Physical examina-tions are best done before the new worker begins employment. Applicants with a questionable physical condition, such as a back problem, should not be allowed to begin work until they are properly cleared. Personal references may have little relevance to real performance and may have little meaning because most applicants can get others to vouch for them. It is worthwhile, however, to check work references. Although former employers seldom verify more than dates of employment, even this information may help establish the credibility of part of the information on the application. The best way, however, to obtain information you can use in making decisions is to use your professional network to learn first hand how an individual performs.

Finally, when you have had the applicants leap all the hurdles successfully, you will choose one and make a job offer.

The hurdles outlined above can help the employer analyze the steps in the employment process to determine whether your institution's selection procedures have an adverse effect on a racial, ethnic, or sex group. You must monitor each hurdle to see if there is a significantly increased rejection rate found at any step. If so, the appropriate action is to identify the causes for that rejection so that solutions can be implemented that will remove any discriminating practices.

However, this analysis is difficult to perform. It is not easy to collect data at each step when you usually do not know the individual's minority status. For example, it is impossible to establish an individual's race or national origin from an application form. It may even be impossible to determine it at the time of interview. Such variables must not affect your hiring decisions, and you are expected to ensure that the process does not adversely affect minority groups, but you do not have good data for analysis—a real dilemma, indeed.

EQUAL EMPLOYMENT OPPORTUNITY AND AFFIRMATIVE ACTION

Equal employment opportunity (EEO) guarantees the right of all persons to work and to advance on the basis of merit, ability, and potential. It is the law as mandated by federal, state, and local legislation; presidential executive orders; and definitive court decisions. EEO ensures fair and equal treatment for all persons, regardless of race, color, sex, national origin, or age, in all employment practices.

Affirmative action (AA) is a positive program intended to carry out the intent of EEO by removing discriminatory practices that still pervade every phase of employment. Many discriminatory practices are still deeply embedded in the institutions of society, and these practices continue to impede the advancement of certain groups of our population. The major thrust of an AA program is the recognition and removal of those barriers that prevent qualified persons from attaining better jobs. The most important measure of an effective AA program is the yearly improvement in the hiring, training, and promotion of minorities.

The following is a summary of laws that in some way apply to EEO and AA:

- *Title VII of the Civil Rights Act of 1964* prohibits discrimination because of race, color, religion, sex, or national origin in any term, condition, or privilege of employment; also established the EEO Commission.
- *EEO Act of 1972 (Amended Title VII)* strengthens the powers and expands the jurisdiction of the EEOC in enforcement of Title VII.
- *Executive Order 11246 (Amended by EO 11375)* requires AA programs by all federal contractors and subcontractors.
- *Equal Pay Act of 1963* requires all employers subject to the Fair Labor Standards Act to provide equal pay for men and women performing similar work.
- *Age Discrimination in Employment Act of 1967* prohibits employers of 25 or more persons from discriminating against persons 40–70 years of age in any area of employment.
- *Title VI of the Civil Rights Act of 1964* prohibits discrimination in all programs or activities that receive federal financial aid.
- *State and local laws* may change/clarify federal mandates.
- *The National Labor Relations Act* prevents discrimination that would be to the detriment of organized union activity.
- *Title IX, Education Amendment Act of 1972* prohibits discrimination on the basis of sex against employees or students of any educational institution receiving federal financial aid.

- *Sections 503 and 504 of Vocational Rehabilitation Act* protects the rights of the handicapped. As an employee you may tell handicapped applicants about the duties of the job and ask them if they feel they can do the job. However, you cannot say that they cannot do the job. The act also provides that employers make "reasonable accommodation" in terms of physical facilities and individual accommodations, such as wheelchairs and visible signals for deaf persons.
- *Public Law 95-555* amended Title VII to prohibit sex discrimination on the basis of pregnancy. Enacted October 31, 1978 by the 95th Congress, this law has substantially affected attitudes toward pregnant applicants and employees. For example, employers now rarely question the legitimacy of using accumulated sick time during maternity leaves.
- *Other laws:* The courts have ruled that discrimination is prohibited by the Civil Rights Acts of 1866 and 1870 and the Equal Protection Clause of the 14th Amendment to the Constitution.

And so you can see that our society's response to removing discriminatory hiring practices is not embodied in only one law. Moreover, court-ordered remedies have been instrumental in prohibiting discrimination. When discrimination cases have been tried, the court decisions that are based on interpretation of law serve as a precedent for future trials. In cases where the courts have found that discrimination exists, they have ruled that there must be equal opportunity for all, and the employer must "make whole" and "restore the rightful economic status" of all of those in the "affected class." These rulings have resulted in extremely expensive assessments for back pay and legal costs. Under Title VII, back pay may be awarded to an entire "affected class" for as long as 2 years before the date of discrimination charge is filed.

An important precedent and guide was the famous AT&T agreement signed with EEOC and the Department of Labor. The agreement awarded millions of dollars in one-time payments to thousands of workers who suffered from discriminatory employment practices. In addition, millions of dollars were set aside for promotion and wage adjustments to minority and female employers. AA plans included hiring and promotion targets for employing males in previously all-female jobs. Hence, we now know that males can fill telephone operator positions, a situation that was unheard of 25 years ago. Because of this and other court decisions, many other employers have modified their employment practices in an attempt to avoid legal actions.

Although change has been slow and discriminatory practices still exist, there has been substantial progress. The legislation and court decisions affecting equal employment opportunity have improved opportunities for minority groups and have made this a better society for all.

In order to ensure that you do not inadvertently violate the intent of the law, certain questions should be eliminated from pre-employment inquiries (application forms and interviews) or carefully reviewed to ensure that their purpose is job-related and nondiscriminatory. Although these questions may not necessarily constitute violations of the law per se, it is usually better not to ask them because, if a charge of discrimination occurs, the burden of proof is on the employer to show that the use of such information is nondiscriminatory and job-related. These considerations include:

- *Race, national origin, religion:* Inquiries about race, color, national origin, or religion do not constitute violations per se (except in some states) of Title VII. However, such inquiries will be carefully examined if discrimination charges should arise. *IT'S BETTER NOT TO ASK SUCH QUESTIONS.* It is not unlawful to ask, but it is unlawful to use this information in the selection process.

- *Education:* The courts have found that non-job-related educational requirements that have an unequal effect on protected groups are a major area of illegal discrimination. Although such requirements would rarely be an issue with hiring of professional staff, they could adversely affect certain ancillary job categories.

- *Arrest and conviction records:* An individual's possession of an arrest record has been ruled by courts to be an unlawful basis for refusal to employ, unless a "business necessity" for such a policy can be established. An arrest is not an indication of guilt, and courts have found that, where minorities are subject to disproportionately higher arrest rates than whites, refusal to hire on this basis has a disproportionate effect on minority employment opportunity. Being convicted of a felony or misdemeanor should not, by itself, constitute an absolute bar to employment, unless there is "job relatedness" between the act and the position.

- *Credit rating:* A negative employment decision based on an applicant's poor credit rating has been found unlawful, where credit policies have a disproportionate negative effect on minorities and the employer cannot show "business necessity" for such rejection. Inquiries about charge accounts and home and car ownership, unless the latter is required for the job, may be unlawful.

- *Sex, marital and family status:* Questions frequently used to discriminate against women that rarely relate to their capacity for job performance include whether the candidate is married or single and the number and ages of her children. The courts have ruled that an employer must not have different hiring policies for men and women with preschool children.

- *Physical requirements:* Application questions and hiring standards related to height, weight, and other physical requirements should be retained only where necessary for performance of a particular job.
- *Experience requirements:* These should be eliminated for those jobs that can be learned quickly.

To avoid other potential areas of discrimination, it is best not to raise questions regarding the following issues:

- *age and date of birth*
- *availability for Saturday or Sunday work:* Title VII provides that an employer must make reasonable accommodations for ''religious observance or practice without undue hardship on the conduct of the employer's business.'' To handle this issue, tell the applicant what the scheduled hours of work are and ask if he or she can meet the requirements.
- *whether friends and relatives are working for the company:* This question may reflect a preference for friends and relatives of present employees or the opposite—that only one partner in a marriage may work for the company.
- *the individual's appearance:* Employment decisions based on length or style of hair, dress, or other aspects of appearance have been found to violate the law. For example, some court rulings have found it is illegal to refuse to hire a male with long hair where similar restrictions are not imposed on females or where hair style requirements can be racially discriminatory.

Generally, the terminology in court discrimination charges is ''individual determination,'' which means that you must look at the applicant as an individual, rather than as a member of a class.

EEOC and the courts have found that many common pre-employment inquiries have the effect of disproportionately rejecting minority group members. Some of these questions have been explicitly prohibited by courts where they have been shown to have a discriminatory effect. The exact legal status of other questions is still to be determined.

The following three pragmatic guidelines are recommended for your consideration in pre-employment inquiries:

1. Does the question tend to have a disproportionate effect in screening out minorities and females?
2. Is this information necessary to judge this individual's competence for performance of this particular job?
3. Are there alternate, nondiscriminatory ways to secure the necessary information?

INTERVIEWING

An interview can be defined as conversation with a purpose. When used to make employment decisions, it is a way of learning more about applicants through purposeful communication. The principles of effective interviewing and the necessary skills apply regardless of what kind of interview is conducted, i.e., an employment interview, patient interview, or counseling interview. All interviewing involves a specialized pattern of communication, initiated for a specified purpose, and focused on a particular subject. Its purpose is to help you select the best applicant possible from among a field of seemingly qualified applicants.

It is generally recognized that the success of the interview in predicting performance is poor. However, to the degree that you apply good interviewing techniques, you can increase the effectiveness of the interview and its outcomes.

The interview is primarily a design to acquire needed information as determined by verbal and nonverbal responses to questions you pose. Two theorists who have greatly influenced how we ask questions are B.F. Skinner and Carl Rogers. Skinner, a well-known behaviorist, believes that behavior that is rewarded tends to be repeated. What kinds of rewards can you give during the interview? You can listen, show appropriate facial expressions of concern or interest, or occasionally nod. Such methods of feedback keep the lines of communication open. Rogers, a humanist, says that judgment is the greatest barrier to communication. Society places value judgments on many things, and if we allow our negative feelings to show it is likely that the interviewee will not disclose more information.

In line with these two theoretical approaches there are two contrasting techniques for asking questions. Directive or Skinnerian techniques obtain information through specific questions, e.g., "Do you have any emergency nursing experience that is not reflected in your application?" Nondirective or Rogerian techniques require more skill because the interviewer tries not to force the answer directly, e.g., "You say that you enjoyed that job, did you?" Generally, you might begin your interview with broad open-ended questions and proceed to more directed questions. Both approaches can provide valuable insight that can help you make your hiring decision.

Actions Performed in the Interview

There are four different actions that you perform simultaneously during the interview:

1. You make *observations* that are purposeful and objective. You observe physical and behavioral responses of the interviewee.
2. Most of your interview time should be spent *listening*. It is well established that our ability to retain what we have heard is very inefficient. You need to

work at getting as much information as possible during a relatively brief
time. Listening as an active process enables you to grasp the facts and
feelings behind what is being said.

3. *Communications,* both verbal and nonverbal, determine whether the flow of
   information is kept open and whether you have obtained the necessary
   information by the end of the interview.

4. *Documentation* or recording of the information exchanged is essential in
   reviewing applicants. It may be helpful to record important observations
   during the interview or immediately after its conclusion. When you allow a
   long time to elapse between observation and recording, you decrease the
   potential for accurate recall of salient points.

Accuracy of Your Ability to Make Judgments

It has already been said that the accuracy of the interview as a predictor of
performance is poor but that you can increase your predictive ability by good
interviewing skills. Some characteristics displayed by the applicant can be more
clearly judged than others. Such characteristics as interviewees' self-confidence,
the effectiveness with which they express themselves, certain attitudes, their
sociability, and a variety of mental abilities can be assessed fairly accurately.
Other characteristics, such as dependability, creativity, honesty, and loyalty, are
not as easily judged. As you prepare to interview a candidate, pursue a line of
questioning that attempts to obtain information about those traits that are easily
judged. Briefly presenting a hypothetical situation to the applicant for consideration and comment is a good way to obtain information about his or her traits and
problem-solving abilities.

A student recently told this author that she was presented the following case by a
nurse manager:

> You are in a patient's room providing care to a patient whom you have
> been taking care of for the past 3 days. A physician enters and notes that
> you are applying betadine to the patient's sacral pressure sore. The
> physician becomes very angered and says loudly, "You nurses are not
> paying attention to this patient. You are responsible for this patient's
> decubitus."

This is a great scenario because it presents many opportunities for you to assess
the applicant's response to the clinical and professional considerations. Does the
applicant's response focus only on the physician's outburst, or are there
expressions of concern for the patient, consideration of the professional nurse's
role in pressure sore management, or attempts to "defuse" the situation? The

applicant's response will give valuable insight into the way he or she may be expected to react to stressful situations.

Conducting the Interview

The following considerations sound like common sense, but are worthy of your review because of the frequency with which they are overlooked.

- *Provide a suitable setting.* An adequate room or space that provides privacy and quiet is essential. It should also be well lit and comfortable in order to facilitate excellent communication.
- *Plan the interview.* Decide clearly on the purpose of the interview and what you want to achieve from it before its conclusion.
- *Study the job description.* Be thoroughly familiar with the content of staff-level job descriptions so that you may pose appropriate questions and respond in an informed manner to any concerns the interviewer may have about performance expectations.
- *Study available information about the applicant.* Before meeting the candidate, be familiar with his or her resume. To read the resume in front of the candidate sends a clear message that you have not prepared for the interview.
- *Study your own prejudices.* Be aware of any biases you may have that may interfere with making a fair decision.
- *Put the applicant at ease.* Applicants' physical and psychological comfort will enhance communication and will help them decide whether this environment is one in which they can be comfortable. Asking a casual question, such as "Did you have any problem finding your way to the hospital?," will go a long way in establishing the right interview environment.
- *Take enough time.* Not allowing adequate time for an interview is a serious mistake many managers make. It would be better to postpone an interview than to do it hurriedly. Conversely, an interview should not take longer than necessary. Too long is equally as bad as too short!
- *Let the interviewee talk.* The purpose is to learn as much about the applicant as possible. The candidate's responses form the substance of the interview.
- *Keep control.* You are in the "driver's seat," and so you need to channel the discussion so that all areas are covered within a reasonable time. Too many interviews tend to ramble on and are largely nonproductive.
- *Avoid any suggestion of discrimination.* Having studied your own biases, you must be clear in your line of questioning in order to avoid any issues that, however well intended, could be in violation of the law. Familiarity with

material presented earlier will help the informed nurse manager avoid potentially discriminatory questions, such as "How many children do you have?"

- *Close in a friendly manner.* Let interviewees know where they stand at that point. If for some reason you will not be considering them any further, then let them know that in a tactful, sensitive manner. In all cases, you should let the applicant know your plans for making a decision and follow-up.
- *Record facts immediately.* Salient facts that will affect your decision must be recorded immediately. if you are recording during the interview, be sensitive to how doing so may affect the interviewee's responses. Let the candidate know that you plan to take notes.

Order of the Interview

It is advisable to proceed in a logical fashion to ensure that all information is exchanged. Although there are no absolutes, you may wish to consider the following format:

- *Introduction:* This is the beginning piece in which you set the mood. Physical setting, salutories, and general conditions can "make or break" the remainder of the interview process.
- *Description of the position:* Although you do not want to "oversell" the position, you do want to present a thorough overview of the position while focusing on nursing philosophy, hours of work, and other performance expectations.
- *Main body of the interview:* Using the directive and nondirective techniques described earlier, you trace the educational and experiential background of the candidate. Your decision will be based largely on the data you glean from this portion of the interview.
- *Discussion of salary and benefits:* This information should be conveyed by the nurse recruiter or personnel department. You should ask if the candidate has any further questions.
- *Closing:* At this time, you tie the interview together and summarize its significant points. Inform the applicant of the next step in the hiring process or when he or she may expect to hear from you.

Asking Questions

You may find the following 12 suggestions helpful for asking questions:

1. Keep them short and simple—an interview is not the time for complex questions.

2. Stick to one idea—pursue one avenue at a time.
3. Use words that the interviewee will understand.
4. Avoid questions that would intimidate the interviewee if he or she were not able to answer them. Many people will answer "yes," rather than appear stupid.
5. Respond to the interviewee's expressed or implied feelings. If he or she says, "I'm nervous", you should not respond by asking "Why are you nervous?" This question can be interpreted as "You shouldn't feel nervous." A better response is, "I understand that you are nervous. Would it help to talk about it?"

    Although you are not conducting a therapy session, you do want to maximize the opportunity to put the individual at ease while at the same time noting that the expression of "nervousness" may be an important indication of his or her ability to handle the job.
6. Avoid such leading questions as "Do you plan to complete your degree requirements within 2 years?" This wording can give a clue to the answer you expect. A better question is, "What plans do you have for the completion of your degree requirements, if any?"
7. On the other hand, you may want to ask a leading question to persuade or suggest an appropriate action. Such a question is, "You can come in Friday morning for your physical, can't you?" You want a "yes" answer so that the individual can start work in the near future.
8. Be careful of gestures and other nonverbal forms of communication—such as grimacing over a disparaging story. Doing so could prevent further meaningful communication.
9. Give the applicant time to think through his or her answers.
10. Rephrase your question, if necessary.
11. Do not assume anything. You should summarize or clarify ("are you saying that . . . ?") by quoting the applicant. Put the statement in his or her own words and add, "Did I state that correctly?"
12. Show the applicant that you are interested in him or her as an individual.

Generally, consciously or unconsciously, interviewees will tend to give the answers they think you expect to your questions. For example, "You have taken your GREs haven't you?" You are subtly telling the applicant that his or her answer should be "yes".

Questions related to the applicant's work experience are the most meaningful for your purpose. You should be looking for relevance of earlier work, sufficiency of work, skill and competence, adaptability, prductivity, motivation, nature of interpersonal relationships, leadership, and growth and development.

Helpful questions related to work experience include:

- What things do you do best? Do less well?
- What things do you like best? Like less well?
- What are your major accomplishments? How did you achieve them?
- What have been the most difficult problems you have faced? How did you resolve them?
- What ways have you found to be most effective with people? Which ways are less effective?
- What is your reason for changing jobs?
- What have your learned from your work experience?
- What are you looking for in a job?

While interviewing, you should be equally aware of what kinds of questions are asked by the applicant. Did they ask about:

- continuing education/orientation
- benefits
- staffing patterns
- the position of nursing in the organization
- nurse-physician relationships
- long-range plans for the hospital/ED
- relationship to the Board of Directors
- system of care delivery

The nature of the applicants' inquiries can tell you a great deal. Are they concerned with the amount of shift rotation they will have to do, or are they more interested in the nursing care delivery system? Which applicant would you prefer?

There are many hazards or potential pitfalls that are easy to fall into while conducting an interview. Some things to watch for during an interview include:

- Avoid being formal or cold, which will inhibit the applicant from talking freely.
- Avoid distractions, such as concentrating on documentation, rather than listening.
- Never "talk down" any other institution.
- Avoid trick questions.
- Don't allow your manner or tone of voice to reveal your real feelings, particularly disapproval.
- Avoid questions that can be answered by yes or no.

CONCLUSION

The interviewing and selection of competent staff members is an opportunity to establish quality nursing care in your ED. By virtue of your position, you have been given the responsibility to make important choices. The intent of this chapter was to familiarize you with the complex circumstances surrounding your decisions and to suggest strategies for conducting effective interviews.

To implement the concept of equal employment opportunity you must exercise a tremendous amount of caution in order to avoid making statements or asking questions that could be interpreted as biased. You are also obliged to ensure fair and equitable consideration for all candidates. Through an informed, wise use of the interview process, you can optimize this opportunity and select the best candidate from among a group of applicants.

The realization that there are potential pitfalls in the process can help you avoid proceeding in a manner that might have negative consequences for you and your employing agency. The wise application of interviewing techniques can help you increase the value of the interview as a selection procedure and make you more effective as a manager in fulfilling your responsibility of selecting qualified staff members.

Chapter 5

Human Resource Management

JOB DESCRIPTIONS AND EXPECTATIONS

A job description describes the position for which the employee is being hired. It includes educational and licensure requirements, general functions, responsibilities, and to whom the employee is responsible. Many hospitals have only one job description for all staff nurses who work in the hospital; it is not specific to the ED staff nurse's functions and responsibilities. Or, in hospitals that utilize a career ladder, there may be separate job descriptions for the different levels. However, these job descriptions often do not reflect the true function of the ED staff nurse. If permitted by individual hospital personnel departments, specific job descriptions should be written for the different levels of staff in the ED.

When a new employee begins work in the ED, review the relevant job description for the position with him or her. Specific expectations of the new ED staff member should be documented and communicated verbally to him or her. Exhibit 5–1 is an example of ED staff nurse expectations.

Employee expectations should be achieved within a specified time limit. A probationary period is a period of time during which the ED nurse manager can determine whether the employee can meet the expectations of the job. Many jobs have a 3-month probationary period. This amount of time may be adequate for a new technician, nurse's aide/orderly, or secretary because their job knowledge and tasks can be learned in 3 months. Exhibit 5–2 describes the responsibilities of an ED nurse's aide/orderly. However, I have found that 3 months is often too short a time to determine the maximum performance level of a new ED staff nurse, because of the extensive learning of ED systems, knowledge, and skills that is required for an RN to perform adequately in the ED. Therefore, I extended the probationary period for staff nurses to 6 months, a period of time that I recommend to other ED nurse managers.

Exhibit 5–1 Expectations of the ED Staff Nurse

At the end of 6 months, the staff RN will:

1. Report for duty on time consistently, have satisfactory attendance, and comply with notification procedures for absence or lateness.
2. Pass IV medication exam and supervision.
3. Pass IV/venipuncture supervision.
4. Complete orientation checklist.
5. Complete basic emergency nursing classes and critical care course.
6. Demonstrate competence in all areas of clinical responsibility in the ED:
   a. Treatment rooms
      1. Maintain specific room supplies and equipment; use and care for equipment properly.
      2. Assist with procedures.
      3. Obtain and send specimens (blood, urine, cultures).
      4. Do appropriate documentation on all ED nursing forms and the ED treatment record.
      5. Institute admission, discharge, and transfer procedures accurately.
      6. Assess patient conditions and responses appropriately.
      7. Administer medications to assigned patients.
      8. Participate actively in patient teaching and discharge planning.
      9. Demonstrate consistently patient advocacy and a warm, caring attitude.
      10. Ensure a smooth, rapid flow of patients from acute treatment rooms.
      11. Ensure that patients receive prompt, appropriate care.
      12. Assist co-workers on own initiative.
      13. Maintain a neat working area.
   b. Holding area
      1. Supervise and administer competent patient care.
      2. Ensure compliance with detaining procedures.
   c. Triage
      1. Determine and document patients' presenting problems, observations, and brief history.
      2. Prioritize patients appropriately according to their level of acuity.
      3. Evaluate and refer patients appropriately.
      4. Administer first aid and lifesaving measures as necessary.
      5. Consistently follow established triage procedure and prioritization categories as outlined in the triage manual.
7. Follow procedures consistently for patient item charging and patient classification.
8. Demonstrate consistently an understanding of policies, procedures, and methods of work organization. Develop technical skills and utilize resources effectively.
9. Demonstrate initiative by assuming responsibility for own learning needs and seeking appropriate assistance when needed.
10. Be able to independently care for all ED patients. Demonstrate an understanding of the pathophysiology involved and its effect on the nursing process.
11. Demonstrate an interest in and enthusiasm for meeting established standards, expectations, and goals.
12. Participate actively in continuing education programs offered by the hospital, ENA, and other appropriate outside agencies.
13. Review one's learning needs with the nurse manager.

Exhibit 5–2 Responsibilities of the ED Nursing Aide

Primary Responsibilities:

Transport of patients, specimens, supplies, and equipment

Maintenance and stocking of supplies and equipment

Examples of Work:

1. Transports patients by wheelchair, stretcher, or bed to other patient care or diagnostic areas. Assists patients with ambulation.
2. Transports specimens to laboratories.
3. Maintains organization and cleanliness of equipment and supply areas and utility rooms.
4. Assists with postmortem care.
5. Retrieves and distributes supplies as needed.
6. Distributes linen.
7. Prepares and maintains linen on stretchers.
8. Maintains an adequate supply of oxygen tanks.
9. Assists nurses with combative patients and with the application of restraints.
10. Maintains a friendly, receptive, and interested attitude.
11. Respects the confidential nature of patient information.
12. Performs related work as required.
13. Signs in and out when leaving and returning to the ED.

The employee's progress should be evaluated continually during the probationary period, with a formal review at midpoint, to determine the employee's weaknesses and need for improvement and to develop specific short-term goals that must be achieved by the end of the probationary period.

ORIENTATION

Hospitals usually offer a general orientation program for all new employees, which includes personnel policies regarding salary, vacation, and sick time accrual; disciplinary procedures; grievance procedures; organization of the hospital; and nursing service policies and procedures.

The general orientation may be relevant to the ED staff if the ED is under the control of the hospital. However, if the ED is controlled by a private physician group, the hospital personnel policies may not pertain to the ED staff. Or, if the ED is under hospital control but authority is decentralized, nursing service policies and procedures may also not be pertinent to the ED nursing staff. In addition, a new ED nurse has different orientation needs than nurses in other hospital areas. ED nursing forms, manuals, responsibilities, required skills, tasks, and relationships are unique to the ED. Therefore, a comprehensive ED orientation is required.

The goal of orientation to the ED is to prepare the new employee to perform the role and responsibilities of the position for which he or she was hired. An orientation program should acquaint the employee with the operations of the ED and the details of the employee's job. Specific training is usually necessary unless the employee has had previous experience in a similar ED. Although the time spent during orientation is not productive time, it helps the employee attain maximum usefulness in a shorter period of time.

A preceptor program is an effective way to orient new staff. A new employee is assigned to an experienced staff member who has demonstrated above-average performance. The preceptor assumes responsibility for training the new employee, helps the ED nurse manager develop specific goals for the employee, and assists in the evaluation of the new employee's progress and performance at the end of the probationary period. The employee begins by observing and helping the preceptor and then working under the preceptor's supervision. The preceptor can slow or speed up the orientation process according to the individual needs of the orientee. Even after the orientee is able to perform without direct supervision, the relationship with the preceptor should be maintained for future learning needs, guidance, and support.

A checklist of responsibilities and tasks required in the ED can help determine the progress made by each new employee and whether expectations are being met. It also ensures that the new employee has received experience in all aspects of emergency nursing. Exhibit 5–3 is an example of such a checklist. The preceptor can utilize the checklist during orientation and assist the employee to complete it by the end of the probationary period.

In addition to on-the-job training, formal basic emergency nursing classes should be considered. Topics that are important to include are:

- assessment of abdominal pain
- assessment of chest pain
- pediatric emergencies, including asthma, epiglottitis, sudden infant death syndrome, and child abuse
- minor and major trauma protocols
- shock (cardiogenic, septic, hypovolemic)
- life-threatening cardiac dysrhythmias
- crisis intervention
- OB/GYN emergencies
- care of the patient with acute asthma, seizures, and ingestion/inhalation/ contact with toxic substances
- triage
- ED equipment, supplies, and trays

Exhibit 5–3 Emergency Department Orientation Checklist

Employee name _____ Employment date _____

Preceptor name _____

	Preceptor initials
1. *Forms*	
ED Treatment record	_____
Nursing record	_____
Trauma record	_____
Critical care flow sheet	_____
Patient item charge form	_____
Discharge instructions	_____
Pre-op checklist	_____
Valuables form	_____
2. *Equipment*	
Cardiac monitors	_____
EKG machines	_____
Monitor/defibrillators	_____
Internal defibrillation paddles	_____
Pediatric paddles	_____
Oxygen: wall units, tanks	_____
Suction: wall, portable	_____
Doppler	_____
Noninvasive blood pressure machines	_____
Infusion pump	_____
Leather restraints	_____
3. *Orthopedic*	
Application/use of:	
ace bandage	_____
splints	_____
immobilizers	_____
crutches	_____
cervical collars	_____
sandbags	_____
ice packs	_____
4. *EENT*	
Eye chart/visual acuity	_____
Eye irrigation	_____
Corneal abrasion	_____
Eye patch	_____
Ear irrigation	_____
Nasal forceps	_____
speculum	_____
packing	_____
Throat cultures	_____

Exhibit 5–3 continued

5. *OB/GYN*
   Pelvic exam   _____
   Cultures   _____
   GYN instruments   _____
   Culdocentesis tray   _____
   Emergency delivery   _____
   Spontaneous abortion   _____
      care of fetus   _____
   Rape victims   _____
   Urine pregnancy test   _____

6. *Urology*
   Clean catch urine   _____
   Catheterization   _____
      straight cath   _____
      indwelling   _____
   Urimeter   _____
   Continuous bladder irrigation   _____
   Urologic manipulation tray   _____
   Suprapubic cystotomy   _____

7. *Cardiac*
   Obtain 12-lead EKG   _____
   Dysrythmia interpretation   _____
      sinus rhythm   _____
      sinus bradycardia   _____
      sinus tachycardia   _____
      atrial fibrillation   _____
      atrial flutter   _____
      paroxysmal atrial tachycardia   _____
      junctional rhythm   _____
      first degree heart block   _____
      second degree heart block   _____
      third degree heart block   _____
      ventricular tachycardia   _____
      ventricular fibrillation   _____
      premature atrial contractions   _____
      premature ventricular contractions   _____
   Idioventricular rhythm   _____
   Paced rhythm   _____
   Monitor lead placement   _____
   Temporary pacemaker   _____
   Esophageal leads   _____
   Code responsibilities   _____
   CPR   _____

8. *Respiratory*
   Airway: oral, nasal   _____
   Ventilation bags   _____

Exhibit 5–3 continued

     Oxygen therapy equipment   _____
        nasal cannula   _____
        mask   _____
        venti-mask   _____
        partial rebreather   _____
        mini-neb treatment   _____
     Ventilator   _____
     Suctioning   _____
        nasal   _____
        endotracheal   _____
     Auscultation of lung sounds   _____
     Arterial blood gases   _____
        obtaining   _____
        interpretation   _____

9. *Gastrointestinal*
     Abdominal assessment   _____
     Tilt test   _____
     Tubes   _____
        nasogastric   _____
        salem sump   _____
        ewald   _____
        Cantor   _____
        Miller-Abbott   _____
        Sengstaken-Blakemore   _____
     Endoscopy   _____

10. *Minor trauma*
     Abrasions   _____
     Hematomas   _____
     Lacerations   _____
        suture tray   _____
     Minor burns   _____
     Bites   _____

11. *Major trauma*
     Peritoneal lavage   _____
     Thoracotomy   _____
     Chest tube insertion   _____
     Thoracentesis   _____
     Tracheotomy   _____
     MAST trousers   _____
     Burn pack   _____
     Major burns   _____
        electrical   _____

12. *Pediatrics*
     Care of pediatric patient   _____
        fever   _____
        asthma   _____

Exhibit 5-3 continued

       seizure   _____
       sudden infant death   _____
       child abuse   _____
       medications   _____
13. *Psychiatric*
    Voluntary commitment   _____
    Involuntary commitment   _____
    Referral   _____
    Care of the violent patient   _____
       suicidal patient   _____
14. *Social*
    Disposition problems   _____
    Abuse   _____
15. *Intravenous therapy*   _____
16. *Phlebotomy*   _____
17. *Hemodynamic monitoring*
    CVP   _____
    arterial pressure   _____
18. *Triage*
    Assessment   _____
    Prioritization   _____
    Documentation   _____
    Interventions   _____
19. *Organ transplant*
    Donor   _____
    Recipient   _____
20. *Miscellaneous*
    DOA: procedure/forms   _____
    Reportable cases   _____
    Postmortem care   _____
    Transfer procedure   _____
    Admission procedure   _____
       safety   _____
    Infection control   _____
    Public relations   _____
    Media   _____

These basic emergency nursing classes can be presented by an ED clinical specialist or staff instructor or by senior members of the staff. You should also take part in presenting this information. Doing so helps acquaint you with the new staff better and vice versa, begins the development of employee trust and respect for you, and aids in the development of good relationships between the new employees and you. If the hospital offers a critical care course, the ED staff should attend it because critical care knowledge is also needed in the ED.

In conjunction with the training and classes, an ED nursing orientation/protocol manual should be developed. The manual helps reinforce what has been taught and serves as a reference for the new employee in the future. It can include ED nursing procedures, established protocols, standards, and a list of approved ED nursing privileges, such as defibrillation, collection of cultures, collection of venous and arterial blood samples, ordering of specific x-ray studies, administration of oxygen and intravenous medications, and initiation of intravenous infusions. The responsibilities and privileges of all levels of ED nursing staff should be described in the manual.

PERFORMANCE APPRAISAL

Reviewing and evaluating employee performance are necessary and important responsibilities of the ED nurse manager. A performance appraisal conference should be a positive and motivating experience for the employee whose performance is being evaluated. Too often, employees view evaluations as a negative experience, characterized by criticisms of their work or themselves, rather than as a means of conveying positive reinforcement, encouragement, and suggestions for growth and development. You must be objective, honest, and fair so the evaluation reflects the actual performance of the employee and not his or her personality.

Purposes of Performance Appraisal

A performance appraisal has the following purposes:

- to identify strengths and encourage and commend good performance
- to identify and correct employee weaknesses
- to provide an opportunity for feedback to the employee concerning his or her work performance
- to provide an opportunity for feedback from the employee to the ED nurse manager concerning departmental issues, individual needs, and management performance
- to create a reasonable degree of competition among staff members
- to determine employee eligibility for merit salary raises and promotion
- to provide an opportunity to discuss employee achievements and personal goals

Types of Performance Appraisals

A performance appraisal can be either informal or formal. Although most employing agencies require at least one formal written performance appraisal for each employee, informal appraisals are just as important. The objectives of informal appraisals are to discuss problems as they occur, to identify strengths and weaknesses, and to assist in employee growth at more frequent intervals than just once a year. Informal appraisals should be done during the entire year before the formal performance appraisal. In that way, when an employee receives the formal performance appraisal, the information communicated has already been discussed with him or her during the year that is being reviewed. Anecdotal notes should be written after each informal performance appraisal conference with individual staff members. These notes can be referred to in the future as you prepare for the formal appraisal.

A formal performance appraisal should rate an employee's knowledge and quality and quantity of work performance as reflected in all areas of his or her responsibilities and skills in the ED. Many hospitals have performance appraisal tools that are developed by the personnel department or nursing services. However, these performance appraisal tools are usually focused on the responsibilities and expectations of the medical-surgical staff member and do not adequately appraise the ED staff member's performance. In addition, one tool or form cannot meet the appraisal requirements of different job levels.

An effective appraisal tool for the ED nursing staff must include emergency nursing functions and nursing needs specific to the individual ED; that is, what the ED staff and you consider to be important. A checklist of specific ED nursing responsibilities, expectations, and skills can be an effective way of evaluating performance. Some broad areas that should be included in the performance appraisal of a staff RN are shown in Table 5–1. Under each topic, specific criteria should be listed with a rating scale. An example is shown in Exhibit 5–4.

Before conducting the appraisal, seek information from assistant nurse managers, preceptors, charge nurses, and co-workers of the employee who is to be appraised so that it is more objective and fair.

In EDs with a large number of staff members, it becomes an almost impossible task for the ED nurse manager to formally appraise the performance of every staff member accurately and fairly. Therefore, delegate some of the performance appraisals to ED assistant nurse managers (or the employee's immediate supervisor), especially for those staff members who work permanent evening or night shifts.

Formal performance appraisals should take into account the employee's performance during the entire review period, not only his or her recent performance or activity in a specific situation. For this purpose, keep and review anecdotal notes from informal conferences.

Performance Appraisal Conference

The employee should be given advance notice of the conference to discuss the written appraisal. Adequate time should be allotted for the conference. The setting

Table 5–1 ED Nursing Areas that Should be Appraised

Functional Performance	Personal Characteristics	Personal Development
Job knowledge	Initiative	Continuing education
Triage	Reliability	Participation in ED, nursing
Data collection	Dependability	service, hospital, and
Assessment skills	Decision making	community activities
Technical skills	Flexibility	Experiences
Assisting with procedures	Adaptability	Professional activities and
Communication skills	Professional appearance	development
Patient teaching	and behavior	
Patient advocacy		
Patient comfort and safety		
Interpersonal relationships		
Clinical judgment		
Documentation		
Medication administration		
Utilization of resources		
Use and care of equipment		
Compliance with policies		
and procedures		
Organizational skills		
Cost efficiency		
Leadership skills		

should be private and permit no interruptions. In the conference there should be two-way communication, from you to the ED staff member and from the ED staff member to you. Encourage the employee to discuss her or his own performance, areas needing further growth, goals, concerns, and feelings about the department and management. Discuss together ways that the employee can improve and/or grow professionally. As ED nurse managers, we not only have the responsibility of evaluating employee performance but also of assisting the employee to achieve expectations and accomplish goals.

THE ROLE OF THE CLINICAL NURSE SPECIALIST IN THE EMERGENCY DEPARTMENT*

In the 1930s and 1940s, with the advent of nurse aides and other ancillary patient caregivers, nursing relinquished its role as the primary providers of care and became managers of care. Since that time, the increase in scientific knowl-

---

*This section was prepared by Margaret Daly McKenna.

Exhibit 5–4 Specific Criteria for Each Area of Responsibility or Skill

	Yes	No
Documentation		
Documents appropriately on ED forms:		
ED treatment record	———	———
Triage record	———	———
ED nursing record	———	———
Trauma record	———	———
Preoperative checklist	———	———
Valuables form	———	———
Incident reports	———	———
Patient item charge form	———	———
Documents consistently:		
Patient history of presenting problem	———	———
Past medical history	———	———
Allergies	———	———
Medications	———	———
Assessment: subjective	———	———
objective	———	———
Procedures	———	———
Patient responses to treatment	———	———
Changes in patient status	———	———
Reporting of changes in status	———	———
Patient/family teaching	———	———
Patient disposition	———	———
Discharge planning/referral	———	———
ED patient classification level	———	———
Times of all nursing interventions	———	———
Times of treatments and procedures	———	———
Signs all documentation	———	———

edge, technology, and specialization in health care has continued to expand the scope of nursing practice. These trends, combined with the plea of nursing leaders to return the nurse to the practice of "laying on hands," resulted in the development of the role of the clinical nurse specialist. Graduate schools of nursing began in the 1960s to use Master's level preparation for the education of designated nursing specialists.

Within the last five years, the number of graduate programs offering clinical specialization tracks in emergency, burn, and trauma care has grown. As a result, an ED clinical specialist is now on the staff of many types of health care facilities. However, I discovered upon entering graduate school that as late as 1983 only a meager amount of literature describing the ED clinical specialist existed. I then took on the challenge of developing this new role by gathering literature references, corresponding with peers, and organizing my own ideas. My goal was to develop an appropriate job description including clinical and research objectives needed as preparation for the role. The original job description conceptualized the ED clinical specialist as fulfilling a multi-dimensional role that incorporated consultation, education, research, personal development, and expert nursing care. Providing care to the population of crisis-stricken emergency patients is an excellent opportunity for achievement of all aspects of this multidimensional career.

On the organizational chart, the ED clinical specialist is a staff position, rather than a line position. The clinical nurse specialist should not be counted as part of the nursing staffing pattern and should be allowed to develop his or her own role in accordance with the specialty. You should allow the ED clinical specialist flexibility in determining work hours. He or she should have the freedom to work throughout the facility and within the community.

The ED clinical specialist must develop "expert" power by serving as an accurate resource, motivational model, and accomplished change agent. By collaborating in both clinical and managerial components, the ED specialist can also establish a pattern of "borrowed" authority for problem solving.

There can be shared responsibilities between the clinical specialist and you. Use a collaborative approach to develop policies and procedures, counsel staff, coordinate quality and appropriateness reviews, and other activities. The alliance allows a pooling of efforts to establish desired outcomes.

A clinical specialist should continuously educate and foster the development of ED staff members. These functions can best be performed informally by being available when and where staff members have questions, usually at the "stretcher-side." In addition, frequent presentations should be made to review protocols or present new treatment or disease entities. By scheduling new staff members on the shift with the clinical specialist, he or she is available to assist in the orientation of new personnel. In addition, the ED clinical specialist should change shifts periodically in order to maintain contact with all the ED nurses.

Educating staff members about trends in the emergency population can increase their awareness of patient needs. A large percentage of patients who come to the ED today are ambulatory and present nonurgent situations. Upon investigation, many patients indicate that the ED is their primary source of health care. Yet, the hospital ED has not typically been regarded as a primary location for patient education activities.

The ED clinical specialist promotes the setting aside of time in a busy ED to provide health care instruction to this emerging population who chooses this alternative in primary health care. Incorporation of health teaching into an area that has been designed to deliver physical care requires the ED staff's understanding of the balance of health and illness instruction. For example, the several minutes it takes to teach a mother to read a thermometer may prevent further risk to the child and decrease her number of visits to the ED.

Direct patient contact can be an avenue for continued proficiency for the clinical specialist as well as a means for staff evaluation. Two ongoing programs at Our Lady of Lourdes Regional Medical Center in Lafayette, LA have helped improve patient care outcomes. Both programs center around patient and nursing feedback. The first is postdischarge follow-up. The ED clinical specialist is in a unique position to follow the hospital and rehabilitative course of the ED patients. He or she first interviews patients and families to determine their perception of their emergency care. The emergency care plan is then compared to the patient outcome, medical diagnosis, and complications incurred. The final product is the written summary or trauma registry, which is available for the ED nursing staff's review.

By identifying specific interventions that affected patient outcome, this analysis of different types of admissions has assisted in developing standards of care. For example, early application of anti-embolism hose on patients with suspected spinal shock was seen to prevent complications of venous pooling. Specific protocols for emergency situations developed from this analysis have proven to be effective.

The other program at the regional medical center relies on immediate staff feedback, which can be provided by the ED specialist. Likewise, the ED specialist's presence at medical and traumatic resuscitations makes possible an expert evaluation of nursing actions. A team forum that would also include the physician can review approaches that were effective and possible actions that would expedite patient recovery or improve the delivery of care.

In summary, the clinical nurse specialist can be a welcome addition to the emergency nursing staff and management. With the scope of nursing practice expanding, preparation in a nursing specialty appropriate to the population of the emergency clientele can expedite the delivery of expert nursing care. In addition to the multidimensional role of education, research, and consultation, the ED specialist can provide collaborative support to the ED director. Staff development can be fostered spontaneously at the "stretcher-side" or through scheduled educational sessions. Education also includes health instruction for the patients who use the department as a primary source of health care. The ED specialist is in a unique position to function as a resource throughout the facility or community who can facilitate the development of new projects to gather, analyze, and improve the quality of emergency care.

CONTINUING EDUCATION FOR EMERGENCY NURSES*

Changes in the health care field are ongoing and frequently difficult to keep pace with. To ensure the delivery of quality care, nurses and other health care profes-

*This section was prepared by Cynthia Possanza.

sionals are encouraged to seek further education. Continuing education department-ments have been developed in hospitals and colleges to address these health care professional needs. Puetz and Peters explain that, "During the 1970's, continuing education in nursing has expanded explosively, fueled by government legislation, professional organization standards and requirements, regulatory bodies such as JCAH, and societal pressures."[1]

Because a nurse is unable to function independently in any setting immediately after graduation, orientation and continuing education programs were developed to bridge the gap between nursing education and practice. According to Nayer, nursing service departments recognized that newly graduated nurses had many inadequacies that jeopardized their ability to provide competent care.[2]

Many colleges and private organizations have assumed responsibility for providing continuing education programs for nurses; however most organized educational programs in the hospital setting are created by hospital staff development ment departments. Although these programs vary from one hospital to another, some similarities can be found. One common thread is the topics covered. The critical care and medical-surgical units are the areas to which most attention is given, because the major needs of the nursing department are general nursing orientation, clinical orientation to medical-surgical areas, provision of critical care courses, and clinical orientation to critical care.

The ED has unique orientation and continuing education needs. Resources for education have been sparse, and even today, remain far below those of other specialty areas because of the nature of the staff members who occupy emergency nursing staff positions and their low turnover rate. Most EDs do not depend upon new graduates for the source of staff. In fact, most emergency nurses have medical-surgical experience, and many have ICU or CCU backgrounds. Turnover is typically low and is spread out over the year. As a result, orientation and continuing education needs may be as readily recognized as they were for the medical-surgical and critical care areas. Providing continuing education was, and in many hospitals still is, the responsibility of the ED nurse manager.

However, in recent years, the ED nursing continuing education needs have become apparent. Trauma designation has increased requirements for trauma education of ED nurses in trauma-designated hospitals. In Pennsylvania, the Pennsylvania Trauma Foundation established specific educational standards for Level 1 and Level 2 trauma designation. The standard for ED nurses is a trauma nursing course of a minimum of 26 hours, plus 8 additional hours of trauma continuing education. This type of educational standard, which requires additional hours of continuing education, may be adopted by more states in the future.

The new graduate or the noncritical care nurse who transfers to the ED has the greatest need for continuing education. Yet, all ED nurses must acquire more skills and competencies than any other nursing specialty, particularly in EDs where medical, surgical, pediatric, gynecologic, psychiatric, and minor and major trauma patients are given care. There are unlimited implications for continuing education.

The practice of triage by emergency nurses has not yet been implemented in all EDs. Appropriate triage requires education and 6 months to 1 year of experience in emergency nursing that should be supplemented by continuing education. Presentation of various triage situations can enable both new and experienced staff members to practice the triage process.

Benefits of ED Continuing Education

Continuing education has several benefits. One obvious benefit is that it may increase the nurses' knowledge and abilities, thus improving patient care. Less apparent is its beneficial effect on retention of staff nurses. In many EDs, the nursing staff members view continuing education as an incentive and benefit of continued employment. Inservice programs are often stimulating and motivating, increase job satisfaction, and represent a change in the everyday routine.

Once the needs and benefits of continuing education specific to emergency nursing are recognized and a resource person is available, the specific needs of the department can be assessed in greater detail.

Needs Assessment

Each nursing care area is different and has different needs. Several sources of information can be used to determine the needs of the particular ED. The first source is the ED staff and managers. Needs assessment tools, to be completed by staff members, should be developed so that the necessary information for planning and justifying future inservice programs can be obtained. Staff members are more likely to attend a program that they identify as meeting their needs. These assessment tools should be tailored to the individual ED, and be easy to complete, and brief so that their completion by staff members can be facilitated. You, as the nurse manager, should also help determine educational needs because the topics requested by staff members may not be the highest priority for continuing education.

Quality assurance reviews that are completed in the ED are a third source of topics for inservices. Problems identified through incident reports and errors made in practice, such as medication errors, patient falls, and nurse injuries are other likely topics.

Program ideas can also be generated by new equipment, techniques, and medications; direct clinical observation; and employee performance appraisals, which identify staff members' weaknesses and need for further education.

It is clear that the essential component in developing continuing education programs is that they are based on staff educational needs identified through as many sources as possible. The planning process requires time and effective communication among educators, staff, and managers if this process is to benefit all the staff.

Resources

Several persons can fill the education role in the ED. ED staff nurses, managers, staff development instructors, and clinical specialists can be called upon to share varying amounts of responsibility for continuing education. A staff development instructor or clinical specialist should be the primary resource, with the ED nurse manager and staff members as adjuncts. However, many EDs do not have a clinical instructor, and so the responsibility for providing continuing education for the ED staff remains that of the nurse manager. Yet, with the increasing managerial responsibilities of the nurse manager, he or she may have little time to devote to continuing education activities. If there is no full time staff development instructor to coordinate and address orientation and continuing education needs, another alternative is to place the ED under the wing of a critical care instructor. Success with this type of arrangement depends on effective planning and utilization of resources, flexibility, and efficient and effective use of time.

ED staff nurses also are a valuable resource in providing continuing education for the rest of the staff. This role needs to be further developed. With your guidance the provision of continuing education can become an expectation for senior staff nurses. In some hospitals, clinical ladders have been instituted to facilitate retention of staff nurses. In these instances, teaching can be incorporated into the job description, and staff members rewarded accordingly, based on these additional responsibilities.

It often takes time for staff nurses to feel comfortable in a teaching role. Practice sessions and informal inservices can help the staff nurse overcome fears and gain confidence. If a staff development instructor is available to the ED, this person can assist staff members to develop objectives, outlines, and audiovisual materials for formal presentations. Participation of ED staff nurses in continuing education provides an increased variety and number of programs, better meets the overall needs for continuing education for ED nurses, and results in increased job satisfaction.

There may also be combined educational programs for the ED physicians and nursing staff. Case reviews in which both ED nurses and physicians participate can be valuable learning experiences.

Material resources are also available for continuing education. Audiovisual materials, such as slide/tape programs and videocassettes, can be purchased, borrowed, or developed. Textbooks and journals concerning emergency care are additional resources. These resources should be available for easy access to the staff members when needed.

Timing of Programs

An important issue is when the educational programs should be presented. Timing depends upon the type of program, availability of resources, and the level of patient care activity in the ED. Inservices should be provided to all shifts, thereby including all or most of the staff. Short inservices, 30–45 minutes in length, are most feasible for the ED where patient activity levels can change quickly. There must be flexibility in rescheduling an inservice if ED patient activity prohibits utilization of the planned time for education.

Specific Programs

Most hospitals offer a critical care course, which should be attended by the ED RN staff because they have to render initial nursing care to patients with critical illnesses and injuries in the ED. Another educational course that can be developed, with participation by experienced staff, and offered to ED nurses after several months of ED experience is an Advanced Emergency Nursing Course. At Albert Einstein Medical Center, Northern Division, such a course is offered to ED nurses with 6 months or more experience in the ED. This course is a 3-day program that is approved for continuing education units (CEUs). The topics covered in this course are:

- triage
- neurologic emergencies
- abdominal emergencies/trauma
- obstetric/gynecologic emergencies
- EENT emergencies
- burns
- chest trauma
- general medical emergencies
- pediatric emergencies
- orthopedic emergencies
- psychiatric emergencies
- legal issues in emergency nursing

The ED staff members have viewed the content and timing of this course positively. They feel that they have gained just enough clinical experience before taking the course to be able to appreciate the classes and to relate them to clinical experiences. Giving the course earlier could overwhelm them with information that they could not yet assimilate.

Other programs of particular interest and need for ED nurses are advanced cardiac life support (ACLS) and a trauma nursing course. Some hospitals offer these types of programs, whereas others do not. If no in-house course is available, staff members should be sent to outside programs, especially for ACLS. Trauma nursing courses and programs are particularly important for trauma-designated hospitals.

Another means of continuing education for emergency nurses is the development, coordination, and teaching of topics relating to emergency nursing in a seminar available to emergency nurses of other hospitals. This seminar would not only meet the educational needs of the particular ED but would also involve nurses in the planning and teaching of the program. If space in the hospital is not available, a room can be rented in most hotels or conference centers. By charging nurses from other hospitals a minimal fee to cover expenses, it is possible to afford the use of hotel facilities, which generally enhance the atmosphere of a professional seminar and offer a change of environment for the staff.

Providing for orientation and continuing education are primary concerns for ED nurse managers. Pressures to provide quality care, changes in clinical practice, and staff turnover necessitate planning orientation and continuing education for the ED staff. The lines of communication between you, the staff, educators, and other resource people need to be open to ensure that educational needs of the ED are addressed. Each institution is different, and your challenge is to tailor the available resources to best serve the needs of your specific ED.

MOTIVATING STAFF

Motivational techniques used by the ED nurse manager should bring out the best in your staff; they should build on individual strengths and avoid weaknesses. Neglecting the important function of motivation may result in low productivity, poor quality of work, and increased absenteeism, conflict, and turnover.

Each ED nurse was initially motivated to work in the ED, possibly because of the rapid patient turnover, the excitement of the ED, the opportunity to provide nursing care to all types of patients, the challenge of not knowing what type of patient would come through the emergency doors next, the decreased rotation, or the current style of the staff and ED manager. However, once a nurse is on board for a period of time, additional motivational factors and techniques are necessary to maintain job satisfaction.

Several motivational theories can aid you in understanding employee needs. Maslow's hierarchy of needs suggests that the following five needs influence motivation:[3]

1. physiologic: hunger, thirst, sleep, and sex
2. security: safety, protection, organized structure, a clear line of authority

3. social: caring, affection, interpersonal relationships, group affiliation
4. esteem: self-respect, respect from others, status
5. self-actualization: meeting individual goals, fulfilling individual potential, and achievement.

Maslow listed these needs in order of importance. Once a need is satisfied, it is no longer motivating. When the lower-order needs are met, the higher-order needs become more important.

According to Douglas McGregor, there are two types of employees.[4] Theory X employees are not willing to work or accept responsibility. They need to be directed, driven, and tightly controlled. In contrast, Theory Y employees want to work, have responsibility, and achieve. Theory Y managers rely on participative techniques and solicit and accept the opinions and ideas of their employees.

Frederick Herzberg divided job factors into hygienic factors and motivating factors.[5] His hygienic factors are very similar to Maslow's lower-order needs and include safety, salary, interpersonal relationships, job security, working conditions, and tasks. Motivating factors correlate with Maslow's higher-order needs and include; personal goals, responsibility, personal achievement, recognition, advancement, status, and power.

Vroom's expectancy theory of motivation is based on satisfaction of needs and job performance incentives; it concerns the success resulting from performance and the degree and/or value of the reward for performance.

It is necessary to keep all these motivational theories in mind, because individuals are motivated in different ways and for different reasons. Emergency nurses remain in the same nursing specialty and in the same hospital longer than most other nurses. Therefore, because of their experience and longevity, motivating the ED nurse becomes more of a challenge for you. The experienced ED nurse may eventually become dissatisfied at work and become less productive without the presence of additional motivating factors. To motivate the staff to peak performance, set and enforce high standards for expected performance and keep the employees informed. They will develop a sense of pride and accomplishment if allowed to participate actively and responsibly in the determination of their own work.

The following are some suggestions that I found helpful to motivate emergency nursing staff:

- Ensure a safe, clean, and pleasant-appearing working environment. The ED doors should be observed by a security guard 24 hours a day. It cannot be predicted who will come through those doors and for what purpose and with which state of mind. It is also important to have regular housekeeping services to keep the area clean. Prints or posters placed over a fresh coat of paint on the walls may help improve the appearance of the ED.

- Provide time for and assign meal breaks.
- Communicate job descriptions and expectations clearly. Define standards and personal goals for each individual nurse.
- Provide a comprehensive orientation that is flexible enough to meet individual needs.
- Be fair with shift rotation and scheduling of holidays, personal time, vacations, and assignments.
- Promote team building and a sense of autonomy. Encourage staff members to assist you or to plan on their own social functions outside the hospital for all the staff.
- Maintain open communication, confidence, trust, honesty, concern, and caring, and be understanding of the staff.
- Promote staff participation in problem solving and planning through small staff committees, during staff meetings, and with individual staff members. Ask for suggestions, alternatives, and ideas from the staff, but be sure to follow through with what they offer.
- Give positive feedback. Recognize and reinforce positive performance and behavior, achievements, and contributions. Too often, employees receive documentation only for negative performance. Positive aspects are just as important to document and place in the employee's folder. It is very important that staff members are not only told when they do a good job but also that they see it in writing. Give them credit for what they do, and show appreciation for it. Emphasize their positive points during routine performance appraisals.
- Offer merit salary raises for job performance.
- Do not neglect negative performance or behavior. If ignored, it will continue. Respect by other staff members will be lost, and individual and group motivation to perform as expected will decrease.
- Be a role model; set an example. The staff will usually follow an effective, motivated leader. Invite staff members to work with you on special projects and hospital committees and to accompany you to certification examinations and professional organization meetings and programs.
- Meet the personal needs of staff members if they do not interfere with unit function.
- Involve senior staff with teaching new employees as clinical preceptors or through teaching formal classes in emergency nursing.
- Offer new opportunities and challenges, such as formal teaching in and outside the hospital, committee membership, and participation in special projects. Encourage and provide educational and research experiences.

Allow time for new or interesting experiences, such as staying with a patient in the OR during surgery or special diagnostic studies, and observing new procedures done in other parts of the hospital. Assign and suggest special projects, with guidance and/or assistance within set time frames. Give additional responsibility.

- Promote and encourage leadership. Allow staff involvement with some managerial tasks.
- Encourage other hospital nurses to utilize the ED staff members as resources.
- Provide inservice programs specific to emergency nursing.
- Reimburse staff financially for taking the CEN examination.
- Provide funding for outside continuing education.
- Offer fair and competitive salaries and promotional opportunities.
- Decrease shift rotation as much as possible.
- Promote and upgrade quality patient services, equipment, and care on an ongoing basis.
- Involve staff in planning and presenting emergency nursing programs for other health care providers.

STAFFING

EDs are usually staffed by nurses who prefer to work in the emergency care setting. The staff may be made up of RNs, LPNs, EMTs, and/or physician assistants. Due to the broad range of knowledge, skills, and responsibilities required of the ED nurses to perform adequately in the ED, it is difficult for the ED nurse manager to supplement staff during unusual situations and staffing short-ages. Rotating or floating nurses from other hospital nursing units to the ED is rarely the answer. Nurses who are not educated and experienced in emergency nursing lack the required assessment and technical skills for emergency patient care. The stress level of the rotated or floated nurse is often very high due to the vast differences in ED routine, activity, pace, and types of patient illness and injury. Many nurses have difficulty dealing with the unknown. In the ED, the unknown is always a given, whether it is not knowing who will come through the ED doors next or not knowing the patients' diagnoses. Quality care is sacrificed and can even be dangerous if a nurse is put into a situation where specific emergency nursing assessment knowledge and skills are necessary, but have not yet been learned or acquired by the nurse. For example, a nurse who is not experienced in the ED may not possess the assessment skills to recognize signs and symptoms of the patient with an undiagnosed ectopic pregnancy or epiglottitis and may not be able to initiate lifesaving actions.

In decentralized organizations in which emergency nursing is not a part of the hospital department of nursing services, the option of rotating or floating nurses from other units does not even exist. Therefore, the following staffing alternatives should be developed:

- Tell all prospective employees during the interview process that it is an expectation of all the ED staff to assist in self-coverage for staffing, because the ED is self-contained and specialized emergency nursing knowledge and skills are required for appropriate patient care.
- Establish a voluntary or mandatory on-call system, especially for the night shift.
- Increase and/or delegate responsibilities.
- Adjust scheduled staff working hours to provide for the most staff coverage during the busiest hours, which usually are from 12 noon until 8 P.M.
- Develop and utilize a pool of experienced ED nurses during immediate and short-term staffing shortages.
- Use agency nurses with emergency nursing experience.
- Orient a small group of nurses from other units as a backup. These nurses should be interested in earning overtime pay in the ED and should already be skilled in some aspect of emergency patient care. The most likely nurses to orient and utilize are critical care nurses, who already have experience with venipuncture, EKGs, starting intravenous fluids, and nursing care of the acutely ill. A pediatric nurse may also be able to supplement staffing in an ED in which a large number of children are treated. The pediatric nurse can be assigned specifically to children. Doing so relieves some responsibility from the ED nurses during staffing crunches.

Staffing levels and patterns must meet the nursing care requirements in relation to census, nursing responsibilities, patient care needs, patient acuity levels, and patient length of stay in the ED.

- *Total Patient Visits:* An ED with 200 patient visits per day obviously requires more staff than one with only 50 patient visits a day. However, staffing according to ED patient visits only may either result in understaffing if acuity levels of the patients are high or in overstaffing if most of the patients have nonacute illness or injuries. There is also a tendency to understaff the night shift, because the number of patient visits dramatically declines between midnight and 7 A.M. Only assigning one nurse to the night shift, no matter how low the average number of patient visits, is dangerous if two emergency patients arrive simultaneously or a multiple trauma victim or code arrives in the ED.

- *Nursing Responsibilities:* Some EDs have available supportive services, such as an EKG technician, technicians for venipuncture and intravenous lines, a full-time social worker, and the like. These EDs may require less nursing staff than those in which nursing staff carry out all these tasks. In some teaching hospitals, medical students and residents carry out some of the responsibilities that are done by nursing in nonteaching hospitals. A triage program requires additional nursing staff as well. In very active EDs, a charge nurse who does not have a patient assignment is often needed to maintain organization and patient flow.

- *Patient Acuity Levels:* Increased patient acuity requires increased nursing time and therefore additional staffing. Some EDs serve as the evaluation and stabilization area for all critical care patients being admitted to the hospital. If critical care patients are transferred directly to critical care units, bypassing or only staying a brief time in the ED, less staff will be needed based on patient acuity.

- *Patient Length of Stay in the ED:* Average patient length of stay varies from ED to ED. In some there is rapid patient flow and turnover, whereas in others patients are detained or held for several hours for stabilization or while waiting for an available inpatient bed. Holding areas require additional staff. Holding areas vary from 2–12 patient spaces; their size must be considered when determining how many nurses are needed for those patients. Whether the patients held are medical-surgical or critical care, additional nursing care is required.

- *Geographical Layout of the ED:* The setting also affects staffing requirements. When I moved from one ED facility to a new, much larger facility in the same hospital, additional staff members were needed to manage patient care over the bigger area. It is possible to observe a larger number of patients in a more confined area than if the distance between patients is great and there is decreased visibility.

There is no standard number of required nursing staff for an ED because of the great variability in the educational backgrounds of the staff members and all the factors mentioned above. No two of the over 150 EDs from which I obtained information regarding patient visits, nursing responsibilities, patient acuity levels, average patient length of stay, holding areas, and triage systems are exactly the same.

To determine efficiently and objectively how much staff is required for each individual ED, use a patient classification tool that measures nursing time. A patient classification system specific to the ED is discussed in detail in Chapter 6.

In addition to the responsibility of nursing staffing, many of you are responsible for staffing secretarial and/or clerical employees. The number of nonnursing employees in the ED is primarily determined by the actual number of patient visits. However, keep in mind that lack of a secretary or clerk adds more responsibility to the nurses. Again, the night shift is often neglected and usually does not have the support of a secretary to register patients or of a medical clerk. This shift already has a drastically reduced number of staff members, yet the nurse(s) is expected to take on additional responsibilities of the nonnursing functions. This lack of supportive staff can not only overload the night shift nurse but it can also delay patient registration, treatment, and patient flow.

You are responsible and accountable for determining and providing adequate, safe nursing care. Appropriate staffing should facilitate the provision of quality nursing care by the smallest number of staff members to ensure high productivity and cost efficiency. You also have the responsibility of determining the number of full-time equivalents (FTEs), proving the need for and requesting additional FTEs, and recognizing and adjusting overstaffing by decreasing FTEs and increasing productivity of the staff.

When changing the type of nursing assignments, such as from task-oriented or functional nursing to primary nursing, staffing adjustments may be necessary.

Staffing Patterns

Staffing patterns in the ED should meet the needs of patient care and be consistent with activity levels. Tables 5-2 to 5-6 show several patterns with their required FTEs of staffing nurses 24 hours a day, 7 days a week, including coverage of vacations, holidays, personal time, and absent days.

The ED nurse manager is not included in the staffing patterns and should not be counted as a patient care provider. In very busy EDs with large numbers of staff, the assistant nurse manager (ANM) should also not be counted as a direct patient care provider. The assistant nurse manager becomes essentially a supervisor and clinical organizer of daily operational patient and nursing activities. In the staffing patterns including a nurse's aide, that employee also does not provide direct patient care. A nurse's aide does not have the educational background, skill, or judgment to provide direct patient care in the ED environment. Rather, he or she

Table 5–2 Staffing Pattern

	Day	Evening	Night	Total FTEs
Nurse manager	1			
RN	3 (4.8)	3 (4.8)	2 (3.2)	12.8
LPN	1 (1.5)	1 (1.5)	—	3.0
Secretary	1 (1.5)	1 (1.5)	1 (1.5)	4.5

Table 5–3 Staffing Pattern

	8 A.M.-4 P.M.	12 noon-8 P.M.	4 P.M.-12 A.M.	Midnight-8 A.M.	Total FTEs
ANM	1		1		2
RN	6 (9.6)	2 (3.2)	6 (9.6)	2 (3.2)	25.6
EMT/LPN	1 (1.5)		1 (1.5)	1 (1.5)	4.5
NA	1 (1.5)		1 (1.5)	1 (1.5)	4.5
Sec./Clerk	2 (3.0)		2 (3.0)	1 (1.5)	7.5

Table 5–4 Staffing Pattern

	8 A.M.-4 P.M.	10 A.M.-6 P.M.	12 noon-8 P.M.	4 P.M.-12 A.M.	12 A.M.-8 A.M.	Total FTEs
ANM	1			1	1	3
RN	4 (6.4)	1 (1.6)	2 (3.2)	5 (8.0)	2 (3.2)	22.4
EMT/LPN	1 (1.5)		1 (1.5)	1 (1.5)	1 (1.5)	6.0
NA	1 (1.5)			1 (1.5)	1 (1.5)	4.5

Table 5–5 Staffing Pattern

	8 A.M.-4 P.M.	10 A.M.-6 P.M.	12 noon-8 P.M.	4 P.M.-12 midnight	6 P.M.-2 A.M.	12 midnight-8 A.M.	Total FTEs
ANM	1			1		1	3.0
RN	7 (11.2)	2 (3.2)	2 (3.2)	7 (11.2)	1 (1.6)	3 (4.8)	32.0
NA	1 (1.5)		1 (1.5)	1 (1.5)		1 (1.5)	6.0
Sec./Clerk	2 (3.0)		1 (1.5)	2 (3.0)		2 (3.0)	10.5

Table 5–6 Ten-Hour Shift, Four Days a Week

	8 A.M.-6 P.M.	2 P.M.-12 midnight	10 P.M.-8 A.M.	Total FTEs
ANM	1		1	2
RN	5 (9.0)	5 (9.0)	3 (5.4)	23.4
NA	1 (1.7)	1 (1.7)	1 (1.7)	5.1

can transport patients and specimens, maintain and stock supplies and equipment, and assist the professional nurse in selective situations. Even though I personally do not advocate hiring EMTs or physicians' assistants in the ED, they do form part of the staff of many EDs. However, they should not replace an RN. Therefore, I placed them in the sample staffing patterns in the place of LPNs.

The ideal staffing pattern would be an all-RN staff who have the educational background, assessment skills and knowledge, and scope of practice as allowed by most state Nurse Practice Acts to render unfragmented quality patient care, with increased productivity and decreased legal risk for overall patient care and nursing practices.

SCHEDULING

The primary purpose of scheduling is to provide adequate staffing for patient care needs, 24 hours a day, 7 days a week. An important factor that should be considered is the personal needs and preferences of the staff whom you are scheduling. It would be very easy to prepare a schedule if the human factor was not of concern. However, it is to your benefit to note staff preferences and requests when preparing time schedules in order to enhance employee job satisfaction and facilitate recruitment and retention. Unfortunately, it is not possible to always satisfy staff members' requests and still meet the staffing needs for patient care. This should be made clear to the staff. If schedules are fair, staff members are more likely to understand when a request must be denied.

A major goal of staffing and scheduling is to create permanent shifts, which decreases or completely discontinues shift rotation. Rotation is a major cause of job dissatisfaction. Until permanent shifts are established, shift rotation is needed to staff the evening and night shift because most nurses prefer to work day shift. Rotation should be fair, with input from the staff on how and how often they prefer to rotate. Try to allow the staff to choose which shift they prefer to rotate to, if more than one shift has to be covered. Staff members usually have different preferences, depending on their family, school, and personal responsibilities and obligations. On occasions when my staff members only had to rotate to one shift other than the day shift, they chose to work two shifts of rotation a week, rather than 1–2 weeks straight on each shift. Even though they rotated more frequently, their personal lives were less disrupted. Some of the reasons they chose to rotate this way included:

- Several were attending evening school, 1–2 nights a week.
- Those who had children would have less babysitting problems and would be able to spend some of the evenings during the week with their children, rather than not seeing them for longer periods of time.

- Those who were married could spend some evenings at home with their spouse, instead of not seeing their spouse all week.
- The unmarried staff members wanted to maintain some social life during the week, with family, friends, and dates who are not available during the day.

When unconventional shift hours need to be covered, again individual staff members may have preferences. A nurse who prefers to sleep later in the morning may be willing to work a permanent 10 A.M. or 12 noon shift. Or, a parent may prefer to work a 6 P.M. shift so that children are only left with a babysitter for a short time until the spouse arrives home from work. These options will help meet staff members' needs and lead to the creation of permanent shifts, resulting in decreased rotation for other staff members.

Permanent shifts are ideal and greatly promote retention because staff members can plan their personal time on a long-term basis, instead of having the job plan their lives. Also because ED nurses generally remain in the same job for several years, it becomes personally and physically more difficult to continue rotating work hours with no relief in sight. It is sometimes better to keep a position unfilled for a while until it can be filled by someone preferring to work a permanent shift other than the day shift. Some EDs have a waiting list of nurses who want to work there and are willing to wait their turn for an open day shift position. The night shift is usually more difficult to staff with permanent employees. Incentives should be considered to attract nurses to work night shift hours. Some incentives are (1) a Friday/Saturday weekend so that the nurse has at least every other Friday and Saturday night off when the weekend policy is to work every other weekend, (2) a shift differential, (3) a monetary bonus, (4) a Monday-to-Friday work week, or (5) night shift only on weekends, possibly as 12-hour shifts.

Post schedules well in advance, at least 6–8 weeks before the working date. Doing so assists you in planning and allows the staff members to plan their personal lives in advance, with time to make schedule changes with less difficulty. When scheduling, take in account days off, vacations, holidays, personal time, and time required for specific educational requirements or certification, such as BCLS and ACLS, that takes nurses away from patient care. Schedule appropriate numbers of staff members during the busiest hours, which are usually between 12 noon and 8 P.M. Weekend activity rarely decreases in the ED, and in many instances, patient visits actually increase during the weekend. Therefore, staffing levels cannot be reduced on weekends, as is common on medical-surgical units. Part-time nurses may need to be scheduled on weekends to complete the staffing complement required. It may also become evident that a particular day of the week is busier on a regular basis than the other days of the week; for example, Wednesday, when most private physicians do not have office hours. Monday may also be a busier day because patients wait over the weekend to see their private physician in the office on Monday, and by that time their illness has worsened to a degree that they require referral to the ED for evaluation or emergency admission. If one day of the week is consistently more busy than the other days, increase the number of staff scheduled for that day.

Creating unconventional shifts—work hours other than the standard day, evening, or night shift—has both advantages and disadvantages. Its advantages are increased staff productivity, appropriate staffing levels that meet patient activity levels, and flexible staffing for staff members who cannot work traditional hours. The disadvantages include fragmented and/or loss of continuity of patient care, confusion, and less control because nurses come and go and report on and off at meal breaks and at the end of their shift at different times. In addition, increased rotation is required if no one volunteers to work the odd shifts permanently. To meet ED hours of highest activity at least one to three additional shifts are required. However creating more than five to six different shifts can create more problems than benefits.

Scheduling should be flexible enough to utilize the nurse who can only work a 4–6 hour shift, but is able to do so during peak hours of activity. Ten- or 12-hour shifts, in addition to 8-hour shifts, may also help provide additional coverage. This staffing pattern may be a solution for weekend staffing.

Preparing time schedules can be extremely time consuming and burdensome until there is a system or cycle to the scheduling and you can maintain a degree of control over it. A time-request book can help the staff and you prepare the time schedule in advance. It can be referred to as you prepare a particular time schedule. Posting schedules in advance allows the staff members the opportunity to plan their own time or switch time with co-workers. However, a time limit should be set when no more changes will be accepted except for emergency situations.

The staff should also be responsible for keeping track of their own accrued and used personal time. They should be expected to request personal time in advance so that it is used within the time frames determined by hospital policy and not at the expense of staffing needs in the ED. Although you should try to meet their requests for time off, patient care needs are foremost. If staffing requirements will fall below acceptable levels, the request must be denied. Explain the reason for denying a time request to the employee.

You must be aware of and comply with hospital personnel policies regarding employee accrual and usage of personal time, working weekends, and the like. It is also important to plan working schedules for the staff that do not result in their working too many days in a row without a day off.

ASSIGNMENTS

Nursing assignments in the ED can be either functional or task oriented, team nursing, or primary nursing. Staffing levels determine the type of nursing system used.

Functional Nursing

Functional or task-oriented assignments are based on a division of work according to patient care tasks that have to be completed. One nurse may do all the venipunctures and intravenous starts, whereas another nurse may do all the vital signs or EKGs. Another form of functional nursing in the ED is when the nurse who is available or closest to the physician after a particular patient is examined carries out the physician's order for that patient. Although functional nursing requires fewer nurses to take care of larger numbers of patients and is the most economical nursing system, its disadvantages outweigh its advantages. It has the following drawbacks:

- leads to poor job satisfaction due to repetition, which causes boredom
- prevents development of nurse/patient relationships
- does not allow for nursing assessment, judgment, or decision making
- does not promote individual growth and development
- causes important nursing responsibilities, such as documentation, teaching, communication, awareness of patient status and responses, and discharge planning, to be overlooked
- results in fragmented nursing care
- leads to an unequal distribution of work
- fosters disorganization and confusion

Team Nursing

In team nursing, the staff is divided into teams, each of which is responsible for smaller numbers of patients. Patients are usually assigned to teams on a geographic basis. Advantages of team nursing over functional nursing are:

- Nurses experience increased job satisfaction.
- Tasks are carried out for fewer patients in a more limited geographic area.
- Nurse/patient relationships can develop because nurses handle a smaller number of patients.
- Several different tasks are carried out by the same nurse for a limited number of patients.
- Patient communication and awareness of patient status and responses improve.
- Documentation is more complete.
- Each nurse assumes more responsibility.

Some of the disadvantages of team nursing are:

- Teams must be evenly composed of different levels of staff in regard to educational preparation and scope of practice. This composition may be difficult to achieve. An RN must lead the team and delegate tasks to the other levels of staff.
- Increased time is required for coordination of nursing activities within each team. Priorities must be determined and carried out without duplication or overlooking of tasks.
- One team may not be busy while another team is. There is often lack of initiative or motivation to assist co-workers on the other team.
- Team nursing requires more staff.
- It is more costly.

Primary Nursing

A primary nursing system in the ED can be organized in two ways: either by triage or geography. In the first system, the patients are assigned to an available RN upon arrival by the triage nurse or charge nurse. In a geographical primary nursing system, an RN is assigned to an area in the ED and all patients assigned to the treatment spaces or rooms in that area become the responsibility of that nurse. The latter system seems to work more effectively in EDs with a large number of patient visits and a continuous and simultaneous inflow of patients. It also works more smoothly when there are different levels of staff. Figure 5–1 shows an example of a geographic primary nursing assignment.

In this example, RN "A", who is assigned to rooms 1, 2, and 3, and RN "E", who covers rooms 10–12, are the primary nurses for all patients assigned to their rooms by the triage or charge nurse. The RN delegates tasks to the EMT (or LPN) while maintaining responsibility and accountability for patient care. When the patients leave the treatment rooms to go to x-ray or to wait for results of diagnostic studies, the primary nurse still has responsibility for the patients.

Advantages of a primary nursing system include:

- Increased nurse and patient satisfaction results.
- RNs assume responsibility and accountability for patients.
- There is comprehensiveness and continuity of patient care.
- Utilization of nursing knowledge and skills increases.
- The number of medication errors decreases.
- Nurse/patient relationships develop with improved communications.
- There is improved follow-through, teaching, and discharge planning.

Figure 5–1 Geographic Primary Nursing Assignments

		Critical care		Shock/trauma		
	4	5		6		

3	EENT			General	7
2	Minor trauma/			General	8
	suture			General	9
1	Cast			General	10
	Room			Gynecology/ urology	11
		15	14	13	Gynecology	12

Pediatrics

Assignments

Rooms 1, 2, & 3	RN "A" and EMT (LPN)
Room 4 & 5	RN "B"
Room 6	RN "C" (assists RN "B" p.r.n.)
Rooms 7, 8, & 9	RN "D"
Rooms 10, 11, & 12	RN "E" and LPN
Rooms 13, 14, 15	RN "F"
Triage	RN "G"
Charge nurse	RN "H"

- Nursing actions are more timely in regard to priorities of patient needs.
- Organization of nursing activities and patient care improves.
- Work distribution is more equal.
- There is better tracking of all ED patients.
- ED confusion decreases.
- Physician/nurse collaboration and decision making for patient care improve.
- There is increased patient advocacy by individual nurses for their patients.

The chief disadvantage of a primary nursing system relates to cost; more RNs are required, which increases the cost of primary nursing. LPNs and EMTs cannot be utilized as primary nurses because only the RN has the educational background and scope of practice according to nurse practice acts and JCAH requirements to meet the complex needs and deliver comprehensive nursing care to the ED patient. However, an LPN or EMT can be assigned to an RN, who may then be given a larger number of less acutely ill patients. The RN assumes responsibility for the patients, but can delegate tasks appropriately to the LPN or EMT. In many systems, the LPN or EMT is called the "associate nurse." The primary nurse maintains responsibility and accountability for nursing care for assigned patients from entry into the ED department (after triage) until discharge.

Other assignments needed in the ED are triage and possibly a charge nurse role. The triage role is performed by one RN, or in very busy EDs where 200 or more patient visits occur daily, two or three RNs can fulfill this role. This assignment may be for the entire shift or half the shift, with switching of assignments with another RN. Because of the stressful atmosphere that can exist during triage, some nurses prefer not to do triage for more than 4 hours at a time.

Alternation of Nursing Assignments

Whatever form of assignments is used, emergency nurses prefer diversity of patient care, which is one of the reasons they chose to work in the ED. To provide variety in required knowledge and skills, it is beneficial to alternate nursing assignments, which will give the nurses an opportunity to use different nursing skills as they care for different types of patients. If a nurse consistently performs as the triage nurse, he or she may lose some of the skills required to care for a multiple trauma patient or other critically ill patients. If a nurse is assigned to the surgical area one day, the next day the assignment can be changed to the medical, GYN, or pediatric area. Change of patient care assignments promotes increased job satisfaction and maintenance of all of the nursing skills required for all ED patients.

NOTES

1. Belinda Peutz and Faye Peters, *Continuing Education for Nurses* (Rockville, MD: Aspen Publishers, 1981).

2. Dorothy Nayer, "Unification: Bringing Nursing Service and Nursing Education Together," *American Journal of Nursing*, June, 1980, p. 1110.

3. Abraham Maslow, *Motivation and Personality*, 2nd edition (New York: Harper and Row, 1970).

4. Douglas McGregor, personal communication.

5. Frederick Herzberg, Bernard Mausofer, and Barbara Snyderman. *The Motivation to Work* (New York: Wiley, 1959).

REFERENCES

Anderson, Carl. *Management—Skills, Functions, and Organization Performance*. Dubuque: Wm. Browne Publishers, 1984.

Andreoli, Kathleen, and Musser, Leigh Anne. "Challenges Confronting the Future of Emergency Nursing." *Journal of Emergency Nursing* (JEN) 11(1):16–20, 1985.

Burns, Helen; Kirilloff, Leslie; and Close, John. "Sources of Stress and Satisfaction in Emergency Nursing," *JEN* 9:329–335, 1983.

Case, Bette. "Moving Your Staff Toward Excellent Performance." *Nursing Management*, December, 1983, pp. 45–48.

Catellani, Constance, and Hanashiro, Paul. "Advanced Cardiac Life Support Training Course for Emergency and Critical Care Nurses." *Heart and Lung* 13(4):387–388, 1984.

Chesney, Alan, and Beck, Shevaun. "Assessing the Need for Continuing Education for Registered Nurses." *Journal of Continuing Education in Nursing* 16(2):39–43, 1985.

Clayton, G. "The Clinical Nursing Specialist as Leader." *Topics in Clinical Nursing* 6(1):17–27, 1984.

Hall, Mary Martha. "A Clinical Nurse Specialist for Your Emergency Department." *JEN* 10(3):175–177, 1984.

Herzberg, Frederick; Mausofer, Bernard; and Snyderman, Barbara. *The Motivation to Work.* New York: Wiley, 1959.

Jenkins, Ruth, and Henderson, Richard. "Motivating the Staff: What Nurses Expect from their Supervisors." *Nursing Management*, February, 1984, pp. 13–14.

Jones, Susan L., et al. "The E.D. Nurses Dilemma: Implications for Continuing Education." *Journal of Continuing Education in Nursing*, November 3, 1984, pp. 97–98.

Klein, Janice A. "Why Supervisors Resist Employee Involvement." *Harvard Bus. Rev.* 84:89, 1984.

Maslow, Abraham. *Motivation and Personality,* 2nd edition. New York: Harper and Row, 1970.

Milde, F. et al. "Continuing Education Needs of Registered Nurses in Iowa Hospital Emergency Departments." *Journal of Continuing Education in Nursing* 11(1):29–35, 1980.

Miller, Margaret. *The Nurse Manager in the Emergency Department.* St. Louis: C.V. Mosby Co., 1983.

Molitor, Lisa. "Triage Dilemmas and Decisions: A Tool for Continuing Education." *JEN*, January/ February 1985, pp. 40–41.

Murphy, Emmett. "What Motivates People to Work?" *Nursing Management*, February 1984, pp. 58–63.

Nayer, Dorothy D. "Unification: Bringing Nursing Service and Nursing Education Together." *American Journal of Nursing*, June, 1980, p. 1110.

"Nursing: A Social Policy Statement." Kansas City: The American Nurses' Association, 1980, pp. 21–29.

Pisarcik, Gail. "Why Patients Use the Emergency Department." *JEN* 6(2):16–21, 1980.

Powers, M.; Reichelt, P.; and Jaloweic, A. "Use of the Emergency Department by Patients with Nonurgent Conditions." *JEN* 9(3):145–149, 1983.

Peutz, Belinda E, and Peters, Faye L. *Continuing Education for Nurses.* Rockville, MD: Aspen Publishers, 1981.

Rowe, Eleanor, L. "Providing Effective Inservice Training." *Journal of Continuing Education in Nursing* 16(4):119–120, 1985.

Sheehy, Susan Budassi, and Barber, Janet. *Emergency Nursing, Principles and Practice,* 2nd edition. St. Louis: C.V. Mosby Co., 1985.

Chapter 6

Emergency Department Patient Classification System[*]

Until recently, ED patient activity was estimated on the number of patient visits. Therefore, staffing levels were based on the number of patients seen yearly. However, higher levels of patient acuity require more nursing time. Even if the total visits do not increase significantly, there may be too few full-time equivalents (FTEs) to deliver the more intensive nursing care needed by the acutely ill or injured emergency patients.

Because of cost-containment measures instituted by third party payers, the total number of patients admitted into hospitals and the length of stay of admitted patients have decreased. At the same time, outpatient areas and emergency services have become more active. For economic reasons, some patients wait longer to see their physicians, and others hesitate to enter the hospital. When outpatient treatment is no longer an option, these patients, who are already more acutely ill than if they had sought treatment earlier, present themselves to the ED.

A patient classification system (PCS) aids in measuring nursing workload and productivity, which is essential for planning for future staffing requirements. Development of an acuity tool may be necessary to secure appropriate reimbursement from third party payers who require justification for the level of costs directly related to the nursing care required by the patient in the ED.

Due to the unique nature of the ED, with its great diversity in daily patient volume, acuity, type of illness or injury, and length of stay, a PCS specifically related to emergency nursing activities and time is necessary. With no references or systems available for an emergency department PCS, I began in 1979 to keep statistics regarding acuity levels and nursing time required.

---

* Adapted with permission from "Adapting PCS to Emergency Services" by Linda Buschiazzo in *Nursing Management,* Vol. 16, No. 5, pp. 34B–34H, © May 1985.

PROVING INCREASES IN ACUITY

I began by keeping statistics of ED patients at Albert Einstein Medical Center, Northern Division, who required intensive or coronary care beds. Because our critical care beds were usually filled, patients needing those beds remained in the ED for several hours and sometimes as long as 24 hours. The nursing workload was much higher than could be estimated based on daily patient visits alone because of the additional nursing time required to provide intensive nursing care. Because of problems in the hospital system that prevented timely transfer of these patients and because of the insufficient number of critical care beds, the numbers and total hours of critical care in the ED continued to climb. The overall increased acuity levels of patients added to the increased nursing requirements. Additional FTEs were needed to meet the increasing demands.

Until 1980, the number of ED patient visits increased each year. However, in 1981 and 1982, census decreased (Figure 6–1). Because there was a 2-year decline in annual patient visits, the hospital administration assumed that less nurses were needed in the ED and emergency nursing FTEs were reduced. Yet, although the total number of patient visits decreased, the time required for nursing care of the critically ill patients almost doubled. The nursing staff became overworked, and the overall quality of emergency patient care declined. Also by the time the

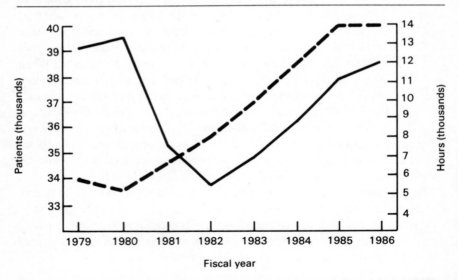

Figure 6–1 Patients Treated in the Emergency Department at Albert Einstein Medical Center, Northern Division

The solid line denotes the total number of patients treated (walkouts not included); the dashed line denotes the hours of critical care patients in the ED.

decision was made to reduce the number of FTEs and the adjustment was actually made, the total number of patient visits began to increase, and has continued to increase since.

It would seem logical that on a day with 90 patient visits, for example, less nursing time would be required than on a day with 120 patient visits. Yet, if 15 of the 90 patients require critical care nursing, and only 2 or 3 of the 120 patients require the same level of care, the day with the smaller number of patient visits would actually require more nursing time.

In addition to analyzing the critical care patient population, I began to examine changes in acuity levels of all the ED patients, according to how they were prioritized by the triage nurse upon arrival. I found that the number of emergent and urgent patients was increasing, whereas the nonurgent patient population was declining, as shown below:

| | Percentage of the Patient Population | | | |
	1982	*1983*	*1984*	*1985*
Emergent	16.5	18	20	23
Urgent	51.5	52	54	55
Nonurgent	32	30	26	22

Because of the overall increase in ED patient acuity, an objective, reliable, and simple acuity tool had to be developed to measure nursing care time and so justify the need for additional FTEs. As there was no available PCS for an ED, a new system had to be developed and revised until it was reliable, produced objective data, and yet was flexible enough to categorize appropriately all types of patients in the ED and demonstrate the nursing time that they required.

DEVELOPMENT OF THE PCS

A factor-type classification system that would have been complete enough to use with the very diverse ED patient population was identified as impractical; it would have been too time consuming to use in the ED environment that is characterized by rapid turnover. For this reason, a prototype system, with isolated factors identified, was developed and supported by work/time studies.

Because the amount of nursing time relates to the expectations and responsibilities of the nursing staff, it may vary in different EDs. Availability of such supportive services as an I.V. nurse, EKG technician, social worker, transport service, and medical students or residents who may perform certain tasks instead of the nurse, reduces nursing time. Time must also be allotted for nursing planning, assessment, interventions, teaching, discharge planning, and documentation. Triage programs and holding areas require additional nursing hours.

The first step in developing a PCS is to explain and discuss with the staff its purpose and benefits. The staff must understand how the development and use of such a tool would, in the end, document *their* workload, productivity, and possibly the need for additional FTEs, if the current number is insufficient. In these times of rigorous cost containment, it may even be necessary to prove that the current number of FTEs is needed and should not be reduced. With support and participation of the staff in the developmental stage, the staff will be more positive about the responsibility and time required to complete the necessary work/time studies.

The next step is to determine the amount of direct patient care time spent with patients; direct care was broken down into the following tasks:

- doing an assessment
- providing physical care
- planning care
- monitoring the patient
- obtaining laboratory or radiology results
- accompanying and monitoring patients during special studies outside the ED, such as a CT scan
- writing documentation on patient records
- teaching of patient or significant other
- providing psychological support of patient or significant other
- providing social support of patient or significant other
- transferring patient to inpatient unit
- giving report to receiving nurse
- discharge planning

During a 2-week period, all the nurses carried and filled out 3 by 5 cards for each assigned patient, with direct care criteria listed on each card. Times were filled in for the total care given, by hour. The cards represented all shifts and all days of the week.

The 1500 completed cards were then divided into 4 categories: Category 1 = 1-20 minutes/hour, 2 = 21-40 minutes/hour, 3 = 41-59 minutes/hour, and 4 = 60 minutes/hour or more.

An average time for each category was then determined (Exhibit 6–1). An analysis of the cards revealed that specific medical diagnoses routinely required similar amounts of nursing time, and that the four categories were closely

Exhibit 6–1 Emergency Department Patient Classification Guidelines

All patients will be classified into one of four categories at the time of discharge by the nurse assigned to the individual patient. The charge nurse will monitor the ED records and ensure that each patient chart has a classification level documented.

Category 1 (average of 14 minutes nursing time)
Patients with minor illnesses or injuries. These patients are examined and/or treated and discharged. No invasive procedures are required.
Examples include: sore throat, mild URI or UTI, sprains, abrasions, viral syndromes, simple toothache, otitis media, conjunctivitis, cast or wound checks, dressing changes, minor chronic headache

Category 2 (average of 53 minutes of nursing time)
Patients who require a moderate amount of nursing care or procedures before admission or discharge.
Examples include: minor lacerations, fractures requiring casting, nosebleeds, first- and second-degree burns, major abrasions or contusions, minor head injuries, pelvic inflammatory disease, patients requiring minimal laboratory studies or consults

Category 3 (average of 228 minutes of nursing time)
Patients requiring extended nursing care. These patients generally require a second nurse initially and are detained for observation or admitted.
Examples include: acute asthma; COPD; threatened, incomplete, or complete abortions; head injuries; seizures; alcohol or drug intoxication; overdose requiring gastric lavage; GI bleeding; TIA; CVA; allergic response; diabetic reaction; pyschiatric (uncooperative); high fever with sponge bath; child abuse; fractured hip; rape; patients requiring OR preparation; patients and/or family requiring extensive psychological or social intervention or extensive teaching

Category 4 (average of 383 minutes of nursing time)
Patients requiring intensive nursing care. These patients always require a second nurse, and sometimes a third nurse is required initially.
Examples include: GI hemorrhage, status seizures, status asthma, overdose (unconscious), acute MI, life-threatening dysrhythmias, pulmonary edema, pulmonary embolism, ARDS, any patient in acute respiratory distress, major burns, dissecting aneurysms, shock, spontaneous delivery, multiple or major system trauma, patients requiring intubation and or hemodynamic monitoring, code blue

associated with discharge or admission medical diagnoses. This was built into the PCS for determining appropriate classification categories. Separating admitted patients from discharged patients is unnecessary because total nursing time is calculated in the PCS, which is not effected by whether the patient is admitted.

Because an ED has no standardized patient day, the PCS system incorporates the patient length of stay as a second time determinant. This information was concurrently gathered on the cards used to identify direct nursing care hours, but it also could have been part of a separate time study.

Indirect Care Time

It soon became obvious that a portion of nursing time—indirect care time—was not accounted for in the tool. Indirect care time includes nursing activities that must be carried out by the emergency nurses every shift, every day, such as:

- serving as the charge nurse (administrative responsibilities)
- counting narcotics
- taking or giving reports at change of shift and meal breaks
- checking equipment and code carts
- stocking treatment rooms with supplies
- returns from in-house transfers
- making transfers to and from another facility
- code response outside the ED
- doing errands to labs, central supply, etc.
- phone calling to verify readiness of an inpatient bed
- making repeat calls for test results
- making phone calls to escort service, pharmacy, page physicians, the patient's family, or community agencies
- doing housekeeping tasks
- serving as the triage nurse

Indirect hours were recorded by each nurse during their shift for 1 week. On each card the identified indirect tasks were listed (Exhibit 6–2). The nurses filled in how many minutes they spent for each indirect activity and totaled each time at the end of the shift. At the end of a 24-hour period, a total indirect time was tabulated from all of the cards and calculated into hours.

The self-reporting was verified and/or adjusted by two assistant nurse managers and me. We found that the staff either reported their time accurately or had a tendency to underestimate their time.

An average time was calculated from all the cards and multiplied by the average number of nurses working during a 24-hour period.

Indirect Time Calculation

Day and Evening Shift	
15 hours triage	15.0
7.5 hours × 2 charge nurses	15.0
1.75 hours × 12 nurses	21.6
Subtotal	51.6 hours
Night shift	
1.75 hours × 3 nurses	5.2
5 hours charge nurse	5.0
(administrative duties)	10.2 hours
Total indirect time =	61.8 hours

After indirect time studies were repeated 2 more times, it was recognized that hours of indirect care remained consistent with little variance.

IMPLEMENTATION OF THE PCS

A thorough inservice training program preceded implementation of the PCS. Each staff member received guidelines and examples of each category. At the time of patient discharge from the ED, the nurses were instructed to categorize each patient as a level 1, 2, 3, or 4 and indicate the level on the top of the ED patient record.

Exhibit 6–2 Indirect Time and Tasks

	Minutes
Count narcotics	_____
Shift report	_____
Phone calls	_____
Return from transfer	_____
Code out of ED	_____
Transfer to other hospital	_____
Housekeeping	_____
Equipment check	_____
Stocking rooms and carts	_____
Errands	_____
DATE _____	TOTAL MINUTES _____
NAME _____	HOURS _____

To ensure compliance and accuracy, the first 2 weeks of using the PCS were not measured for statistical purposes. The two assistant managers and I reminded the staff members on each shift to classify their patients. We also reviewed charts for accuracy of classification levels. Inappropriate classifications were discussed with individual nurses, as well as with the entire staff to ensure that everyone was classifying patients similarly.

To determine and document total nursing care hours required, the total number required by each category was documented on a worksheet. This was done by reviewing each patient record during the previous 24-hour period and obtaining the category number (1, 2, 3, or 4) written on the top of the patient records. At the same time, the nursing documentation was reviewed for the accuracy of each assigned category. The number of patients in each category was then multiplied by the average number of minutes predetermined for each category. The total number of minutes of each of the four categories was then added together and calculated into hours to give the total required nursing hours. The total direct time was then added to the predetermined amount of indirect care time to give an accurate number of hours of nursing time required during a 24-hour period, as shown on the worksheet in Table 6–1.

To ensure consistent monitoring of productivity and required staffing, an additional column was added to the worksheet. To determine the required number of staff for the 24-hour period, total required hours were divided by 7.75 hours, the actual work time per nurse on an 8-hour shift. For example, if there were 200 hours of patient care, then 25.8 nurses were required during that 24-hour period.

At the end of each month, daily required nursing hours were tabulated and divided by the number of days in the month, which gave an average monthly required nursing care hours. To determine required FTEs, the average number of monthly hours was divided by 7.75 work hours per nurse and then multiplied by 1.6 FTEs. Because of days off and holiday and vacation time, 1.6 FTEs are actually needed to cover the hours of one nurse.

$$\text{FTEs required} = \frac{\text{total direct hours} + \text{indirect hours}}{7.75} \times 1.6$$

During the developmental and implementation phases the PCS was a priority for the assistant nurse managers and me. It took our commitment and additional hours of work on all shifts to monitor and help the staff complete the time studies.

Time studies were repeated after 6 months and again at 6-month intervals for 2 years. The only variation in direct time seen in the repeat studies related directly to changes in average patient length of stay and bed availability. The amount of indirect time did not vary. Minor adjustments were made when we moved to a new ED facility that was three times the size of the old ED. The larger space of the new facility slightly increased the time needed to provide patient care. In addition,

Table 6–1 Emergency Department Patient Classification Worksheet

Category 1 = 14 min. × 1 hr. = 14 min.
Category 2 = 24 min. × 2.2 = 53 min.
Category 3 = 53 min. × 4.3 = 228 min.
Category 4 = 85 min. × 4.5 = 383 min.

Month Nov.1985
Average daily hours required 227
Required FTEs 46.9

Date	Cat. 1	Total Min.	Cat. 2	Total Min.	Cat. 3	Total Min.	Cat. 4	Total Min.	Total Hrs. Direct	Average Indir.	Total Req. Hrs.	Req. Staff
9/1	27	378	56	2968	19	4332	5	1915	160	62	221	29.3
9/2	51	714	43	2279	18	4104	12	4596	195	62	257	33.2
9/3	33	462	30	1590	10	2280	6	2298	111	62	173	22.3
9/4	74	1036	32	1696	12	2736	12	4596	166	62	228	29.4
9/5	25	350	52	2756	18	4104	5	1915	152	62	214	27.6
9/6	29	406	52	2756	29	6612	3	1149	182	62	244	31.5
9/7	33	462	44	2332	12	2736	12	4596	169	62	231	29.8
9/8	28	392	41	2173	11	2508	9	3447	142	62	204	26.3
9/9	21	294	40	2120	17	3876	13	4979	188	62	250	32.3

Month required average hours   6810 ÷
Days in month   30
Average daily hrs.   227

there was a slight increase in time required for the highest acuity level because hemodynamic monitoring capabilities became available in the ED, and the ED nurses assumed responsibility for this select group of patients.

Random sampling is still done to revalidate or readjust time parameters.

COMPUTERIZED PCS

In the spring of 1985, the PCS at the Albert Einstein Medical Center was computerized, and the manual tabulations and worksheets are no longer used.

Computerization was possible because the ED had access to the computerized hospital patient entry system. Menus (screens) were developed that included an ED patient log. Arrival, treatment, and discharge times of each patient are part of the log, giving one continuous access to data verifying length of stay. The ability to enter each patient's classification level was added to the computer entry system. Working closely with the data processing staff and using the original manual formulas for the system, we developed a computer program to organize the PCS data and produce the daily worksheet and monthly summaries complete with FTE calculations.

SUMMARY

Manual calculations for a PCS may be initially time consuming, but they are very worthwhile and should be done continuously. Doing so is the only means of measuring and monitoring nursing workload, productivity, and required FTEs for the ED. A PCS can help you budget for increase or the same number of FTEs. It can also be used to determine costs of emergency nursing services and eventually charge fees for nursing care.

REFERENCES

Buschiazzo, Linda. "Patient Classification in the Emergency Department." *Journal of Emergency Nursing (JEN)* 10:7–8, 1984.

Buschiazzo, Linda. "Patient Classification in the Emergency Department." *JEN* 10:183–184, 1984.

Buschiazzo, Linda. "Adapting PCS to Emergency Services." *Nursing Management* May, 1985, pp. 4B–34H.

Curtin, Leah. "DRG Creep, DRG Weights and Patient Acuity." *Nursing Management* October, 1984, pp. 7–9.

Giovannetti, Phyllis, and Meyer, Gloria G. "Building Confidence in Patient Classification Systems," *Nursing Management* August, 1984, pp. 31–34.

Grant, Susan; Bellinger, Arnold; and Sweda, Barbara. "Measuring Productivity through Patient Classification." *Nursing Administration Quarterly* Spring, 1982.

Henninger, Dawn, and Dailey, Chris. "Measuring Nursing Workload in an Outpatient Department." *Journal of Nursing Administration* September, 1983, pp. 20–23.

Johnson, Katherine. "A Practical Approach to Patient Classification." *Nursing Management* June, 1984, pp. 39–46.

Chapter 7

Patient Care Management

HUMANIZING PATIENT CARE

Anytime that a patient is in the ED, the patient and family feel stress and anxiety. With increasing demands on the nursing staff, increasing technology, and increasing patient activity, high levels of staff stress can often result in a lack of sensitivity toward the ED patient population and their families. The ED nurse manager must ensure the provision of humanized patient care by the ED nursing staff so that basic and psychological needs of patients, as well as their physical needs, are considered and met.

Causes of ED Patient Discomfort and Stress

ED patients have various psychological needs, in addition to the need for treatment of the problem that brought them to the ED.

Privacy

Lack of privacy increases patient discomfort and stress. Therefore, patients should be ensured of privacy during interviews and examination. Separating one patient from another by only a curtain, interviewing in a hallway or waiting room, or having a patient in a hospital gown in the view of others or lying in a hallway on a stretcher deprive the patient of privacy. When it is necessary to place patients in similar conditions due to lack of space in ED, every attempt must be made to provide as much privacy as possible. For example, if a private room is not available for triage, the triage area should be partitioned by privacy room dividers and should be far enough from other patients that conversation cannot be overheard. If the treatment areas are separated by curtains, conversing with and

143

interviewing the patient must be done more quietly. At times a patient has to be taken out of a treatment area quickly to provide room for a newly arrived patient who has a greater need for that treatment area. The patient taken out of the room then ends up in a hallway on a chair or stretcher in clear view of others. This type of situation, which occurs frequently in most busy EDs, robs patients of their dignity. It is important to explain to them why they were moved and ensure that they are completely covered with a sheet or blanket. If possible, provide a less obvious area for patients to wait. When interviewing and patient teaching are done, the patient should be moved to a more private area. Physicians often attempt to examine a patient in an ED hallway, oblivious to the privacy concerns of patients. This must be discouraged, or portable dividers must be available if there is insufficient space to return the patient to a treatment area. Lack of privacy due to a large number of patient visits and treatment needs greater than can be handled by an existing ED facility is a good reason for ED expansion. Provision for physical privacy is essential.

Communication

Often, the staff's top priority is the provision of physical care of patients. Because of the many physical care demands placed on the nursing staff, the nurses may run from room to room carrying out tasks, with little communication with the patient or family. ED patients, more so than any other hospital patient, need to know what to expect, why they are being moved to another area, what they are waiting for, and what is their progress or cause of their current condition. Many patients have fears: fears of hospitals, of diagnostic procedures and treatment, of disability, diagnosis, surgery, or death. They need to communicate these feelings and to receive reassurance. Other patients are unable to communicate effectively due to language barriers. Use translators when possible. Maintain a list of hospital personnel that speak foreign languages so that they can be called upon for translation when needed. Some patients require written rather than verbal communication. Obviously, deaf patients experience less stress if communications are written. Many foreign-speaking patients can understand written English better than the spoken language.

Communication with the patient's family and/or significant other is also essential and must be an expectation of the nurse caring for the patient. Patient and family anxiety levels increase if the family or significant other is not told about the patient's progress and condition. A volunteer, patient/staff liaison, or social worker can assist with these communication needs. Communications with patients and family members must be done honestly and courteously. Discussions between physicians and/or nurses should not be held where patients can overhear and/or misinterpret what is being said.

Comfort

In the ED, patients experience various discomforts, many of which can be easily alleviated. ED stretchers are difficult to lie on for long periods of time. Mattresses are thin and often slide, stretchers are narrow, and a single sheet is often used to cover a patient who is clothed only in a short hospital gown. The nursing staff must be aware of patient comfort and try to increase it by changing the position of patients who cannot do so on their own, elevating the heads of stretchers or offering a pillow, keeping patients warm by using blankets, and providing nourishment for patients who are in the ED for an extended period of time or who had not eaten for several hours before arrival and are going to be detained in the ED for any reason. Bathrooms should be clean and accessible to patients. The noise level should be kept to a minimum. Public telephones should be available.

Visitor Policy

Many EDs have a visitor control policy that prohibits the family from remaining with the patient. This type of policy increases patient and family anxiety. Appropriate exceptions to the policy must be permitted if exclusion of a family member is a cause of high anxiety for the patient or family member. These exceptions are particularly important for the pediatric, geriatric, and critically ill patient.

Causes of Dehumanization of Patient Care

Patient care can become dehumanized for the following reasons:

- differences in social class between health care providers and the patient population that lead to differences in thought, language, culture, interaction, responses, and degree of empathy
- standardized instead of individualized approaches by staff
- staff attitudes, morale, and working conditions
- physical design of the ED
- patient overload
- hospital system problems
- lack of supportive services
- exclusion of the patients from decision making concerning their care (This has been increased by HMOs and PPOs that do not allow patient choice of the hospital or physician)
- teaching environment in which patients are subjected to multiple questioning and examinations by various levels of physicians and nurses

- the ED environment
- increasing technology

Summary

The ED nurse manager, who serves as a role model to the staff, must maintain an awareness of the emotional, psychological, and physical needs of the patients. Attempts must be made to change the physical environment, systems, supportive services, working conditions for the staff, and staff attitudes to humanize patient care. Patient care must be personalized and individualized. The staff members must be aware and sensitive to all patient needs and perform as patient advocates. Increased sensitivity can be achieved by group discussions with the staff or by utilizing a resource person trained for this purpose. Behavioral expectations of the staff must be defined, communicated, and enforced.

As I tell my own staff, "Put yourself or a loved one in the place of your patient." Then, sensitivity and humanization of patient care will surely increase.

PATIENT TEACHING IN THE EMERGENCY DEPARTMENT

Patient teaching is a major part of the ED nurses' role. The ED nurse must be highly trained, with a broad range of knowledge and skills to be able to meet the learning needs of all ED patients with their varying illnesses and injuries. The ED nurse must have expertise in the care of the orthopedic, surgical, trauma, gynecologic, obstetric, medical, psychiatric, and pediatric patient. In order to provide effective teaching to patients, the ED nurses must continually update their knowledge and skills and use good communication skills.

Patient education in the emergency department is also a necessary component of JCAH *Standards for Hospital Accreditation* and the Patient's Bill of Rights. The ENA has included a standard for patient education in their *Standards of Emergency Nursing Practice* (Exhibit 7–1).

As health care costs continue to rise, there is an increasing emphasis on preventive health education and self-care. Many patients utilize the ED as their only source of health care. Their educational needs may be as basic as learning to read a thermometer or may be involved, such as teaching specific instructions for cast care or crutch walking.

Patient teaching begins when the patient is initially assessed by the triage nurse. A patient who presents with a laceration of the hand may need to be taught to put direct pressure over the wound to stop bleeding when a laceration occurs or may require teaching for a problem unrelated to the presenting condition. For example, when vital signs are taken, the patient may be found to be hypertensive. During the history, the patient may reveal that he discontinued his antihypertensive medica-

Exhibit 7–1 Standards of Emergency Nursing Practice

EDUCATION   Comprehensive Standard I   Provision of Information

EMERGENCY NURSES SHALL ASSIST THE PATIENT AND SIGNIFICANT OTH-ERS TO OBTAIN KNOWLEDGE ABOUT ILLNESS AND INJURY PREVENTION AND TREATMENT.

Rationale: Emergency nurses have the professional responsibility to promote good health practices of the public by meeting the learning needs of patients, families, and communities. Emergency nurses are in the unique position to interact with consumers, both in the emergency setting and in the community.

Outcome: Learning needs are addressed to maximize coping mechanisms and participation in care.

COMPONENT STANDARDS

A. Patient and significant other teaching: Teaching shall be an ongoing process that includes provision of information about the patient's condition, patient and significant other responsibilities and options, and recommendations for appropriate follow-up.

OUTCOME CRITERIA

A.1. Emergency nurses offer information about the patient's condition to the patient and significant others in a way that is consistent with their intellectual and emotional capabilities.

2. Emergency nurses offer explanations about treatments before their initiation whenever possible.

3. Emergency nurses involve patients and significant others in the decision-making process related to therapeutic intervention whenever possible.

4. Emergency nurses explain or ensure explanation of medications, treatment, self-care, referral, and/or prevention.

5. Written follow-up instructions regarding aftercare follow-up, and/or referral are provided and explained.

B. Prevention: Epidemiological trends shall serve as a basis for identification of individuals at risk of illness or injury.

B.1. Emergency nurses assist patients and significant others in the identification of factors that place them "at risk" for illness or injury.

2. Appropriate methods for illness or injury prevention are explained.

3. Early detection and intervention strategies are explained.

C. Public education: Public education regarding emergency care and the emergency care system shall be a responsibility of emergency nurses.

C.1. Emergency nurses disseminate information concerning access and utilization of the emergency care system.

2. Emergency nurses provide health education to facilitate appropriate decision making about self-management or needed intervention.

Source: Reproduced by permission from *Standards of Emergency Nursing Practice* by Emergency Nurses Association, pp. 45–46, The C.V. Mosby Company, St. Louis, © 1983.

tion on his own because he felt better. This situation is a perfect opportunity to begin patient teaching about hypertension and the need for consistent use of medication and for follow-up.

Patient teaching interventions occur throughout the ED patient visit. Patients are taught about their treatment, procedures, and the like. ED nurses give explanations for various measures done to or for patients.

To meet the learning needs of patients effectively, those needs must be identified and organized into an individualized teaching plan. There are several ways to identify these needs. Patients may verbalize them, they may be apparent and specific to an illness or injury, they can be determined through development of nurse/patient relationships, and they can be identified through observations of nonverbal communications. The patient's capacity and receptiveness for learning must also be assessed. Explanations and teaching must be done in language and terms that the patient can understand.

Factors that influence the patient's ability to learn include age, educational background, socioeconomic and cultural background, religious influences, motivation, anxiety level, mental status, and communication barriers. A patient who is deaf or speaks a foreign language requires a translator. A child may not understand or retain what is being taught. Often the nurse must assess the extent of the patient's knowledge of even the simplest of terms. If an ED nurse is trying to teach a patient how to obtain a clean catch urine sample but the patient does not understand the word "urine," the nurse must discover the word that the patient uses for urine and explain the procedure in words that the patient can understand. Patients who are anxious or fearful, as they often are in the ED, will have difficulty paying attention to or understanding what is being taught to them. The ED nurse must assess the patients' understanding of teaching efforts by asking them to repeat to the ED nurse, in their own words, what was taught.

Patient teaching must be reinforced verbally and in writing so that patients can refer to the written instructions at home after discharge. It may be helpful to call some patients at home to evaluate their retention and follow-up of patient teaching.

Patient teaching and the patients' response to teaching must be documented. The documentation can be done on the ED medical record, or a special form for teaching interventions and patient responses can be developed to be included with the ED record.

Teaching plans and aids can be developed by the staff, with you as a consultant. Some types of teaching aids to consider are translation cards, instructions with pictures, multiple specific discharge instruction sheets, pamphlets, medication handouts, and videotapes that can be shown in the waiting room. Teaching aids developed by such organizations as the American Heart Association can be ordered and given to patients.

Patient teaching concerning patient illness and injury, preventive health care, self-care, and discharge instructions and follow-up is a responsibility of the ED nursing staff. You should involve the staff in planning patient educational programs.

NURSING DIAGNOSIS*

Federal deregulation has forced health care institutions to become more competitive in their delivery of health care services. At the department head level, this competitive environment has stimulated health care managers to develop methods to operate their departments more cost effectively while maintaining the quality of the service. In order to develop high-quality, cost-effective delivery systems, nurse managers must first address the question of "What service do they provide?," or, stated more conceptually, "What is nursing practice?" This question is particularly difficult for an ED nurse manager to answer because of the nature and scope of emergency nursing practice.

This difficulty in defining nursing practice arises because patients seeking emergency treatment have identified a need for health care that in most instances is physical in nature. Consequently, the focus of the emergency nurse and the expectation of the patient are that his or her physical needs will be met. The nurse's role in these situations is often assistive in nature. If emergency nursing practice focuses only on the physiologic needs of the patient, the question then becomes: "Can this service be provided more cost effectively by a paramedic who is trained in short-term emergency interventions?"

It is my belief that emergency patients have additional health care needs that must be recognized by the emergency nurse. These additional needs stem from the physical problem, but are less apparent and can remain unidentified by both the patient and nurse. Use of nursing diagnosis encourages the nurse to focus on the nursing needs of the patient for which he or she can independently plan interventions. Nursing diagnosis provides an effective tool with which you can define emergency nursing practice and develop methods for cost-effective delivery of the service.

Nursing Diagnosis—A Definition

The concept of nursing diagnosis has been discussed and debated within the profession since the early 1960s. Although some opposition to the development of nursing diagnosis still exists, a great majority of nurses support the need to develop clear diagnostic labels that are descriptive of the patient's nursing care needs.

There is no universally accepted definition of the term "nursing diagnosis." However, a review of the literature indicates that the definition proposed by

---

*This section was prepared by Eileen C. Alexander.

Gordon is widely used. She describes a nursing diagnosis as an "actual or potential health problem which nurses, by virtue of their education and experience, are capable and licensed to treat."[1] Although several definitions are found in the literature, there is consensus among authors that a classification system of nursing diagnoses must include patient problems or conditions for which the nurse can independently prescribe an intervention.

Because much of the practice of the emergency nurse deals with assessment, rapid planning, and interventions to meet the physiologic needs of patients and medical orders are frequently required for intervention, nursing diagnosis can be viewed as having no application in the ED. When applying nursing diagnosis in settings that are very physiologically oriented, it is helpful to focus on the patient's *responses* to their physical problems and the alterations in their ability to function either physically, psychosocially, emotionally, or intellectually. This focus assists in identifying independent nursing functions and formulating nursing diagnoses.

This concept can be illustrated by the patient who presents to the ED with a chief complaint of substernal chest pain, a pulse of 48, and a blood pressure of 80/60 mm Hg. The medical diagnosis of myocardial infarction with bradycardia describes the physiologic problem. Several nursing diagnoses could be used to describe the nursing care needs of this patient. "Alteration in comfort due to myocardial ischemia" describes the patient's response of pain, which is not addressed in the medical diagnosis. However, administration of a pain medication and oxygen, which are the most immediate interventions needed, requires a physician's order. "Decreased cardiac output" is another acceptable nursing diagnosis that describes an altered ability to function physically, but administration of atropine is another interdependent nursing action. However, "anxiety or fear related to pain" is a *response* to a health problem for which a nurse can independently intervene. Nursing actions are frequently implemented to reduce fear and anxiety, but are not routinely identified as nursing care in acute settings and are rarely documented. In emergent situations, the emphasis is on the physical problem that must be treated first, but nurses must also recognize and document the nursing care that they diagnose and treat from an independent practice base.

Relevance to Emergency Nursing

The trend in health care toward increasing technology and increasing specialization is still continuing. Nurses practicing in specialty areas that use advanced technology must maintain the ability to develop their independent nursing practice base, in addition to the interdependent functions that are needed in collaborative practice areas, such as critical care and EDs. The nursing focus, the *care* aspect, frequently goes unrecognized in these highly physiologic practice environments. This is particularly evident in emergent situations where rapid lifesaving interventions are necessary. In this setting, much of the nurse's role involves interdependent functions that require medical orders.

In 1985, the ENA made a commitment to the use of nursing diagnosis as part of the role and responsibility of the emergency nurse and plan to include it as part of the core curriculum for emergency nursing.[2] Nursing diagnosis has been included in the *Standards of Emergency Nursing Practice* since 1983[3] and the American Nurses Association (ANA) supports the use of nursing diagnosis in the ANA guidelines of professional practice.

Because the use of nursing diagnosis is being recognized by our professional organizations as a component of professional nursing practice, there will be future legal implications requiring its use. Fortin and Fabinow state, "At this time, nurses do not appear to be under any legal compulsion to diagnose their patients formally or to record their diagnosis although the law should change as the ANA guidelines on nursing practice become more widely implemented."[4] Given these commitments by our professional organizations and the practice recognition that may be derived from the use of nursing diagnosis, it seems that future efforts of ED nurse managers, clinical specialists, and clinicians should be directed toward developing practical methods for implementation of nursing diagnosis in the ED setting.

Application in the Emergency Department

The nature and scope of practice inherent in emergency care require the nurse to refocus his or her perspective and maintain flexibility in that focus in order to apply nursing diagnosis in emergency nursing.

Unlike the critical care nurse, the scope of practice of the emergency nurse is very broad and covers many continua of care. One example is the degree of urgency continuum. At the nonurgent end is the patient who needs a new prescription written; at the opposite emergent end is the very critical multiple trauma or unstable cardiac patient. This broad scope of practice requires nursing flexibility to change from a physiologic focus in the emergent setting to a psychosocial or teaching focus in the nonurgent setting.

Other continua within the scope of emergency practice are age related: newborn to geriatric. At the pediatric end of this continuum, the nurse may recognize an "alteration in parenting" and intervene with emotional support, community referral, or specific health teaching; at the geriatric end, a "self-care deficit" may require similar interventions, but with a different focus and goal.

The wide spectrum of clinical specialties is another example of the need for flexibility. The emergency nurse must have a basic knowledge base in all clinical disciplines from gynecology to cardiology; however, his or her area of expertise is identification of the true emergency, implementation of the correct interventions, and referral to the most appropriate source for follow-up care. Consequently, many of the nursing diagnoses frequently used in emergency nursing are related to crisis intervention, knowledge deficits, or altered ability to function due to the physiologic problem.

Patients presenting with nonurgent clinical problems are the largest percentage of an individual ED's census. However, these patients frequently have the least documentation of nursing care on the ED record. Much of the nursing care delivered to these patients is in the form of health teaching related to their chief complaint.

For example, this type of nursing care is given to the patient who receives medical treatment for a simple laceration. The nursing care after the initial triage assessment and wound cleaning includes providing the patient with information about the suture procedure. After the wound has been repaired, discharge instructions are given that describe any specific wound care needs, signs and symptoms of infection, and referral information indicating when and where to return to have the sutures removed. If this patient had sustained an extensive laceration requiring hospitalization, these nursing interventions—providing wound care and observing for signs of infection—would be the responsibility of the nurse. In the outpatient setting, the nurse's responsibility is to educate the patient concerning the observations and interventions that must be done in order to provide quality health care. The nursing diagnosis of "knowledge deficit" would describe this patient's nursing needs.

Although discharge teaching aimed at prevention is routinely done in EDs, it is not well documented as a nursing function. In many cases, documentation of teaching consists of completing a checklist indicating which pamphlets were given or a notation in the nurse's notes that wound care instructions were given. It is rare that the patient's response or acceptance of the teaching is charted.

Crisis intervention for patients and their families is frequently the role of an emergency nurse, but often is not identified as an independent nursing function. With a patient who is dead on arrival in the ED, the nursing time spent with the patient is minimal and may consist only of postmortem care. However, nurses provide support and direction for the family to assist them in the grieving process and in making necessary funeral arrangements. These interventions help the family develop effective coping patterns. Because these independent nursing functions are interventions with the family, they are rarely documented on the patient's medical record.

Implementing nursing diagnosis in an ED requires some modification. Formulation of the nursing diagnosis in other less urgent settings is done after a comprehensive nursing history and physical assessment. In the ED setting, the usual process of collecting a holistic data base must be abbreviated due to time constraints imposed by the need to set priorities.

Novotny-Dinsdale describes her implementation of nursing diagnosis in an ED.[5] She uses modified SOAP charting and an adaptation of the Problem,

Etiology, Symptoms (PES) format developed by Guzzetta and Dossey to formulate the nursing diagnosis. The examples in her article clearly identify the nursing care responsibilities of the emergency nurse. The methodology she describes is a practical approach to the use of nursing diagnosis in the ED setting.

Relevance to Emergency Department Management

Implementation of nursing diagnosis can benefit individuals by improving the quality of care to the patient and increasing the professionalism and accountability of the nurse. Nursing diagnosis promotes professionalism and accountability by assisting the nurse to recognize those aspects of emergency care, both interdependent and independent, that are the responsibility of the nurse as a member of the emergency care team. Quality of care is increased because the nurse must focus on patient's *responses* to the physical problem, as well as the problem itself. This added focus identifies additional health care needs for which the nurse can independently plan interventions, thereby increasing the level of care provided by the emergency care team.

Nursing diagnosis can assist both the development of emergency nursing as a clinical specialty and nursing management because it can be used as a method to identify and document the scope and practice of an emergency nurse. You can develop quality assurance programs that incorporate nursing diagnosis as a mechanism for the evaluation of nursing care in your ED. This data base can be used to facilitate nursing care evaluation at the individual or overall department level.

Nursing diagnosis can also help you identify the nursing needs of your specific patient population. A chart audit incorporating nursing diagnosis as a component of the data collection may indicate that ''ineffective coping'' is a patient need frequently identified by the nursing staff. This data can be useful for making staffing decisions. When it can be demonstrated that the nursing staff is spending a significant percentage of nursing care hours performing crisis intervention techniques, the nurse manager may use this information to demonstrate a need for a psychiatric nurse clinician in the ED.

''Knowledge deficit'' is a patient need in all EDs. Nursing documentation, which indicates that discharge teaching is not readily understood and requires frequent repetition by the nurse, can be useful in demonstrating that health care education is a significant need for this patient population. When triage nurses and primary nurses must spend additional time in assessment and teaching roles in order to ensure that information is understood, there is a direct impact on staffing. This information can be useful in preparing justifications for additional nurse staffing to meet the educational needs of the patient population. Nursing diagnosis can be used as a first step in developing measures of nursing intensity.

When valid indicators of nursing intensity are developed, reliable productivity measures can be instituted. The specific identification and measurement of nursing services delivered to individual patient populations can provide a framework for third party reimbursement.

In summary, nursing diagnosis is relevant to emergency nursing because it provides a tool to identify the specific role of the emergency nurse. This tool can be used to develop measures of nursing intensity and to justify the need for a professional clinician to provide nursing care.

In our current health care environment, alternative, cost-effective delivery systems, such as urgicare centers, are becoming more common. EDs must now provide emergency services in a competitive environment. In order to meet this challenge, nursing must have the methodology to identify the specific service we provide and to quantify the utilization of the service. Development of this methodology will enable us to provide our professional services in a competitive health care environment.

STANDARDIZED CARE PLANS IN THE EMERGENCY DEPARTMENT*

"Standards" has been a word used quite liberally by nurses with various interpretations to fit their particular purposes. One traditional application of nursing standards has been the standardized care plan (SCP), which refers to a predefined level of care for a selected patient problem. When developed specifically for the ED, the SCP can be useful in several ways. At the Boston City Hospital ED, SCPs are used to orient new staff members and to teach all staff a uniform and comprehensive approach to a particular patient problem. They can also be used as an objective measure for performance evaluation of individual nurses or as the foundation of an audit tool for quality assurance studies for the entire department.

SCPs can also be of assistance to others in the professional community. Has a nurse colleague from another facility ever contacted you for advice on managing a particular patient problem? The SCP can be a positive means of sharing treatment methods and expanding a network of nurse collaboration (Exhibit 7–2).

Development of a Standardized Care Plan

At the outset, there were two issues to address. The first was to find clinical nurses who were interested in becoming involved in the development of a SCP, and the second issue was to encourage them to develop a standardized care plan of their own.

The Boston City Hospital ED SCP committee consists of clinical nurses who agree with the need to provide standardized care in the department and are willing

*This section was prepared by Joseph Blansfield.

Exhibit 7–2 Standardized Care Plan, Boston City Hospital Emergency Nursing Service

STANDARD CARE PLAN FOR ASTHMA

Purpose: To provide a systematic and organized approach to foster continuity, consistency, and excellence in the nursing care given to the adult with an acute onset of asthma

Definition: A reversible clinical syndrome characterized by episodes of wheezing and dyspnea separated by intervals of normal breathing

ASSESSMENT	DIAGNOSIS

I. *Triage and Initial Assessment*
Breath sounds
Respiratory effort (mild, moderate, severe)
    including accessory muscle use
Skin color (cyanosis)
Peak flow with spirometer
Vital signs, noting pulsus paradox
Onset and duration of SOB
Cough (productive? describe)
Perception of problem; compare with
    usual attack (not as bad/same/worse)
	Respiratory dysfunction
	Asthma

PLAN/INTERVENTION	EVALUATION/REASSESSMENT

Position of comfort (semi-fowlers or seated)
Hydration PO/IV (D_5W)
Medications (as ordered)
  Bronchosol 0.5 mg/2.5 ml 0.9% saline
    via nebulized O_2/Air @ 5 Liters flow
  Epinephrine 1:1000 0.2–0.4 mg sc
  Aminophylline 5–6 mg/kg loading
  Aminophylline 0.5–1.0 mg/kg/hr
    maintenance infusion
Methylprednisolone
Encourage sputum production.
  correct coughing/suction
Teach effective breathing (slow deep breaths).
Consider cardiac monitor/EKG if:
  Aminophylline toxic (or possibility)
  rate 140 and age 35 or older
  Hx of cardiac asthma
Diagnostic studies (as ordered)
  CBC & differential
  Theophylline level
  Chest x-ray, blood gases
	Elicit patient level of comfort.
	
	Check breath sounds and other
	  assessment criteria for improvement
	  after each medication or treatment
	  and every hour thereafter and record.
	
	Check vital signs (BP,P,R) with each
	  medication or treatment and every
	  hour thereafter and record.
	
	Document study done and results
	  when available.

Exhibit 7–2 continued

ASSESSMENT	DIAGNOSIS
II. *Continued Assessment*	
Precipitating factors/stressors (What do you think triggered this attack?)	
A. *Environmental (Extrinsic)*	If knowledge deficit, see also #IV.
1. Pollens	
2. Humidity	
3. Pollution	
4. Smoking	
5. Fires/Fumes	
6. Allergens	
7. Exertion	
B. *Psychosocial (Intrinsic)* (Any unusual stressors or changes in your life right now?)	Either 1. Inadequate coping or 2. Anxiety
Can patient identify source or stressor?	
C. *Physical*	
1. Infection (respiratory, nosocomial)	Indicate the physical factor.
2. Compromised airway/partial obstruction	
3. Medication sensitivity (allergic reaction)	

PLAN/INTERVENTION	EVALUATION/REASSESSMENT
A. *Environmental (Extrinsic)*	
Teach methods of minimizing stressors and preventing future attacks (or refer for teaching):	Patient states means of incorporating plan into ADL based on individual need.
(Pollens) 1. Air cleaners/seasonal therapy	
(Humidity) 2. Dehumidifier	
(Pollution) 3. Air conditioning/note weather	
(Smoking) 4. Abstinence	
(Fires/Fumes) 5. Avoidance	
(Allergens) 6. Avoidance/immunization	
(Exertion) 7. Staging exercises	
B. *Psychosocial (Intrinsic)*	
1. Involve support group (family and friends) in management of disease	Supports increased.
2. May refer to Psych./Soc. Service	Patient identifies stressor.
3. May begin to teach/assist patient to problem solve	Patient states short-term plan to begin to manage psychosocial stressors.
4. Explanations and rationale for intervention	Patient states willingness to seek follow-up appointment.
5. Reassurance	

Exhibit 7–2 continued

C. *Physical*

1. Rest, hydration, analgesia and antibiotics (as ordered)	Physical precipitating factor alleviated
2. Relieve/clear (support airway as necessary)	Patient response to treatment recorded
3. Avoidance (Medic-Alert bracelet)	

ASSESSMENT	DIAGNOSIS
III. *Grave Change in Condition*	
Decreased air exchange	Acute change in respiratory
Fatigue	system; decreased ventilation
Cyanosis	and perfusion
ABGs poor	
Cardiac or Respiratory compromise	

IV. *Disposition*

A. *Discharge*

1. Knowledge of disease and Treatment regimen	1. Knowledge deficit
Have you ever had asthma before? Do you have any questions about your disease?	
2. Potential for compliance	2. Noncompliance (with adequate knowledge base)
Do you have any difficulty following MD orders?	

B. *Admission*

1. Same as above	1. Same
2. Same as above	2. Same

PLAN/INTERVENTION	EVALUATION/REASSESSMENT
III. *Grave Change in Condition*	
Ensure/support ABCs	Document condition change and
Move to trauma room	transfer to trauma room.
Notify MD, summon arrest team	

IV. *Disposition*

A. *Discharge*

1. Identify readiness and level of learner.	Readiness and level are identified
Begin explanation of disease process and treatment regimen (when appropriate).	Patient can repeat definition of asthma and purpose of treatment.
Explain in writing and/or brochure.	Patient states misconceptions are corrected.
Provide follow-up for further teaching	Rationale for noncompliance is
2. Ascertain reason (financial, etc.)	explored.
for noncompliance if any.	Patient states willingness to seek
Monitor compliance as outpatient.	follow-up.

B. *Admission*

1. Provide reassurance.	
Give report to inpatient nurse as to teaching needed and teaching done.	Document accordingly.

Source: Developed by J. Blansfield. C. Fackler. K. Bergeron, and P. Rice, Standards Committee, Boston City Hospital.

to join a committee and work toward the development and implementation of these standards. It was important that experienced clinical nurses be involved because their knowledge of clinical practice was helpful in determining appropriate, realistic levels of care and ensuring compliance. Communication among peers is more effective and less authoritative than from management, which simplifies implementation and evaluation of the SCP.

The leader of our group is a clinical nurse specialist. Any ED senior staff or nurse manager with a strong practice base, familiarity with the patient population and common patient conditions, and a knowledge of group dynamics and the committee process could chair the SCP committee. Standards written solely by administrators or educators would probably achieve limited success. The concept of "writers are doers" is considered essential by the members of our committee.

Each SCP committee should develop a format that is suited to its ED. Many care plan manuals and reference books contain valuable information, but unfortunately are of limited use to emergency nurses because they usually have a broad focus and are meant to apply to an inpatient setting. Also, traditional care plans are derived from a problem list and are meant to have a general application. SCPs for the ED must focus on the presenting problem or symptom and include content specific to ED nursing, such as triage, initial assessment and management, and planning for the patient's ultimate disposition, whether admission or discharge.

The ENA *Standards of Emergency Practice* define general standards of practice, research, education, and professionalism. Included in a practice standard is a statement that SCPs should identify priorities for nursing actions; reflect considerations of environmental, physical, and psychological stress factors affecting emergency health care providers; be based on current scientific knowledge; and incorporate teaching-learning principles. An SCP is included in the appendix as an example.

A review of the literature shows a paucity of information on SCPs for specific areas, such as the ED. Heister et al. developed protocols for audit purposes in the ED that, among other things, are described as achieving a minimum standard of patient care.[6] However, developing SCPs was not their primary intention.

Upon reviewing various types of formats and considering the merits of each, we decided to adopt a slightly modified nursing process (assessment, diagnosis, plan/intervention, evaluation/reassessment) to form the outline of our plans. The nursing process is universally understood by nurses with different educational preparation and practice levels. Therefore, it is easy to remember, and we feel will be more readily used.

Other aspects of our particular format are that horizontally it follows the nursing process, which by design is meant to be continuous and ongoing. The nursing process is a very effective tool for problem solving, and when care is re-evaluated and revised it keeps the plan dynamic and prevents the nurse from being stymied. Vertically, the format follows a logical progression of care through the ED. Our

SCPs have evolved to include the triage assessment, any further continued assessment, acute care including any potential grave change in condition, and disposition planning for admission or discharge.

We also surveyed formats from other EDs that included such additional content as necessary equipment and teaching rationale. Although it may be valuable information we decided not to incorporate this material into our SCPs because it would make them too cumbersome and it did not correlate well with the nursing process.

Committee Process

It is advisable that the SCP committee begin with the most prevalent patient problems that would benefit most from a SCP. We found it helpful to list our most common patient problems, rank them, identify committee members who had a particular interest or expertise in them, and then delegate responsibility for one SCP to each member.

First drafts were developed based on clinical experience, the consultation of experts in the area, and a review of current literature. Drafts were circulated in advance of a committee meeting, and then the members met to discuss and decide the final content. The group process included a good deal of negotiation to achieve consensus. The clinical nurse can be the best judge of whether a suggested standard of care is too ideal or unrealistic or if most nurses can and will comply with it.

Implementation Strategies

After a standard had been developed, it was introduced to the staff. Various strategies were used to introduce the SCP to as many nurses as possible, but we found that the unpredictable pace of the clinical setting, inconsistent staffing, and distractions within the ED (intercoms, phones, ambulances, etc.) made such an introduction difficult. Some of the strategies we tried included small group clinical conferences, postings on the bulletin board and in the clinical area, and individual notification in each nurse's mailbox. These tactics were effective in disseminating the SCP to all the staff, but did not allow time for questions and clarification.

Eventually, we learned that we had to utilize all the strategies at different times. In small groups we presented actual case studies as examples and discussed application of the SCP and any additions or revisions in patient care. An SCP was distributed to each nurse and a notebook was created to hold all SCPs and to be kept in the patient care area for reference. After sufficient inservice training, the committee would choose and publicize a date when the SCP would become effective.

We have discovered that SCPs need to be regularly reinforced, or compliance will begin to decline. We have attempted to address this problem by including a brief review of old standards and introduction of new ones at each monthly staff meeting. There are often areas of concern about or deficiencies in existing standards, and the staff meeting provides a regular forum for discussion. Once a SCP has been implemented and a documentation audit performed, the results are presented to the staff at this time.

Educational Appendix

Subsequent standards have been longer than earlier ones and have included an appendix that serves as an educational component. This appendix may contain operational definitions, charts or diagrams, and references used in the preparation of the SCP. Some appendixes have included descriptions of heart sounds, an explanation of the Glasgow Coma Scale, and illustrations of ischemic changes on EKGs. The nurses have been appreciative of these additions, which add the attraction of learning new material to the expectation of consistent care delivery.

Conclusion

The intent of the SCP committee in instituting SCPs was to describe a uniform, understandable, and acceptable level of care for patients with certain common problems. One method of evaluating its effect is documentation, and according to chart audits it has improved substantially. Even though this is still an area that needs further improvement, we have made real progress.

There have been some additional unexpected benefits, as well. When individual nurses increase their knowledge about a particular patient problem, they gain more recognition from their peers and are used as a resource, which in turn increases clinical confidence.

An additional element is also important to the committee members. The responsibility for largely defining the quality of care that a patient with a certain problem would receive is taken very seriously. Many of the committee decisions ultimately become an expectation of care. This opportunity to define care gave us a sense of control over our practice and was also a source of higher morale.

NOTES

1. Marjory Gordon, *Nursing Diagnosis: Process and Application* (New York: McGraw-Hill Book Co., 1982), p.2.

2. Emergency Nurses Association, "Nursing Diagnosis." *Etcetera* 9, no. 4, (1985):3.

3. Emergency Department Nurses Association, *Standards of Emergency Nursing Practice* (St. Louis: C.V. Mosby Co., 1983), p.17.

4. Jacqueline D. Fortin and Jean Robinow, "Legal implications of nursing diagnosis." *Nursing Clinics of North America* 14, no. 3 (1979):558.

5. Valerie Novotny-Dinsdale, "Implementation of Nursing Diagnosis in One Emergency Department." *Journal of Emergency Nursing 11,* no. 3,(1985).

6. K. Heister, B. Johnson, and L. Trimberger, "ED Standards and Audit Criteria." *Journal of Emergency Nursing* 8, no. 2 (March/April 1982):83.

REFERENCES

American Hospital Association/Center for Disease Control. "Patient Education in Emergency Departments." Atlanta: AHA/CDC Health Education Project, Center for Health Promotion and Education, 1982.

Blansfield, J.; Fackler, C.; and Bergeron, K. "Developing Standardized Cure Plans: One Emergency Department's Experience." *Journal of Emergency Nursing* 11(6):304–309, 1985.

Carpenito, Lynda J. "Is the Problem a Nursing Diagnosis?" *American Journal of Nursing* 84(11):1418–1419, 1984.

Clark, Sharon R. "Nursing Diagnosis: Its Application in an Ambulatory-Care Setting." *Topics in Clinical Nursing* 5(4):57–62, 1984.

Emergency Department Nurses Association. *Standards of Emergency Nursing Practice.* St. Louis: C.V. Mosby Co., 1983.

Emergency Department Patient Questionaires. Philadelphia: Albert Einstein Medical Center, Northern Division, 1985.

Hauck, Mary R., and Roth, Deborah. "Application of Nursing Diagnosis in a Pediatric Clinic." *Pediatric Nursing* 10(1):49–52, 1984.

Heister, K.; Johnson, B.; and Trimberger, L. "ED Standards and Audit Criteria." *Journal of Emergency Nursing* 8(2):83–87, 1982.

Hickey, Mairead. "Nursing Diagnosis in the Critical Care Unit." *Dimensions of Critical Care Nursing* 3(2):91–97, 1984.

"Hospital tackles Patient Concerns during Emergency Department Waits," *Hospitals,* February 16, 1984, p. 40.

McDonnell, Lee. "Emergency Room Follow-up Program for Discharged Elderly," *Health Progress,* June, 1985, p. 24.

Murphy, Emmett C. "High Touch Techniques for Managing the Environment," *Nursing Management,* November, 1984, pp. 79–81.

Parker, Janet Glen. *Emergency Nursing; A Guide to Comprehensive Care.* New York: John Wiley and Sons, 1984.

Sheehy, Susan Budassi, and Barber, Janet. *Emergency Nursing Principles and Practice,* second edition. St. Louis: C.V. Mosby Co., 1985.

Steele, Drue. "A Proposal for Two New Nursing Diagnoses: Potential for Organ Failure and Potential for Tissue Destruction. *Heart and Lung* 14 (5):426–430, 1985.

Stewart, Margie; Hefferman, Kellee; and Smith, Lorraine. "ED Patient-Family Advocacy Experience for Nursing Students." *Journal of Emergency Nursing* 9(5):268–271, 1983.

Tanner, Christine A. "Symposium on Nursing Diagnosis in Critical Care, Overview." *Heart and Lung* 14 (5):423–425, 1985.

Targolia, Michael J. "Nursing Diagnosis: Keystone of Your Care Plan." *Nursing 85, 15* (3):34–37, 1985.

Turner, Gerald P., and Mapa, Joseph. *Humanizing Hospital Care*. Canada: McGraw-Hill Reyerson Limited, 1979.

Wake, Madeline, M., and Gotch, Pamela M. "Nursing Diagnosis in Critical Care: Reflections and Future Directions." *Heart and Lung* 14(5):444–448, 1985.

Chapter 8

Financial Responsibility and Accountability

Lynnette Holder

The word "budget" is derived from the Middle English word "bougette," which was a small leather bag or pouch used to carry items of value needed for daily business. When a trip was planned, the bougette was packed with essentials for the journey. Thus, a budget came to be a collection of items needed for carrying out some planned business or activity.

For the hospital and its constituent units, a budget is a comprehensive operational plan or guide for the allocation of resources based on preconceived needs for a proposed series of programs to deliver patient care for one fiscal year. It is based on predetermined hospital goals and plans for future operations and incorporates estimates of all expenditures during the period, as well as proposals for financing them. Because the budget is usually expressed in dollars, it can be described as the expression of a hospital's or unit's goals and objectives in financial terms.

THE EFFECTIVE BUDGETING PROCESS

The budgeting process is a tool for planning, monitoring, and controlling costs. Effective budgeting provides an institution's management with several benefits directly related to planning and control. First, it forces hospital management to reconsider and evaluate institutional and departmental objectives and policies on a regular basis. All levels of managers are required to participate actively in the establishment of objectives and in determining appropriate courses of action. The budgeting process provides a continuous check on the progress being made toward the achievement of hospital objectives.

Second, effective budgeting requires that the activities of all departments be coordinated into an overall plan. It requires an analysis of historical data and performance and correlates that analysis with future projections. Effective budgeting leads to consistency and cohesiveness among departmental plans and with the hospital's overall objectives.

Third, effective budgeting provides standards against which actual performance can be measured to determine variances that require investigation and corrective action. Both efficiency and inefficiency are pinpointed, which stimulates a high degree of cost consciousness and cost containment throughout the entire organization.

An important prerequisite to effective budgeting is a sound organizational structure, which is necessary to provide patterns of responsibility that facilitate budgeting. This structure should include well-defined work units with clearly designated levels of authority. Areas of responsibility, or management centers, should coincide with cost centers. A *cost center* is the smallest functional unit for which expenses and revenues, if any, can be accumulated and reported. Ideally, each separate unit in the nursing department should have its separate account. This promotes fiscal control and accountability at the unit level.

Another prerequisite for an effective budgeting process is the availability of accurate statistical data at the institutional, departmental, and unit levels. These historical data are needed to identify past goal attainment and to measure past activity or work output levels. These statistics serve as the keystone for projections of future activities, expenses, and revenues. These data should include volume, units of service used to measure outputs, and historical patient mix data collected by Diagnosis Related Groups (DRGs) and payer analyses.

The effectiveness of a budgeting process is enhanced by regular formal budget reports and budget variance analysis. Actual financial status should be compared at regular, established intervals with corresponding budget plans. Thus, any variance between actual and expected fiscal performance can be identified promptly. Through analysis and corrective action, fiscal variance can be minimized and controlled.

IMPLEMENTATION OF THE BUDGET PROCESS

The preparation of a hospital budget requires coordinated teamwork by department heads and managers at all levels. The chief financial officer typically serves as the budget director of the hospital, with department managers assuming the role of budget coordinator and resource agent for their respective departments.

Budget development is facilitated by a clearly delineated and well-understood institutional budgeting plan. This plan includes a definition of the hospital's *fiscal year*, which is the term used to describe an institution's annual budget period. The fiscal year, which may or may not correlate with the calendar year, is used as the base upon which an institutional budget timetable or calendar is established. Such a calendar is a budgetary tool that identifies target completion dates for specific budget-related tasks (Exhibit 8–1). Its use promotes the orderly, institutionally coordinated attainment of the various steps required in the budgeting process.

Exhibit 8–1 Budget Calendar for Fiscal Year Beginning July 1

October 1–15	Definition of key result areas by administration and Board of Trustees.
October 15–31	Preparation of FY _____ institutional, statistical, and economic assumptions.
November 5	Departmental budget kickoff for FY _____ . Distribution of budget plan, calendar, and forms. Dissemination of FY _____ key result areas, historical data, budget assumptions, and instructions.
November 5–29	Development of departmental and unit FY _____ goals and objectives.
November 30	Due date for submission of goals and objectives.
December 1–15	Administrative review and approval of departmental goals and objectives.
December 10	Deadline for submission of FY _____ new program requests.
December 16– January 1	Preparation of FY _____ capital requests by department heads.
January 2	Due date for submission of all capital requests.
January 3–23	Preparation of FY _____ expense budgets by department heads.
January 24	Due date for submission of all expense budgets.
January 25– February 16	Administrators review, analyze, and revise FY _____ departmental expense and capital budgets.
February 1–18	Develop FY _____ revenue budgets.
February 19	Due date for submission of revenue budgets.
February–March	Administrators review and discuss FY _____ budget revisions with department heads.
March–April	Complete preliminary operating budget review by Senior Administration. Review and revision of operating, capital, and new program budgets by Senior Administration.
April 11	Deadline for submission of FY _____ institutional master budget to the Board of Trustees.
April 12–30	Review of budgets by Board of Trustees.
May 1	Approval of FY _____ master budget by Board of Trustees.
May	Communication of FY _____ budget details to department heads.
July 1	Use approved budget to guide, monitor, control, and evaluate spending and income.

The budget plan also includes a group of explicit institutional budget assumptions. What is the anticipated occupancy or patient volume for next year? Will there be changes in services offered? If so, when? With how much and what kinds of activity? How large will salary increases be for the next year? What inflation factors should be used to project the cost of supplies and fringe benefits? Is there any change anticipated in reimbursement timing or amounts? Entire sets of these statistical and economic assumptions are used to guide and coordinate the budget forecasts made throughout the organization by individual departments.

BUDGET STYLES

Finally, the budgeting plan identifies the budgeting style that the institution expects to be used. There are a number of budgeting styles that health care institutions have adopted. The approach used depends on the institutional setting, the type of budget, and individual preference.

Fixed or Static Budgeting

Currently, the *fixed budget* is the most common budgetary approach. Using historical data, this budget is developed on the basis of a single estimate of annual volume or activity, which for an ED would be patient visits. Total visits are spread into 12 parts, one for each month of the year, with expenses and revenues allocated proportionately. Obviously, this is a simple budgetary approach and is relatively easy to prepare. However, it does not incorporate monthly or seasonal variations in activity, nor does it allow for any overall increase or decrease in ED patient visits. Because it does not allow for volume variations in the initial plan, it is difficult to control, evaluate, and relate to the unit's actual performance.

Some institutions have modified the fixed budget approach by developing a series of three or four fixed budgets with relevant ranges of volume or activity. This allows the fiscal plan to be adjusted in increments to the actual activity experienced by the ED. Although this approach reduces the limitations of the traditional fixed budgeting style, it clearly requires more preparation and maintenance time. In addition, this modified approach only reflects broad variations in activity.

Flexible or Variable Budgeting

The flexible or variable budgeting approach is based on the assumption that the amount of resources consumed will vary with the level of activity actually experienced. A formula including predetermined rates is used to develop a budget directly related to volume or activity.

In order to develop a flexible budget, costs are classified into fixed, variable, and semivariable costs. *Fixed costs* are those that are relatively constant and are not related to volume or activity. Examples of fixed costs in an ED may include the salary of the nurse manager, a minimum number of professional nurses, and a clerk. *Variable costs* are those that vary directly in proportion with changes in activity, such as supplies. *Semivariable costs* or step-variable costs are those costs that vary with volume, but not smoothly in proportion as do variable costs. Step-variable costs include equipment and the remainder of personnel costs not designated as fixed costs. (Although personnel costs are expected to reflect volume and productivity, staffing patterns reflect ranges of activity. Extra nursing hours are not hired for each additional patient visit.)

Flexible budgeting is especially effective in such areas as the ED in which workload volume is highly variable. The health care industry has been slow to adopt this budgeting approach probably because of the time and effort required to prepare and maintain it. However, as cost control becomes increasingly emphasized in hospitals, we can expect to see more use of this technique.

Zero-Base Budgeting

Zero-base budgeting is an annual budgeting approach that presumes that no monies are automatically allocated. Rather than basing future budgets on past allocations, all expenditures in the proposed budget must be justified. The budget proposal for each program or unit prioritizes its objectives, identifies the consequences of not funding the program or unit, and establishes ways for the costs and benefits of the program to be measured. In addition, the budget proposal identifies alternative ways to attain the purpose or objectives of the program, including alternative quality and quantity outcomes.

Zero-base budgeting is a sophisticated method to compare programs on the basis of cost-benefit relationships, and it ensures that program funding is not based on tradition. With zero-base budgeting, established programs must compete with new programs for available funding and are thus required to maintain their productivity and credibility.

OBJECTIVES

Every unit or cost center exists as part of a whole institution, which in turn exists in relation to an outside community and environment. The budget planning process begins at the institutional level with an assessment of the environment and a determination of the hospital's particular role or mission. Based on this determination and the hospital's competitive standing, overall institutional goals and objectives are established to enhance the comparative strengths of the organization and to minimize its weaknesses. These institutional goals, often called *key result areas*, are broad, long-term objectives that establish the directions in which the organization plans to move.

From the key result areas are derived departmental and unit objectives. *Unit objectives* are specific statements of goals that a nurse manager plans to accomplish. They are action commitments related to institutional objectives, and they define the planned performance of a unit or cost center over a designated period of time. To avoid overemphasis on any one key result area, objectives should address a variety of unit and institutional goals and be balanced by both short-range and long-range considerations. At the same time, objectives should be measurable, realistic, and achievable in the performance of routine unit activities. When identifying unit objectives, exercise caution to challenge but not overextend yourself and your staff. Set realistic objectives that are achievable in the light of available resources of time, money and personnel (Exhibit 8–2). In order to facilitate the allocation of resources, organize the objectives on the basis of institutional priority.

After unit objectives have been established, translate them into specific activities that will lead to goal attainment. Establish target outcomes as a mechanism for identifying the successful accomplishment of an objective, and include specific work assignments with clearly designated accountability.

Action plans also delineate the time frame in which activities and related objectives will be accomplished. These time constraints help establish work priorities and enforce accountability. Finally, action plans include estimates of the amount and cost of the resources required to carry out the plan. It is these estimates that are consolidated into a comprehensive financial description of unit activities, the unit budget (Exhibit 8–3).

MANAGEMENT BY OBJECTIVES

Clearly, a health care institution achieves its mission and goals through the combined efforts of its operating departments. Management by objectives (MBO) is a system of goal setting and evaluation that focuses on the results desired in pursuit of a defined mission. MBO programs use participation of managers at all levels within the organization to provide goal-oriented direction and coordination to the numerous actions undertaken throughout the organization. Using the MBO approach, first determine the desired end results, then plan a sequence of action to produce the desired results in a given time frame, and finally estimate the resources necessary to carry out the plan to completion. Use a regular periodic review, evaluation, and reports to note progress and to make revisions in plans to achieve continued progress.

MBO is also tied into the evaluation process for managers at all levels in the organization. With MBO, the effectiveness of a manager is measured by his or her ability to set realistic objectives, to delegate responsibility for specific actions appropriately, to monitor progress regularly, and to complete an objective as scheduled. Attainment of objectives is directly linked to the salary compensation system of the organization.

Thus, MBO programs are integrated management systems that include setting of objectives, evaluation of accomplishment, and compensation based on goal attainment. Because the MBO system is designed for continuous monitoring and reviewing of goals and performance toward those goals, it provides a flexible way

Exhibit 8–2 Unit Objectives

_____ Medical Center

FY _____ Statement of Objectives

| Department: | Emergency | Date of Approval: | December 12, | Date: | November 26, |
| Cost Center: | 3677 | Approved by: | | Submitted by: | |

OBJECTIVE	AS MEASURED BY	PRESENT LEVEL	DESIRED LEVEL
1. Maintain Emergency Department Nursing patient advocacy and guest relations	1. Patient surveys	1. 83% positive response of random sample	1. 90% positive response, with all patients receiving questionnaire
2. Increase number of RNs certified as ACLS providers and CEN	2. Number and percent of RN staff certified	2. 6 (29%) RNs CEN certified 11 (52%) RNs ACLS certified	2. 15 (71%) RNs CEN certified 19 (90%) RNs ACLS certified

Exhibit 8–3 Unit Budget

_____ Medical Center

FY _____ Action Plan

Department _____ Emergency _____ Cost Center _____ 3677 _____ Date Submitted _____ 12/20

Objective 1. Maintain ED Nursing Patient Advocacy and Guest Relations

MILESTONES	ACCOUNT-ABILITY	J	A	S	O	N	D	J	F	M	A	M	J	RESOURCES NEEDED
1. a. Inservice staff regarding plan and method for distributing patient survey at time of patient discharge	a. Staff Development Instructor	X												5 RN Hours 1 LPN Hour
b. Begin distribution at patient discharge	b. Staff		X											
c. Monthly tabulation of positive response rate	c. ED Quality Assurance Committee		X	X	X	X	X	X	X	X	X	X	X	4 RN Hours 1 LPN Hour
d. Review of response rate with corrective action as indicated	d. Nurse Manager		X	X	X	X	X	X	X	X	X	X	X	
e. Evaluate compliance with distribution plan	e. ED Quality Assurance Committee			X			X			X			X	4 RN Hours

Exhibit 8-3 continued

Objective 2. Increase number of RNs certified as ACLS providers and CEN

MILESTONES	ACCOUNTABILITY	COMPLETION DATE												RESOURCES NEEDED
		J	A	S	O	N	D	J	F	M	A	M	J	
1. a. Staff Application (9) for CEN exam	a. Staff					X					X			$900
b. Staff (9) complete Advanced Emergency Nursing Course	b. Staff Development Instructor, Staff							X					X	180 RN Hours
c. Staff (9) sit for CEN exam	c. Staff	X							X					
d. Schedule staff (8) for ACLS	d. Nurse Manager		X		X				X	X				$1200
e. Staff attend ACLS program	e. Staff			X		X				X	X			128 RN Hours

of managing change as it occurs within the organization and environment. Proponents maintain that MBO clarifies the direction in which the organization is moving, not only for top administrators but also for individuals throughout the organization. This clarity of direction, coupled with increased individual involvement, results in increased effectiveness and productivity at the individual, departmental, and organizational levels.

BUDGET DEVELOPMENT

From a unit perspective, the term ''budget'' is often used to refer to the operating budget, which is the unit's plan for day-to-day operating expenses and revenues. However, from an institutional perspective, the term ''budget'' more correctly refers to the master budget, which includes the hospital's operating, long-range, capital, program, and cash budgets. Because the nurse manager is usually not involved in the development of long-range or cash budgets, only operating, capital, and program budgets are discussed in further detail.

Operating Budget

The operating budget of a unit or cost center consists both of the planned expenses that will be incurred in the operation of that unit during the next fiscal year and the corresponding planned revenues that will result. In accordance with the institutional budget calendar, formulation of the operating budget should start several months before the beginning of the new fiscal year to provide sufficient time for budget planning, forecasting, review, and revision. Using institutional budget assumptions and unit objectives as a foundation, you identify the factors that will affect the activity of the unit and therefore its operating budget. Begin preparing the operating budget with an analysis of current and historical data, which may include:

- census or patient visits
- unit activity trends
- patient acuity
- average length of stay
- patient mix by illness, DRG, or payer status
- admission/treatment/discharge patterns
- unit routines
- hospital or unit policy
- modification in support services
- unit geography

- new services or programs
- expansion of services or programs
- patient teaching/discharge planning
- staff mix
- staff orientation and education
- expense budget for current fiscal year
- revenue patterns and status

Using institutional budget assumptions, unit objectives, and analysis of the above data will enable you to anticipate the activities, workload, and associated resource utilization that will occur on the unit in the next fiscal year. These estimates can then be translated into realistic projections of required resources, associated expense, and anticipated income.

As previously described, the operating budget is the fiscal plan for both income and expenditures resulting from the operation of a unit or cost center. However, in many institutions, operating budgets for nursing cost centers consist entirely of an expense budget. In these institutions, the nursing department and its cost centers are not designated as revenue producing, because the revenues derived from nursing service are included in overall reimbursements for room and board. In EDs, both expense and revenue portions of the operating budget usually exist. However, because the revenue may not be considered to be directly related to nursing service, you may not be at all involved in preparing the revenue side of the budget. For ease of presentation, the two components of an operating budget, the expense budget and the revenue budget, are discussed separately.

Expense Budget

The expense budget includes the direct personnel and nonpersonnel costs associated with the routine operation of a unit or cost center. These expenses include the costs of all employees, supplies, nourishments, and minor equipment used by the unit. Examples of items that may be included in an ED expense budget are:

- personnel salaries: wages, and fringe benefits
  - administrative (salaried)
  - physician (may include percentage of salary)
  - staff (hourly wage)
- education
  - tuition reimbursement
  - orientation
  - inservice
  - continuing education; registration, travel expense

- uniform purchase or lease
- laundry
- nourishments
- medical and surgical supplies
- drugs and pharmaceuticals
- laboratory reagents
- IV solutions
- small equipment purchase
- equipment lease and rental
- repair and maintenance
- office supplies
- forms/printing
- housekeeping supplies
- membership fees
- books and periodicals
- meeting expense

Operating expenses are usually charged directly to the unit or cost center on the hospital's general ledger in discrete groupings called *line items*. Entire lists of line items for each cost center are referred to as a *chart of accounts* (Exhibit 8–4). In addition to direct costs, the chart of accounts may include a portion of indirect unit operating expenses that are allocated to each cost center. A complex formula is used to calculate each cost center's share of indirect expense, such as heat, light, electricity, and housekeeping. Because a unit or cost center has very little control over indirect expenses, the amount to be budgeted in each cost center is usually determined by the institutional fiscal officer.

Personnel Budget. Preparation of the personnel budget, which is the largest component of the expense budget, begins with a determination of projected unit workload. In order to determine correctly the personnel resources that will be required, it is essential to describe unit workload accurately. However, doing so is especially difficult for EDs where patient acuity, volume, and length of stay are extremely variable. Certainly, the number of patient visits is woefully inadequate as an indicator of ED workload. How many hours of direct and indirect nursing care are required by various emergency patients? How many additional hours are required for managerial activities that support patient care?

EDs should implement systems that quantify patients' nursing care needs as the basis for workload measurement. These systems, known as patient classification

Exhibit 8–4 Chart of Accounts

Cost Center 3677	Emergency Department
Account Number	*Account Description*
	Personnel
3677-004	Salaries/Wages—Physician
3677-010	Salaries/Wages—Nurse Manager
3677-011	Salaries/Wages—Assistant Nurse Manager
3677-012	Salaries/Wages—Registered Nurse
3677-013	Salaries/Wages—Licensed Practical Nurse
3677-014	Salaries/Wages—Nursing Assistant
3677-016	Salaries/Wages—Secretary/Clerk
	Nonpersonnel
3677-102	Tuition reimbursement
3677-217	Direct purchase—Instruments
3677-219	Direct purchase—Other medical supplies
3677-301	Inventory—Reagents and chemicals
3677-302	Inventory—Other lab supplies
3677-303	Inventory—Pharmacy supplies
3677-306	Inventory—IV solutions
3677-310	Inventory—Sutures
3677-311	Inventory—Syringes
3677-312	Inventory—Surgical needles
3677-314	Inventory—Other surgical supplies
3677-319	Inventory—Other medical supplies
3677-400	Direct purchase—Forms
3677-401	Direct purchase—Office supplies
3677-404	Direct purchase—Uniforms
3677-417	Direct purchase—Minor nonmedical equipment
3677-418	Direct purchase—Other nonmedical supplies
3677-503	Inventory—Cleaning supplies
3677-509	Inventory—Plastics and glassware
3677-518	Inventory—Other nonmedical supplies
3677-612	Maintenance service contract
3677-614	Outside maintenance and repair
3677-702	Books and periodicals
3677-703	Education—registration
3677-704	Education—travel
3677-712	Equipment lease and rental

systems (PCS), use evaluative criteria to assign patients to acuity categories that have been closely correlated with required nursing care hours (see Chapter 6).

By using a PCS, determining the annual nursing care hours required in the ED becomes a simple mathematical process. Each patient classification category correlates to a predetermined number of nursing hours per patient day (NHPPD).

(NHPPD includes time spent on both direct and indirect nursing care activities for patients.) The number of NHPPD is multiplied by the number of patients in each category for the entire fiscal year, yielding the number of annual nursing care hours required for each patient classification category. The categories are combined, resulting in the total number of nursing care hours required by the ED for one fiscal year (see Table 8–1).

Computation of required nursing care hours using a PCS is based on the actual historical activity of the ED. With a PCS, both patient volume and acuity are considered, resulting in a more accurate prediction of the number of nursing care hours that will be required to care for a particular patient population. This historical data can then be adjusted to account for any change in activity projected by the unit or institution.

Although a PCS is currently the most accurate method of projecting workload, the number of nursing care hours required annually in an ED can also be calculated by other means. If the staffing pattern is perceived to be fairly adequate, it can be used to determine the required hours of nursing care. With this method, the number of staff members desired per shift is multiplied by the length of the shift times 365 days per year (Table 8–2). This method is based on historical data and is useful if there is little or no projected change in staffing requirements. In addition, it incorporates planning for the various categories of the work force (staff mix) and for staffing needs on the different shifts (shift mix). However, the staffing pattern is only roughly correlated to past unit activity and is not based on objective determinations of workload.

Another method that can be used to calculate required personnel resources uses accepted patient/nurse ratios to compute the number of nursing hours required in an ED. Gross acuities of patients are first estimated and used to establish accepted ratios between patients and staff. In effect, staffing patterns are established for

Table 8–1 Computation of Required Nursing Hours Using Patient Classification Data

Patient Classification Category	Percentage of Total ED Patients	Number of Patients	Average Number of Hours per Patient	Nursing Hours Required per Category
Level 1	36.1	10,830	.67	7,256
Level 2	40.5	12,150	1.32	16,038
Level 3	16.2	4,860	4.23	20,558
Level 4	7.2	2,160	6.82	14,731
TOTAL	100.0	30,000		58,583

Table 8–2 Computation of Required Nursing Hours Using Established Staffing Pattern

Job Category	Days	Evenings	Nights	Total Shifts	Hours per Shift	Days per Year	Annual Required Hours
NM	1			1	8	365	*
ANM	1	1	1	3	8	365	8,760
RN	4	4	2	10	8	365	29,200
LPN	1	1	0	2	8	365	5,840
NA	1	1	1	3	8	365	8,760
MC	1	1	0	2	8	365	5,840
				TOTAL ANNUAL REQUIRED NURSING HOURS:			58,400

*The nurse manager represents fixed nursing care hours contributed by one individual who is not included in the staffing requirements.

small subsets of patients or small geographical areas in the ED. Conversion into required nursing care hours can then be accomplished as outlined above. However, this method is not very useful in the emergency setting, where patients are continuously entering and leaving. It is more useful in inpatient units where a patient's length of stay is measured in days. In addition, this method is highly subjective, and thus the established ratios may be incorrect. It is not recommended as a reliable method for projecting the ED workload.

Computation of the required annual nursing care hours for an ED can also be based on a standard target number of nursing hours per patient day (NHPPD). In the emergency setting, patient length of stay is less than a day, so NHPPD is the same as nursing care hours per patient visit (NHPPV). Based on historical data, the ED can identify a NHPPV goal. This number is then multiplied by the anticipated patient volume to arrive at the projected total number of nursing hours required to provide care for that patient volume.

Approved NHPPV = 1.95
30,000 projected annual patient visits × 1.95 NHPPV =
58,500 required annual nursing hours

Because this method is volume related, it can be used even when there are great variations in the number of patient visits. The difficulty with this method lies in establishing a NHPPV goal that is both realistic and reflective of actual patient acuity. Because there is such marked variability in the acuity of ED patients, any deviation from planned acuity patterns can result in substantial errors in determining nursing workload.

After the required annual hours of nursing care have been identified, a determination must be made as to how to allocate these hours to the different types of staff members assigned to the ED. This staff mix can be based on past staffing proportions, historical data, and/or subjective determinations. Staff mix is usually described as a percentage of the total number of annual required nursing hours (Table 8–3).

The next step in preparing the personnel budget is to determine the number of employees necessary to meet the workload. It is important to differentiate between position and full-time equivalent (FTE). A position is the same as a worker: one job for one person, without regard to scheduled hours of work. An FTE is a standard measure that correlates to a "full-time worker": one employee working 8 hours per day, 5 days a week, 52 weeks per year. Thus, an FTE is the equivalent of an employee paid for 2080 hours annually.

However, all hours paid to employees are not productive ones for the institution. In order to determine the number of FTEs needed to provide a specified number of nursing care hours, consider only the productive hours per FTE. In an ED, productive hours are those hours that are directly or indirectly used to produce patient care. Nonproductive hours are all other paid hours, which include vacation, sick, and holiday time and educational or inservice time planned or allocated per employee. Because the bulk of nonproductive time is benefit time, it is specific to each institution and job category and must be calculated for each category of employee (Exhibit 8–5). The number of annual productive hours per FTE equals the annual paid hours minus the annual paid nonproductive hours allocated per FTE. It is this number, the annual productive hours per FTE, that is divided into

Table 8–3 Staff Mix Calculation

Patient Classification Category	Nursing Hours Required per Category	Percentage RN Care	RN Required Hours	Percentage LPN Care	LPN Required Hours
Level 1	7,256	45	3,265	55	3,991
Level 2	16,038	85	13,632	15	2,406
Level 3	20,558	100	20,558	0	0
Level 4	14,731	100	14,731	0	0
TOTAL HOURS BY SHIFT MIX	58,583		52,186		6,397

Exhibit 8–5 Computation of Productive Hours per FTE

	RN			LPN	
1. Identify nonproductive hours planned per FTE:					
Vacation	20 days × 8 hours =	120	10 days × 8 hours =		80
Holidays	11 days × 8 hours =	88	11 days × 8 hours =		88
Sick time	8 days × 8 hours =	64	8 days × 8 hours =		64
Inservice		48			24
Nonproductive hours per paid FTE	=	320		=	256
2. Calculate productive hours per FTE:					
Annual paid hours per FTE	=	2080		=	2080
Minus nonproductive hours	−	320		−	256
ANNUAL PRODUCTIVE HOURS PER FTE	=	1760		=	1824

the annual required nursing care hours to determine the total number of FTEs required to support the unit activity for the next fiscal year (Exhibit 8–6).

The next step in preparing the personnel budget is to allocate the required FTEs into work shifts (shift mix). Because many institutions pay a differential to employees who work evenings or night shifts, shift mix has a definite financial impact and must be considered when preparing the budget. Shift mix can be identified using patient classification data or any other determinant of activity trends by shift.

Exhibit 8–6 Determination of Required FTEs

$$\frac{\text{Required Nursing Hours}}{\text{Productive Hours per FTE}} = \text{Required FTE}$$

$$\frac{52{,}186 \text{ Required RN Hours}}{1{,}760 \text{ Productive Hours/RN}} = 29.7 \text{ RN FTE}$$

$$\frac{6{,}397 \text{ Required LPN Hours}}{1{,}824 \text{ Productive Hours/LPN}} = 3.5 \text{ LPN FTE}$$

The shift mix is often expressed as a percentage, which is applied to the unit's total number of FTEs to determine shift staffing levels (Table 8–4).

After identifying the required number of FTEs, staff mix, and shift mix, you can begin to convert these figures into dollars. To do this, you will need the following information: current employee salaries, differential rates, planned merit and cost of living or general salary increases, overtime payment practices, and fringe benefit costs. All this information is necessary to calculate salary expenses that will reflect the costs in effect at the beginning and throughout the fiscal year.

Using a worksheet, determine the combined base salary for workers in a particular job category. Then the actual dollar amounts required by planned merit and cost of living raises, resulting in a new base salary for that job category for the upcoming fiscal year. Referring to the shift mix previously determined, add the costs incurred due to shift differential. This results in an amount often referred to as *regular salary*, or the salary that it will cost to pay employees to work their regularly scheduled hours and shifts of work (Table 8–5).

However, many institutions also include provisions for a specific amount of overtime to be included in planned budgets. Planned overtime hours may be added early in the budget preparation process to the unit's required hours of nursing care. Using this approach, the overtime hours are included in those that are converted into the FTEs required to support the unit's activity. Or, overtime allocations can be included in the budget by determining the planned cost of overtime hours and adding them to the regular salary amount that has been calculated for the fiscal year. Either method will result in a total adjusted salary for the next fiscal year for each job category.

Employee fringe benefit cost may be included as part of the unit salary expense, as a separate line item on the unit expense budget, or incorporated into the hospital operating expense as a discrete item budgeted elsewhere. It is usually calculated as a specific percentage of regular salary expense.

Table 8–4 Calculating Shift Mix

	RN			LPN		
Shift	Percentage of RN Staff	Required Hours	Required FTE	Percentage of LPN Staff	Required Hours	Required FTE
Days	38	19,831	11.3	60	3,838	2.1
Evenings	40	20,874	11.9	40	2,559	1.4
Nights	22	11,481	6.5	0	0	0
Total	100	52,186	29.7	100	6,397	3.5

Table 8-5 Salary Worksheet

Job Title	Number of FTE	Average Hourly Rate	Base Salary	Merit Raise[a]	Cost of Living Raise[b]	New Salary Base	Evening 10% Differential	Night 10% Differential	Regular Salaries	Overtime	Total Adjusted Salaries	Fringe Benefit Expense[c]
HN	1.0	14.90	31,000	1,550		32,550			32,550		32,550	5,534
RN	29.7	12.82	791,968	27,719	29,699	849,386	33,975[d]	18,686[d]	902,047	5,034	907,081	153,348
LPN	3.5	9.54	69,451	2,431	2,604	74,486	4,469[e]	0[e]	78,955	1,690	80,645	13,422
NA	4.5	8.47	79,279	2,775	2,973	85,027	2,834[f]	2,834[f]	90,695	828	91,523	15,418
MC	3.0	8.34	52,042	1,821	1,952	55,815	2,791		58,606	504	59,110	9,963
TOTAL	41.7		1,023,740	36,296	37,228	1,097,264	44,069	21,520	1,162,853	8,056	1,170,909	197,685

[a]Merit raises affecting individuals at various times throughout the year have a net annual budget effect of 3½ percent increase.

[b]This allows for a 5 percent cost of living adjustment that takes effect on October 1, which is three-quarters of the fiscal year.

[c]The total cost of the fringe benefit package for employees is approximated at 17 percent of the regular salary expense.

[d]This allows for the differential for the 40 percent of the RN staff who will be scheduled on evening shift and the 22 percent scheduled for night shift.

[e]This allows for the differential for the 40 percent of the LPN staff scheduled for evening shift.

[f]This allows for the differential for one-third of the NA staff to be scheduled for evenings and one-third to be scheduled for night shifts.

The procedure for salary computation outlined above is followed for each category. When all job categories have been completed, total the amounts reflecting total employment or personnel costs for the cost center.

Nonpersonnel Budget. The second part of the expense budget is the nonpersonnel section, which includes the financial plan for those unit expenses that are not related to employment. These expenses include medical supplies, equipment, and services that are not charged directly to the patient. For the most part, nonpersonnel expenses are variable costs and thus are closely tied to volume of service. If patient volume is projected to remain stable, nonpersonnel expenses can be calculated at the current cost adjusted for inflation. Projected activity increases or decreases can be captured by proportionally increasing or decreasing related nonpersonnel expense (Table 8–6).

A second way to estimate nonpersonnel expense in an ED is to identify historical nonpersonnel costs per patient visit. Because expenses are closely related to unit output, costs can be easily adjusted for expected change in patient volume. Using this method, nonpersonnel costs are projected as the cost per visit times the anticipated number of patient visits.

Some nonpersonnel costs, however, are fixed or semivariable costs and thus are not dependent on unit activity or output. These expenses, such as educational, equipment lease, and maintenance agreement costs, must be calculated directly.

Revenue Budget

The revenue budget for a given unit or cost center reflects the income that is anticipated as a result of that unit's operation. Revenue budget forecasts are obtained by applying the rates to be charged for various units of service to the volume of activity anticipated and adding some excess of revenues over costs for other needs, such as capital purchases.

In the ED, revenue is generated by the provision of direct patient care and is referred to as *patient revenues*. These revenues are based retrospectively on charges for hospital and professional (physician) services, which include both actual incurred costs plus an amount for overhead and profit. The ED revenue budget thus can be calculated by projecting patient visits or units of service, such as lab test, case application, EKG, and the like, and multiplying that by anticipated charges.

Since the advent of the prospective payment system, reimbursement for all Medicare and many other groups of inpatients is based on the patient's discharge diagnosis. Hospitals receive reimbursement on a per case basis, with no consideration of actual costs incurred or services provided for an individual patient. Although, as of 1986, EDs do not fall under prospective payment determinations, they may be subject to them in the future. If so, ED patient revenues will be determined by the number of patients discharged and the corresponding rates for each diagnosis group.

Table 8–6 Nonpersonnel Expense Calculation

Account Number	Account Description	Previous Year Actual	+	3% Activity Increase	+	FY Inflation Factor	=	FY Requested Amount
3677-102	Tuition reimbursement	2400		—		—	=	2400
3677-217	Direct purchase—Instruments	1647		—		7%	=	1762
3677-219	Direct purchase—Other medical supplies	1969		+ 59		6%	=	2150
3677-301	Inventory—Reagents and chemicals	1520		+ 46		3%	=	1613
3677-302	Inventory—Other lab supplies	6430		+ 193		5%	=	6954
3677-303	Inventory—Pharmacy supplies	200		+ 6		7%	=	220
3677-306	Inventory—IV solutions	150		+ 5		7%	=	165
3677-310	Inventory—Sutures	1280		+ 38		0%	=	1318
3677-311	Inventory—Syringes	4106		+ 123		0%	=	4229
3677-312	Inventory—Surgical needles	1710		+ 51		0%	=	1752
3677-314	Inventory—Other surgical supplies	14,516		+ 435		4%	=	15,549
3677-319	Inventory—Other medical supplies	27,857		+ 836		4%	=	29,840
3677-400	Direct purchase—Forms	468		—		0%	=	468
3677-401	Direct purchase—Office supplies	570		+ 17		3%	=	605
3677-404	Direct purchase—Uniforms	375		—		5%	=	394
3677-417	Direct purchase—Minor nonmedical equipment	50		—		7%	=	54
3677-418	Direct purchase—Other nonmedical supplies	175		+ 5		4%	=	187
3677-503	Inventory—Cleaning supplies	84		—		4%	=	87
3677-509	Inventory—Plastics and glassware	520		+ 16		9%	=	584
3677-518	Inventory—Other nonmedical supplies	3248		+ 97		4%	=	3479
3677-612	Maintenance service contract	250		—		—	=	250
3677-614	Outside maintenance and repair	273		—		10%	=	300
3677-702	Books and periodicals	120		—		—	=	120
3677-703	Education—Registration	1423		—		5%	=	1494
3677-704	Education—Travel	236		—		—	=	250
3677-712	Equipment lease and rental	432		—		—	=	432
3677	Cost Center Total Nonpersonnel	72,009						76,656

Capital Budget

The *capital budget* is the institution's plan for major purchases, improvements, or projects during the budget period. Capital expenditures are defined in each individual institution on the basis of cost and expected life-span. For example, a hospital may define capital items as those that exceed $500 and have a life expectancy of 2 years or more.

Capital requests are usually triggered by new technology, new or expanding programs, the need to replace antiquated or poorly functioning equipment, or a desire to improve current equipment availability. In such patient care areas as the ED, nurse managers should collaborate with the medical staff to identify capital request items. Because of the high cost of new technologies and major equipment, no institution can afford to purchase all the capital items it would like to have. When participating in the development of the capital budget, you must judge the worthiness of individual purchases or projects and prioritize them accordingly.

Capital purchase requests must be based on sound criteria that permit the administration to compare requests and make knowledgeable choices in the allocation of the hospital's resources. These requests typically include the following information:

- department name
- name and quantity of the item
- description of the item
- function of the item
- nature of request (new or replacement)
- cost
- name of supplier
- proposed purchase date
- justification for the request
- resulting change in current operation
- impact on revenues or operation costs
- source of funding
- priority

Most institutions provide specific guidelines and forms to be used in the preparation of capital budget requests. These forms often contain capital purchase plans for a 3- to 5-year period (Exhibit 8–7).

New Program Budgets

A program budget is often developed as a financial plan for a specific new program or service. Program budgets focus on one service and identify its

Exhibit 8–7 Guidelines for Preparing Capital Budget Request

FY _____ CAPITAL BUDGET SUMMARY

Department _____   Cost Center _____

CAPITAL FINANCING

Cost Estimates:

Purchase price	$ _____
Installation cost	_____
Renovation	_____
Trade-in or salvage	_____
Cost per square foot	_____
Square footage	_____

Source of Funds:

Unrestricted capital funds	$ _____
Restricted grants, gifts	_____
Lease/purchase	_____

NET CAPITAL REQUEST $ _____   TOTAL FUNDING SOURCES $ _____

CAPITAL PURCHASE REQUEST	BUDGET YEAR ONE	BUDGET YEAR TWO	BUDGET YEAR THREE	THREE-YEAR TOTAL
Equipment				
Patient care	_____	_____	_____	_____
Other	_____	_____	_____	_____
Equipment total	_____	_____	_____	_____
Renovation/construction	_____	_____	_____	_____
External agencies	_____	_____	_____	_____
TOTAL	$ _____	$ _____	$ _____	$ _____

objectives, target patient population, and planned outcomes. In addition, detailed information is included about the program's estimated operating costs, capital requirements, anticipated revenues, and benefits to the institution. These costs, revenues, and benefits may involve numerous departments and so are best presented in a coordinated manner.

Program budgets are used to evaluate the overall costs and benefits of a proposed program to the institution and are usually developed separately from the annual budgetary process. Although the time period defined in a program budget may be the anticipated life of the program, it is usually expressed in terms of budget years. New program budgets in effect use a zero-base budgeting style, although historical data are interpreted and applied in making the budget projections. When the new program is approved, its costs and revenues are integrated into the other operations and budgets of the organization.

BUDGET SURVEILLANCE

As with any process, the final step in fiscal management is evaluation. To budget is not only to make plans but also to use the plans that have been developed to control operations. The budget is only an effective instrument for planning and control if it is compared with actual results on a regular basis. Periodic evaluation provides a mechanism for measurement and feedback to the manager about goal attainment. With regular budget review, unanticipated results are brought to your attention. Corrective action can then be initiated in a timely manner to foster attainment of unit objectives and compliance with the planned budget.

The reporting tools used to provide budget control information use data similar to that of the budget development process. This facilitates comparison of actual and budgeted data as the fiscal year progresses. Performance reports collect and organize information at cost center, departmental, and institutional levels. Usually first-line managers receive reports for only their own area of responsibility, with supervisors and department heads receiving overall summaries of the units under their supervision. Generally included in the performance reports are personnel utilization information and expense statements (Exhibits 8–8 and 8–9). Revenue statements are also provided if applicable to the cost center.

Performance reports used for budget control are usually distributed on a monthly basis. Most show actual, budgeted, and variance amounts for both the current month and the fiscal year to date. You can use this information to analyze actual activity and resource utilization, to identify problem areas and unfavorable trends, and to develop alternative correcting strategies.

Variance Analysis

Analysis of variances or deviations between budgeted and actual operating results should be made in detail after receipt of performance reports. To ensure

Exhibit 8-8 Unit Labor Variance Report

LEVEL IV
COST CENTER: EMERGENCY DEPARTMENT
ACCOUNT NO. 3366

PAY PERIOD ENDING 12/31/
PAY PERIOD NO. 13
SUPERVISOR: L. HOLDER

ACTUAL PAYROLL EXPENSES

| | | PRODUCTIVE | | | NONPRODUCTIVE | | | | |
| | | | | OVERTIME | OVERTIME | | | | | |
		REGULAR	SHIFT	REGULAR	SHIFT	OTHER	HOLIDAY	SICK	VACATION	TOTAL
CURRENT	HOURS	2,356	3,712	16	60	160	16	24	152	6,496
YEAR TO DATE	HOURS	15,886	21,132	115	163	760	208	416	2,080	40,760
CURRENT	$	32,445	50,495	268	1,107	1,954	205	281	1,809	88,564
YEAR TO DATE	$	202,041	354,740	1,928	2,807	3,536	2,389	4,618	26,403	598,462

ACTUAL LABOR EXPENSE VERSUS BUDGET

		PRODUCTIVE TIME	NONPRODUCTIVE TIME	TOTAL PAID TIME	BUDGET	VARIANCE	PERCENT VARIANCE
CURRENT	HOURS	6,144	352	6,496	7,228	732 +	10.1 +
YEAR TO DATE	HOURS	37,296	3,464	40,760	43,368	2,608 +	6.0 +
CURRENT	$	84,315	4,249	88,564	97,576	9,012 +	9.2 +
YEAR TO DATE	$	561,516	36,946	598,462	585,455	13,007 −	2.2 −

SICK AND OVERTIME HOURS PERCENTAGE

	% SICK/PAID HOURS	% OVERTIME/PAID HOURS
CURRENT	.0037	.0017
YEAR TO DATE	.0121	.0060

Exhibit 8–9 Monthly Unit Expense Report

COST CENTER: EMERGENCY DEPARTMENT
ACCOUNT NO. 3366

PERIOD ENDING 12/31/
SUPERVISOR: L. HOLDER

Personnel	CURRENT PERIOD				YEAR TO DATE			
	ACTUAL	PLAN	VARIANCE	VAR%	ACTUAL	PLAN	VARIANCE	VAR%
010 Salaries/Wages—Nurse Manager	2712	2713	1	0	16275	16275	0	0
012 Salaries/Wages—Registered Nurse	71750	75590	3840	5	466672	453540	13132–	3–
013 Salaries/Wages—Licensed Practical Nurse	5542	6720	1173	17	42719	40323	2396–	6–
014 Salaries/Wages—Nursing Assistant	6145	7627	1482	19	45033	45762	729	2
016 Salaries/Wages—Secretary/Clerk	2410	4926	2516	51	27763	29555	1792	6
SUBTOTAL—SALARIES	88564	97576	9012	9	598462	585455	13007–	2–
Nonpersonnel								
102 Tuition reimbursement	540	200	340–	170–	1125	1200	75	6
217 Direct purchase—Instruments	223	147	76–	52–	859	881	22	2
219 Direct purchase—Other medical supplies	175	179	4	2	983	1075	92	9
301 Inventory—Reagents and chemicals	247	135	112–	83–	822	807	15–	2–
302 Inventory—Other lab supplies	649	580	69–	19–	3212	3477	265	8
303 Inventory—Pharmacy supplies	36	18	18–	100–	123	110	13–	12–
306 Inventory—IV solutions	20	14	6–	43–	90	83	7–	8–
310 Inventory—Sutures	98	110	12	11	632	659	27	4
311 Inventory—Syringes	514	352	162–	46–	1876	2115	239	11
312 Inventory—Surgical needles	184	146	38–	26–	823	876	53	6
314 Inventory—Other surgical supplies	1395	1296	99–	8–	7735	7775	40	1
319 Inventory—Other medical supplies	2148	2487	339	14	13662	14920	1258	8
400 Direct purchase—Forms	51	39	12–	31–	230	234	4	2
401 Direct purchase—Office supplies	135	50	85–	170–	472	303	169–	56–

Exhibit 8–9 continued

404 Direct purchase—Uniforms	0	33	33	100	35	197	162	82
417 Direct purchase—Minor nonmedical equipment	0	5	5	100	0	27	27	100
418 Direct purchase—Other nonmedical supplies	0	16	16	100	0	94	94	100
503 Inventory—Cleaning supplies	23	7	16–	229–	47	44	3–	7–
509 Inventory—Plastics and glassware	52	49	3–	6–	290	292	2	1
518 Inventory—Other nonmedical supplies	275	290	15	5	1702	1738	36	2
612 Maintenance service contract	21	21	0	0	125	125	0	0
614 Outside maintenance and repair	0	25	25	100	0	150	150	100
702 Books and periodicals	0	10	10	100	39	60	21	35
703 Education—registration	95	125	30	24	875	747	128–	17–
704 Education—travel	0	21	21	100	100	125	25	20
712 Equipment lease and rental	36	36	0	0	216	216	0	0
SUBTOTAL—NONPERSONNEL	6917	6391	526–	8–	36073	38330	2257	6
COST CENTER TOTALS								

effective control without expending undue effort in analyzing insignificant variances, each institution defines what degree of variance must be analyzed. Significant variances are usually described as both a function of the dollar amount and the percentage of the budgeted amount for the item in question. Thus, a $300 deviation would be significant for an item budgeted at $1000, but not for an item budgeted at $50,000 for the fiscal year.

You should study significant variances indicated by performance reports and be able to explain why variances arose so that you can isolate and correct areas of concern. Causes of variance can include:

- error in budget projections
- unplanned salary adjustments
- use of more expensive item or staff than budgeted
- waste
- theft
- use by other units or departments
- price increase
- change in activity volume or workload
- shift in the quality of care delivered
- change in policy or procedure
- modification in technology
- altered efficiency of nurses
- reclassification of item in chart of accounts
- lost charges
- unforeseen events

Through timely variance analysis, you can locate the causes of inefficiencies and identify justifiable variances. With prompt investigation and intervention, you can effect changes in spending patterns, thereby promoting cost containment and unit efficiency.

Productivity

Any discussion of fiscal accountability and responsibility must include a commentary on productivity. When resources are limited, organizations must promote effectiveness and efficiency, which enable it to provide a stable amount and quality of patient care at a lower cost. Productivity enhancement has become a key strategy for institutional survival and is an essential element of your role.

Simply put, productivity is the ratio of output (goods and services produced) to input (resources used). ED nursing productivity can best be measured by comparing required nursing hours (based on acuity-adjusted patient visits) to the total number of nursing hours utilized by the department.

Because the efficient allocation and use of resources is a managerial function, today's nurse manager is challenged to improve productivity without reducing the quality of care delivered. Productivity can be enhanced by any action that either increases the output or decreases the input of an ED. Strategies that might be used to improve ED outputs include:

- marketing effectively to increase volume, thereby spreading fixed costs over patients
- modifying the physical layout of the ED
- improving the admission systems, thereby enhancing patient flow to inpatient areas (work flow)
- increasing employee autonomy and motivation through participative management techniques, quality circles, committee activity, and rewards

Unit productivity can also be enhanced by reducing input. Approaches that may reduce resource utilization in an ED include:

- decentralization to reduce layers of management
- organized delivery of supplies and support services to minimize the erosion of delivered nursing hours
- clearly defined responsibilities to avoid duplication of effort
- an objective review of routine orders and practices
- streamlined documentation
- the use of highly qualified staff who are efficient and adept
- creative staffing patterns, designed to match resource availability to activity trends
- an increased professional staff mix, which results in less time spent instructing or supervising others
- cross-trained staff, who can function effectively in several clinical areas
- redefined work period lengths for nursing assistants or unit clerks who are not needed for an entire shift, especially during periods of lesser activity
- the use of management principles to reduce high absenteeism, attrition, and overtime
- expanded roles for nurses, reducing fixed costs by having them do activities previously performed by separate categories of workers

- the use of alternative educational strategies, such as self-paced learning programs, to reduce orientation time

Perhaps the most effective strategy to improve productivity is to increase staff awareness and involvement. If provided with information and opportunity, ED nursing staff can contribute substantially to a productivity improvement program. Together, managers and staff can use their multiple perspectives and collective creativity to generate, assess, and implement successful productivity enhancement techniques.

CONCLUSION

The utilization of resources within health care institutions has increasingly become a key function of any manager. Your role in institutional fiscal accountability is easily established. As the manager of a large labor body that is the predominant user of supplies, you have great potential in controlling and influencing spending patterns. With today's great emphasis on cost containment, the ED nurse manager must be a truly professional manager with fiscal expertise.

Fiscal accountability and responsibility begin with the definition of realistic, attainable unit objectives. These are translated into financial terms and expressed as the unit's annual budget, with clear delineations of amounts allocated for each resource. This budget is used to guide and control unit activity throughout the fiscal year.

Fiscal accountability is further established as you monitor and adjust spending in order to stay within defined budget parameters. Monthly performance reports are carefully reviewed, with prompt and appropriate adjustments made to maximize their effect. Productivity is evaluated regularly, and creative approaches are used to enhance unit productivity levels. The ED nurse manager who regulates resource utilization from day to day will have no quarterly surprises. Wise financial management and fiscal accountability must be put into practice daily.

REFERENCES

Althaus, Joan Nietz; Hardyk, Nancy McDonald; Pierce, Patricia Blair; and Rodgers, Marilyn S. "Decentralized Budgeting: Holding the Purse Strings, Part 1." *The Journal of Nursing Administration* 12(5):15–20, 1982.

————. "Decentralized Budgeting: Holding the Purse Strings, Part 2." *The Journal of Nursing Administration* 12(6):34–38, 1982.

Deegan, Arthur X. II, and O'Donovan, Thomas R. "Budgeting and Management by Objectives." *Health Care Management Review* 9(1):51–59, 1984.

Drucker, Peter F. *Management: Tasks, Responsibilities, Practices.* New York: Harper Colophon Books, 1974.

Edwardson, Sandra R. "Measuring Nursing Productivity." *Nursing Economics* 3(1):9–14, 1985.

Finkler, Steven A. *Budgeting Concepts for Nurse Managers*. Orlando, Florida: Grune and Stratton Incorporated, 1984.

Fuller, Mary E. "The Budget." *The Journal of Nursing Administration* 6(4):36–38, 1976.

Goetz, Joseph F. Jr., and Smith, Howard L. "Zero Base Budgeting for Nursing Services: An Opportunity for Cost Containment?" *Nursing Forum* 11(2):123–137, 1980.

Kelliher, Matthew E. "Managing Productivity, Performance, and the Cost of Services." *Healthcare Financial Management* 39(9):23–27, 1985.

Kirk, Roey, and Dunaye, Thomas M. "Managing Hospital Nursing Services for Productivity." *Nursing Management* 17(3):29–32, 1986.

Meyer, Alan D. "Hospital Capital Budgeting: Fusion of Rationality, Politics and Ceremony." *Health Care Management Review* 10(2):17–27, 1985.

Rowland, Howard S., and Rowland, Beatrice L. *Hospital Administration Handbook*. Rockville, MD: Aspen Publishers, 1984.

————. *Nursing Administration Handbook*. Rockville, MD: Aspen Publishers, 1980.

Schmied, Elsie. "Allocation of Resources: Preparation of the Nursing Department Budget." *The Journal of Nursing Administration* 7(7):33–36, 1977.

————. "Living with Cost Containment." In *Management for Nurses*, ed. Stone, Sandra; Firsich, Sharon Cannell; Jordan, Shelley Baney; Berger, Marie Streng; and Elhart, Dorothy, 224–232. St. Louis: C.V. Mosby Company, 1984.

Stevens, Barbara J. *The Nurse as Executive*. Wakefield, MA: Nursing Resources Incorporated, 1980.

Thibadoux, Greg M., and Greenberg, Ira S. "Standard Costing Method Increase Productivity." *Healthcare Financial Management* 39(9):81–82, 1985.

Chapter 9

Quality Assurance

QUALITY ASSURANCE

The goal of quality assurance is to provide appropriate and accountable patient care in a cost-effective manner. Quality should be identifiable and measurable according to the emergency care standards and expectations established by self-regulation, policies and procedures of the hospital, Emergency Nurses Association standards, the Nurse Practice Act, regulatory agencies, the Patient Bill of Rights, and consumer expectations. Quality assurance in the ED should be an integrated and coordinated approach used to monitor and evaluate quality of care and identify and resolve problems (see Table 9–1).

JCAH emergency services standards require:

- monitoring and evaluation of quality of all major functions of the ED
- routine collection of information about important aspects of emergency care
- periodic assessment by the ED/service of the collected information in order to identify important problems in patient care and opportunities to improve care based on objective criteria that reflect current knowledge and clinical experience
- actions, taken when patient care problems are identified
- evaluation of the effectiveness of the actions taken

The findings, conclusions, actions taken, and the impact of actions must be documented and, as appropriate, reported.

A quality assurance (QA) program in the ED must involve nursing care. To evaluate the quality of emergency nursing care, predetermined standards are necessary. Job descriptions, emergency nursing expectations, and nursing care

Table 9–1 ED Quality Assurance Indicators to be Monitored

Indicator	Comments	How Monitored	By Whom	How Often
Code Cart Inventory	JCAH requirement	Review code cart checklist signatures	*QA committee	Monthly
Labeled IV Bags	P&P—IV therapy	Audit—direct observation all shifts	*QA committee	Monthly
Patient Falls	P&P—prone to fall	Review incident reports	*QA committee	Monthly

Employee Injuries
  Needle Sticks
  Back Injuries
  Other
		Review all employee injury incident reports	*QA committee	Quarterly

Patient Classification Appropriateness	ED standard	Retrospective chart review of all patient records on two randomly selected days	*QA committee	Bimonthly

* Specific members of the QA committee will be assigned (ED nursing managers are members of the QA committee with staff members).

standards must first be developed and communicated to the ED nursing staff so that specific ED nursing actions and behaviors are defined and can be measured.

EMERGENCY DEPARTMENT NURSING PROCESSES FOR A QUALITY ASSURANCE PROGRAM

QA responsibility should not be that of the ED nurse manager alone. The staff should participate in QA activities through a committee consisting of ED nursing management and staff. If the ED has the resource of a clinical specialist, he or she should also participate in the QA program. The committee can assume responsibility for determining QA criteria and the means and frequency of monitoring and evaluating them, compiling and documenting findings, recommending actions to be taken to resolve problems, and providing feedback to the staff.

Quality indicators, which indicate how well or poorly the ED staff is performing, should be identified. Indicators should be meaningful, and there must be the ability to collect data about them.

Key indicators can be derived from such areas as patient safety, care, and satisfaction; nursing policies, procedures, protocols and standards; the ED treatment record, the triage record, incident reports, and other forms. Indicators are usually potential problem areas that have been identified. A few examples of quality indicators for emergency nursing include whether:

- triage priority reflects the seriousness of illness or injury
- RN signature is in appropriate places
- current medications are listed
- allergies are listed or NKA is documented
- complete vital signs are taken
- discharge instructions are noted and signed for
- response to treatment is indicated
- date of last tetanus toxoid is noted when applicable
- LMP is noted for females of childbearing age
- the trauma room is appropriately stocked
- needles are properly disposed of
- code carts are checked each shift
- IV bags are labeled with patient name, date and time, name and amount of additive, rate of flow
- there are patient complaints concerning nursing attitude
- employees are stuck with contaminated needles
- there are patient "walkouts" without treatment

Once the key indicators are identified, then determine measurable standards and objective audit criteria. Determine how to monitor, collect, and record data; how frequently to record information; and who is to be given that responsibility. Direct observation and retrospective audits can both be used to answer these questions: Is there a standard established? Is there compliance? If not, by whom and why not?

Next, develop plans to correct problems or maintain standards. QA can be achieved by re-educating staff through inservice programs or revising audit criteria to correct inappropriate ones. These corrective actions should then be re-evaluated. Throughout this process, provide feedback to the staff.

The following, then, describes the eight steps of a QA program:

1. identification of indicators
2. development of standards and criteria
3. monitoring and data collection
4. analyzing/identification of problems
5. reporting
6. feedback
7. corrective action
8. re-evaluation

You may also need to track ED volume activities. Volume indicators may include the number of patient visits, admissions, number or percentage of all hospital admissions, number of deaths, DOAs, codes, incident reports, patients who walked out without treatment, and various waiting times.

A QA program in the emergency department should be simple in structure and have meaningful outcomes for it to be effective and cost efficient.

Monitoring and Data Collection

Means of monitoring and collecting data for QA must be simple and require minimal time. Checklists are most useful, and completing them can become a routine required responsibility. A checklist of equipment and supplies is a perfect example. Critical care and trauma rooms require that additional and specialized equipment and supplies be available immediately as needed for the care of ED patients. Develop checklists of these supplies, with the expectation that staff are assigned to complete them everyday and on each shift. Code carts are also to be checked each shift, so staff must be assigned routinely to check them and sign a form that it was done. An equipment book can be maintained, with an individual assigned to document routinely the working condition and availability of other ED equipment. This can be done daily or weekly, according to the specific needs of the individual ED.

Criteria reflecting established standards of care should be developed to enable the appropriateness of care to be monitored through a review of documentation on the ED records. Standards of nursing care and audit criteria can be developed for generalized monitoring of patient care or for specific types of patient illness.

The asthma patient is frequently seen in the ED and can be a choice for the development of specific criteria for QA auditing. Criteria could be as follows:

- Diagnosis: Asthma
- Documentation is to include:
  - History
    - presenting complaint
    - precipitating factors
    - length of attack
    - pre-existing medical problems
    - current medications
    - medication allergies
  - Assessment
    - ABCs
    - complete vital signs
    - respiratory assessment

- Interventions
  - monitor vital signs
  - medications given (time and initials noted)
  - treatments
  - change in status
  - response to medication
- Disposition
  - status on discharge or transfer
  - written instructions
  - follow-up care indicated

Criteria should be developed for monitoring the quality of care given for illnesses and injuries that are most commonly treated in the ED. In addition to asthma, other conditions that are often seen are head injury, sickle cell crisis, seizure, and gastrointestinal bleeding.

Assessment of Findings and Plan of Action

QA activities must be measurable in order to determine a percentage of noncompliance with standards. An example of a QA activity sheet is shown in Table 9–2. Those areas with lower percentages of compliance (usually below 80 percent) are identified as problems. Problems must be listed with an action plan to correct them. An example of a problem list and action plan is shown in Exhibit 9–1. The action plan must then be implemented and followed by re-evaluation to determine if the problem still exists.

Evaluation of the QA program

The effectiveness of the QA program should be evaluated at least annually and changes should be made as required. The ED nurse manager should integrate ED nursing QA activities with the overall ED quality assurance activities by working closely with the ED director.

SAFETY

All new employees must be taught ED safety procedures. Safety procedures should also be reviewed with all staff members at least once a year. They must be aware of the locations of fire alarms, fire extinguishers, and emergency exits and

Table 9–2 Quality Assurance Activity Sheet

Criteria	Standard	Yes	No	NA	Comments
Assessment of ABCs	100%				
Complete vital signs	100%				
Respiratory assessment	100%				
History of presenting problem, including precipitating factors and duration	100%				
Current medications noted	100%				
Allergies noted	100%				
Repeat vital signs	100%				
Medications given (includes time and initials)	100%				
Response to medication	100%				
Treatments	100%				
Change in status	100%				
Admitted (include to what unit) or discharged	100%				
Written discharge instructions with patient signature	100%				
Follow-up care indicated	100%				

Exhibit 9–1 Identified Problems

Problems
Complete vital signs not recorded
Time of medication not noted
Discharge instructions not given

Action Plan
Inservice to all nursing staff to remind them to take and document consistently complete vital signs, including temperature, and to document times that medications are administered
Revise the ED record to provide a space for patients to sign for receipt of written discharge instructions

procedures for power failure and evacuation. Internal and external disaster procedures must also be reviewed with them.

Because EDs use stretchers instead of beds, emphasize the importance on keeping siderails up and/or applying safety straps at all times when patients are left unattended. Safety procedures for specific types of patients, such as alcoholic or seizure patients, should be clearly established and communicated. Inservices on dealing with violent behavior and application of restraints should be conducted to ensure patient and staff safety.

You must insist on protection of the ED staff when possible danger to them exists. EDs in some areas require 24-hour security guards for the safety and protection of the ED staff and patients. In some urban EDs, it is not uncommon for fights between patients or visitors to occur, for patients or visitors to enter the ED with dangerous weapons, or for the safety of staff members to be threatened by an agitated, intoxicated, or psychotic patient or family member for various reasons. All ED personnel should be instructed how to protect themselves and the other ED patients in these types of situations.

All electrical equipment must be checked routinely and staff members must be instructed to report any faulty electrical cords, equipment, wires, and outlets.

INFECTION CONTROL

Infection control measures must be established and enforced with appropriate policies and procedures to prevent cross-infection and contamination. When patient treatment is needed quickly, physicians and nurses may tend to ignore infection control measures, such as hand washing and wearing sterile gloves, and masks. Even when rushed, however, staff members must take appropriate infection control measures, except in extreme situations.

REFERENCES

Decker, Christine. "Quality Assurance: Accent on Monitoring." *Nursing Management,* November, 1985, pp. 20–24.

Flint, Loring S.; Hammett, William H.; and Martens, Katherine. "Quality Assurance in the Emergency Department." *Annals of Emergency Medicine* 14(2):134–138, 1985.

Joint Commission on Accreditation of Hospitals. *Accreditation Manual for Hospitals,* American Hospital Association, Chicago, 1986.

Peisert, Margaret. *The Hospital's Role in Emergency Medical Services Systems.* Chicago, American Hospital Publishing, Inc., 1983.

Chapter 10

Forms and Manuals

EMERGENCY DEPARTMENT RECORDS AND FORMS

Emergency Department Treatment Record

JCAH requirements for the ED treatment record* are that, each time a patient visits the ED/service, his or her medical record must include:

- patient identification: when this is not obtainable, the reason is entered in the medical record
- time and means of arrival
- pertinent history of the illness or injury and the physical findings, including the patient's vital signs
- emergency care given to the patient before arrival
- diagnostic and therapeutic orders
- clinical observations, including the results of treatment
- reports of procedures, tests, and results
- diagnostic impression
- conclusion at the termination of evaluation and treatment, including final disposition, the patient's condition on discharge or transfer, and any instructions given to the patient and/or family for follow-up care
- if a patient leaves against medical advice

You should have input into the design and content of the ED treatment record, so that nursing documentation needs are met.

Some EDs use a single-page ED treatment record. Patient identification and billing information frequently fills up one-third to one-half of the space, which

---

*JCAH Accreditation Manual for Hospitals, Chicago, Emergency Services section, pp. 35–36; 1986.

Exhibit 10–1 Sample Triage Record

HUP	HOSPITAL OF THE UNIVERSITY OF PENNSYLVANIA	EMERGENCY DEPT. TRIAGE RECORD
		DEPARTMENT OF NURSING

Date: _____ Time: _____

Name: _____ Age: _____

Allergy _____ Last Tetanus Year _____

Presenting Complaint: _____

_____

_____

_____

Health History   1. _____

2. _____

3. _____

LNMP _____ GCS _____ G _____ P _____ SAB _____ TAB _____

MEDICATIONS DOSE	LAST TAKEN

TIME	TEMP.	P	R	B/P	ASSESSMENT
	P.O.			/	
	R.			/	
				/	
				/	
				/	
				/	
				/	
				/	
				/	
				/	
				/	
				/	
				/	
				/	
				/	

INDICATE LOCATIONS OF INJURIES

Initial Triage Class: _____

Re-triage Class: _____

Time _____

Re-triage Class: _____

Time _____

SPECIAL PROCEDURES		LAB WORK	
☐ Soaks	☐ Ace Applied	☐ Urine	Hct _____
☐ Scrub	☐ Splint	☐ Lab Stix	Hgb _____
☐ Elevations	☐ Sling	Bld _____ Ket _____ Sug _____	
☐ Irrigations	☐ Dressing Applied	rot _____ PH _____	
☐ Ice Applied	☐ Cervical Collar	☐ Capillary Glucose	
		☐ Weight	
Other _____			

Triage Nurse _____

Triage Nurse _____

Source: Reprinted with permission of Hospital of the University of Pennsylvania.

often leaves insufficient room for physician documentation and little to no space for nursing documentation. To meet the nursing documentation needs, separate nursing forms should be developed.

A triage form is necessary in EDs that have or are considering implementing nursing triage. The form must have space for documentation of data collected upon arrival. Exhibit 10–1 is an example of a triage form used in the ED of the Hospital of the University of Pennsylvania. Specific triage documentation is discussed in Chapter 11.

In addition to the triage form, another form is necessary for nursing documentation, or the nursing documentation in the treatment area can be written below the triage note on the same form. A check-off format should be used as much as possible, because it is time saving and also reminds the ED nurse of specific items that must be documented. Spaces should be provided for noting the times that procedures and observations were made and for the nurse's signature. Both of these items are often forgotten when ED nurses are documenting in a hurry. Exhibit 10–2 is the ED nursing documentation form that is used in the ED at Albert Einstein Medical Center, Northern Division, which was developed by the ED nursing staff for everyone but the nonurgent patient.

After many years of using a single-page ED treatment record at the Albert Einstein Medical Center, Northern Division, the ED changed to a two-page form that allows space for triage documentation, a nurse's note, physician documentation, and lab results. The ED registration is computerized, with the triage information as the first data entered into the computer to be printed on the ED record. The ED nursing staff wanted room on the form to document initial patient assessments and to do the necessary documentation of the nonurgent patients who receive minimal treatment or referral. The space that is provided is frequently sufficient for documentation of nonurgent patients, and therefore, the use of an additional nursing form is not always required. However, for those patients who require more extensive nursing care and documentation, the ED Nursing Continuation Record is used. The nurse's note continues from the ED treatment record to this form. We have found that it is more likely that physicians will read the nursing documentation when it is on the same form on which the physician documents. Using one form also prevents duplication of documentation. If the nurse documents the presenting problem and history, the physician does not duplicate what is already written. Other important information, such as allergies, medications, and initial vital signs, is readily available to the physicians and other nurses on one form. Exhibits 10–3 and 10–4 show the two-page ED treatment record.

Exhibits 10–5 and 10–6 are patient item charge forms that are inclusive and easy to complete. All patient items that are chargeable are listed. When items are used, the quantity used is documented on the line next to the appropriate item. This type of form should be reviewed and updated at least once a year.

To facilitate continuity of nursing documentation for critical care patients, it is helpful that the ED nurse begins documentation on the hospital critical care flow sheet, if such a form is used in the critical care units. Using this form is especially important when critical care patients are detained or held in the ED for more than 1–2 hours.

Exhibit 10–2 Sample Nursing Continuation Record

ALBERT EINSTEIN MEDICAL CENTER

EMERGENCY DEPARTMENT
NURSING
CONTINUATION
RECORD

PATIENT'S NAME: _____
NO: _____
Date: _____

NORTHERN DIVISION

MEDICATIONS	DOSE	DIRECTIONS	TIME	INITIALS	Time

INTRAVENOUS SOLUTIONS

IV CAP: _____

Cath Size	Site:		Rate
Volume	SOLUTION		

VENTILATION DATA

O_2 THERAPY VIA _____ AT _____ L/min

TREATMENTS

Time						

INTAKE–OUTPUT

Time	IV SOL	PO	URINE	Tubes	Vomitus
Intake Total			Output Total		

COMA SCALE CODE

Response	1	2	3	4	5	6
EYES OPEN	Never	To Pain	To Sound	Spontaneously		
VERBAL	None	Incomprehensible sounds	Inappropriate Words	Confused Conversation	Oriented	
MOTOR	None	Extension	Flexion Abnormal	Flexion Withdrawal	Localizes Pain	Obeys Commands

NEURO CODE

COLOR CODES
N - Normal
P - Pale
D - Dusky
F - Flushed
J - Jaundice
M - Mottled
C - Cyanotic

Extremities movement
-1 -2 -3 -4

Pupil Reaction
+ - Reactive
- - Nonreactive
D D-ated
C Constricted
Greater than
Less than
Equal
s - Sluggish

Pupils mm
1 2 3 4 5 6 7 8

INITIAL ASSESSMENT

Time	

COLOR: ___ normal ___ other _____

SKIN: ___ normal ___ other _____

PULSES: ___ normal ___ other _____

NEURO: ___ alert & oriented ___ other _____

VITAL SIGNS

Neurological Checklist

Time	TEMP	PULSE	RESP	B P	Color	Right Arm	Left Arm	Right Leg	Left Leg	R. Pupil	L. Pupil	Pupil Reaction	Eyes Open	Best Verbal Response	Best Motor Response	Total

Coma Scale

HEART SOUNDS: ___ normal ___ other _____

LUNGS: ___clear bilaterally___ other _____

ABDOMEN: ___ bowel sounds present; soft, nontender _____
other _____

EXTREMITIES: ___ normal ___other _____

PROCEDURES AND OBSERVATIONS

Time	

R.N. Signature: _____

Source: Reprinted with permission of Albert Einstein Medical Center, Northern Division, Philadelphia.

Exhibit 10–3 Sample Emergency Treatment Record

Northern Division
York and Tabor Roads
Philadelphia, Pa. 19141

EMERGENCY TREATMENT RECORD

BILL NO.

ACCESSION NO.
UNIT NO.

PATIENT NAME

ADDRESS

REG'N DATE	TIME	ARRIVAL CODE	F.C.	ACCIDENT DATE/TIME	VAL. REC. #	TELE. NO. HOME	REG'N CLERK

RACE	MAR.ST.	RELIGION	SEX	AGE	BIRTH DATE	SOCIAL SEC. NO.	OTHER IDENTIFICATION NO.

NEAREST RELATIVE NAME AND ADDRESS

TELE. NO.

RELATIONSHIP

PAT. OCCUPATION

EMPLOYER NAME AND ADDRESS

PHONE

WORK RELATED ILLNESS/INJURY
YES   NO

PAT. BROUGHT TO HOSPITAL BY

NOTIFICATIONS ☐ FAMILY ___
HEALTH DEPT. ☐   POLICE ☐   FIRE DEPT. ☐   MEDICAL EXAMINER # ___

☐ ACCEPTED ☐ REJECTED

PAT. FAMILY PHYSICIAN

ADDRESS

PHONE

STATUS
☐ E ☐ U ☐ N

TIME	TEMP	PULSE	RES	BP

TRIAGE NOTE:

TRIAGE NURSE

ASSIGNED
TO   LOCATION   LAST T.T.   LMP

CURRENT MEDICATIONS

ALLERGIES

NEURO WATCH STARTED? ☐ YES

ADDITIONAL NURSING NOTES:
TIME:

CONTINUATION STARTED? ☐ YES

CLASSIFICATION CATEGORY TRAUMA? ☐ YES

☐ 1 ☐ 2 ☐ 3 ☐ 4 MOST ACUTE

TIME	TEMP	PULSE	RES	BP

PRIMARY NURSE:

✓	ORDERS	DONE	✓		DONE	✓		DONE	✓		DONE	
	CBC & DIFF			ABG			BLOOD CULTURE			TILT-TEST		ACCU CHECK		TIME BLOOD SENT	INIT.
	PT, PTT			SERUM B HCG			U.A.			VISUAL ACUITY		TYPE AND SCREEN			
	PLATELETS			CARDIAC ENZYMES			URINE C & S			EKG		TYPE AND CROSS		TIME URINE SENT	INIT.
	IL 8			LIVER PROFILE			URINE PREGNANCY			MONITOR		_____ UNITS			
	AMYLASE			HEPATITIS SCREEN			STREP SCREEN			INT				ORDERING PHYSICIANS	
	LIPASE			VDRL			GC CULTURE			O₂ AT _____ L/mm					

X-RAY STUDIES

COMPLETE ABDOMEN	C SPINE COMPLETE	L R HIP	B-NUMBER
CHEST PA/LAT			
CHEST PORTABLE	FLAT PLATE ABDOMEN	C SPINE PORTABLE	PELVIS
L R WRIST	L R HAND	L R ANKLE	L R FOOT	X-RAY NOTIFIED TIME
SKULL	CT SCAN	B SCAN	

OTHER ORDERS:

Exhibit 10–3 continued

AUTHORIZATION FOR EMERGENCY SERVICE

I consent to undergo such examination, diagnostic procedures and curative emergency treatment prescribed by the physicians of the Albert Einstein Medical Center, or their delegated assistants, for the condition described on this sheet as Provisional Diagnosis for which I voluntarily came to the Albert Einstein Medical Center for medical care; such consent to include the administration of blood and medication as may be deemed necessary by the responsible physician, with the exception of:

_____

(State: Non-Spinal Anesthesia, Allergic Drug or other Medication)

I certify that I understand the risks involved in the diagnostic procedures and treatment I am to receive, and I waive any claim that my consent is not an informed consent. I also acknowledge that no guarantee or assurance has been made as to the results that may be obtained.

Date _____ Patient _____ Witnessed _____

If the patient is unable to sign or is not legally competent to sign, note reason, therefore, and relationship of person signing for the patient.

Date _____ Reason (Minor, Legally Incompetent, Physical Condition) _____

Authorized Person _____ Relationship _____ Witness _____

NOTE: If telephone consent has been obtained to treat a minor specify:

Telephone Time–Date _____ Authorization Provided By _____ Relationship _____

Authorization Received by _____ Witness _____

ASSIGNMENT OF BENEFITS

I authorize any holder of medical or other information about me to release to the Social Security Administration and Health Care Financing Administration or its intermediaries or carriers, or to the billing agent of this physician or supplier any information needed for this or a related Medicare Claim. I permit a copy of this authorization to be used in place of the original, and request payment of medical insurance benefits either to myself or to the party who accepts assignment.

Signature _____ Date _____ H.I.C. No. _____

REFUSAL OF TREATMENT

I hereby refused the prescribed treatment. I acknowledge that the risks resulting from my refusal have been fully explained to me, that my questions have been answered and that I understand that in all probability my refusal will seriously imperil my/his/her life or health. I hereby release the Albert Einstein Medical Center, its nurses, employees, personnel, other representatives, together with all physicians in any way connected with this medical care, from any and all liability for any injuries or damages resulting from this refusal of treatment.

_____
Signature of Patient or
Representative

_____
Date and Time

_____
Witness

PATIENT LEAVING HOSPITAL AGAINST ADVICE

_____ is leaving from Albert Einstein Medical Center
Name of Patient

contrary to the advice of the physicians in charge of my/his/her care, or their assistants or designees. I acknowledge that the risks resulting from my action have been fully explained to me, that my questions have been answered and that I understand that in all probability my action will seriously imperil my/his/her life or health. I hereby release the Albert Einstein Medical Center, its nurses, employees, personnel, other representatives and all physicians in any way connected with this medical treatment from any and all liability for any damages or injuries which may result from this discharge against advice.

_____
Signature of Patient or
Representative

_____
Date and Time

_____
Witness

Source: Reprinted with permission of Albert Einstein Medical Center, Northern Division, Philadelphia.

Exhibit 10–4 Sample Emergency Treatment Record

EMERGENCY TREATMENT RECORD

PHYSICIAN'S NOTES:

LABORATORY RESULTS					URINE PREG. TEST □ POS □ NEG	X-RAY RESULTS
Hgb	HCT	PMN	BANDS	MONO	UA	
WBC	PLTS	LYMPH	EOS	ATYP		
PT	PTT	AMYLASE			ABG	
PT CONT	PTT CONT	LIPASE			PO2	PCO2	EKG RESULTS
					PH	HCO3	
NA	CI	BUN		GLUCOSE	% SAT	FIO2
K	CO2	CREAT		CALCIUM		

TREATMENT RENDERED/RESULT:

CONSULTATION

SERVICE _____ SPOKE WITH _____ TIME _____ INITIAL _____

CONDITION AT TIME OF
DISCHARGE OR TRANSFER:

☐ GOOD ☐ FAIR ☐ POOR ☐ CRITICAL ☐ TIME EXPIRED _____ ☐ TIME DISCHARGED _____

☐ TREATED & RELEASED ☐ REF. TO AGENCY ☐ REF. TO PRIV. PHYS. ☐ REF. TO OPD ☐ REF. TO OTHER HOSPITAL ☐ AMA TREATED
☐ AMA NOT TREAT. ☐ W/O TREATED ☐ W/O NOT TREATED ☐ DOA ☐ EXPIRED ☐ ADMIT SERVICE OF _____

DIAGNOSTIC IMPRESSION

RESIDENT
SIGNATURE _____

PRINT:

PRIVATE ATTENDING
SIGNATURE _____

PRINT:

EMERGENCY ATTENDING
SIGNATURE _____

PRINT:

REGISTRATION DATE

BILL NO.

ACCESSION NO.
UNIT NO.

PATIENT NAME

ADDRESS

Source: Reprinted with permission of Albert Einstein Medical Center, Northern Division, Philadelphia.

Exhibit 10–5 Sample Supplies Order Form

PATIENT SUPPLIES

PATIENT SUPPLIES: Please enter the quantity for each item provided to the patient.

CODE	QTY	CHARGE ITEM
		ORTHOPEDIC SUPPLIES
01509-9		ACE BANDAGE 2"
01510-7		ACE BANDAGE 3"
01512-3		ACE BANDAGE 4"
01582-6		ACE BANDAGE 6"
01433-2		ARM SLING
01682-4		CRUTCHES
00693-2		CAST SANDLE
01160-1		CERVICAL COLLAR
05304-1		PHILADELPHIA COLLAR
01981-0		CLAVICLE STRAP
		CAST
01410-0		LONG ARM/LONG LEG
01409-2		SHORT ARM/SHORT LEG
		IMMOBILIZER
01400-1		KNEE
01980-2		SHOULDER
01196-5		ACROMIOCLAVICULAR
		SPLINTS
01517-2		FINGER (ALUMINUM)
01401-9		FROG

CODE	QTY	CHARGE ITEM
01450-6		ENT TRAY
01194-0		HEMORRHAGE TRAY
01255-9		IRRIGATION TRAY
01601-4		INCISION & DRAINAGE
03811-7		SHAVE & PREP KIT
01458-9		SIGMOIDOSCOPY TRAY
01140-3		SPINAL TAP
01145-2		SUTURE TRAY
01170-0		SUTURE REMOVAL TRAY
01459-7		THORACENTESIS TRAY
01460-5		THOROCOTOMY
01461-3		TRACH TRAY
01434-0		VAGINAL EXAM TRAY
01462-1		VENOSECTION (CUTDOWN)
01589-1		FOLEY CATH KIT
01809-3		ENEMA
		TUBES AND CATHETERS, DRAINAGE UNITS
01513-1		FOLEY CATH
01583-4		FOLEY CATH 3 WAY
01907-5		SALEM SUMP TUBE
01543-8		LEVIN TUBE
01593-3		SUCTION CATH
01381-1		TROCAR CATHETER (PERITONEAL)
01553-7		CHEST TUBES
01542-0		CANTOR TUBE
01540-4		FOLEY BAG
01992-7		URIMETER DRAIN SET
01449-8		CONTINUOUS BLADDER IRRIGATION SET
01584-2		CONTINUOUS BLADDER IRRIGATION DRAINAGE BAG

CODE	QTY	CHARGE ITEM
		IV SUPPLIES
03831-5		BUTTERFLY INFUSION SET
03832-3		ANGIOCATH
05305-8		DERMICEL TAPE
01899-4		MICROPORE TAPE
00911-8		STANDARD TUBING
00919-1		MICRODRIP
02089-1		BURETROL
00540-5		DIAL-A-FLOW
04546-8		PUMP TUBING
05830-5		50 cc D5W
05831-3		100 cc D5W
00831-8		250 cc D5W
00835-9		500 cc D5W
00827-6		1000 cc D5W
00935-7		1000 cc D5/.45 NSS
03527-9		500 cc D5/.2 NSS
00851-6		1000 cc 10% DW
00814-4		500 cc NSS
00867-2		1000 cc NSS
00883-9		1000 cc RINGERS LACTATE
00890-4		1000 cc D5R.L.
00823-5		IRRIG. NSS
03826-5		IRRIG. WATER
03392-8		BLOOD ADM. KIT
04795-1		BLOOD WARMING COIL
		HEMODYNAMIC MONITORING EQUIPMENT
03928-9		A LINE KIT #1

01398-7 ___ WRIST/FOREARM UNIVERSAL
03890-1 ___ PLASTER - LONG ARM/LONG LEG
01409-2 ___ PLASTER - SHORT ARM/SHORT LEG
05303-3 ___ ALUMINUM - LONG LEG
05302-5 ___ ALUMINUM - SHORT LEG
01385-4 ___ ARM BOARD

___| OTHER
___| OTHER
___| OTHER

SURGICAL TRAYS AND KITS

01142-9 ___ ABDOMINAL TAP TRAY
01909-1 ___ ABG KIT
01390-4 ___ BURNPAC
01542-0 ___ CANTOR TUBE TRAY
01447-2 ___ CARDIAC ARREST TRAY
01144-5 ___ COMBO TRAY
01195-7 ___ CULDOCENTESIS TRAY
01238-5 ___ DELIVERY TRAY (BABY TRAY)
05306-6 ___ SUTURE SET (DISPOSABLE)

___| WOUND CLOSURE TRAY (DISPOSABLE)

AFFIX PATIENT LABEL HERE

03301-9 ___ PENROSE DRAIN
01549-5 ___ LEG BAG
01547-9 ___ BLAKEMORE TUBE
01237-7 ___ LUKENS TUBE
05364-5 ___ COOK CATHETER
00457-2 ___ GASTRIC LAVAGE

___| OTHER
___| OTHER
___| OTHER

OTHER SURGICAL SUPPLIES

01503-2 ___ ADAPTIC
___ DRESSINET
01143-7 ___ NASAL GAUZE
01507-3 ___ IODOFORM PACKING
01423-3 ___ PLAIN PACKING
02772-2 ___ EYE CAUTERY
03804-2 ___ KLING SMALL
03810-9 ___ KLING LARGE
05030-2 ___ NASOSTATS
01602-2 ___ SUTURES (EACH)
01943-0 ___ PLEUREVAC

___| NOZ STOP

04548-4 ___ TRANS DUCER DOMES
05820-6 ___ CATHETER FLOW, DIR THERMODILUTION CATHETER
05819-8 ___ PACING TD CATHETER
05824-8 ___ BIPOLAR TRANSVENOUS PACING ELECTRODE
05823-0 ___ GUIDE WIRE "J"
05825-5 ___ SEMI FLOATING BIPOLAR PACEMAKER
05816-4 ___ PERCUTANEOUS INTRO SET
05821-4 ___ ARROW RADIAL ARTERY CATH SET
01580-0 ___ INTRACATH
03813-3 ___ CVP MONOMETER
01723-6 ___ TRANS MYOCARDIAL PACING KIT

RESPIRATORY

01703-8 ___ ARTERIAL BLOOD GAS
01388-8 ___ ORAL AIRWAY

OTHER

01737-6 ___ CODE BLUE
01749-1 ___ EKG
01748-3 ___ MONITORING
01738-4 ___ OBSERVATION (IN HOURS)
00529-8 ___ B-Hcg

___| BONE MARROW NEEDLE

Source: Reprinted with permission of Albert Einstein Medical Center, Northern Division, Philadelphia.

Exhibit 10–6　Sample Drugs Order Form

PATIENT DRUGS

PATIENT DRUGS: Please enter the quantity for each item provided to the patient.

CODE	QTY.	CHARGE ITEM	CODE	QTY.	CHARGE ITEM	CODE	QTY.	CHARGE ITEM
		MEDICATIONS						
		IV/IM	71209	__	TETANUS TOXOID	62612	__	DIGOXIN .125mg
60996	__	ADRENALIN 1:1000 1ml	69146	__	TETANUS IMMUNE GLOBULIN 250U	62653	__	DILANTIN 100mg
62976	__	ADRENALIN (INTRACARDIAC) 1:10,000 10ml	60004	__	VITAMIN K 25mg/2ml	69658	__	FLEXERIL 10mg
61101	__	ALDOMET 250mg/5ml	69401	__	VISTARIL 100mg/2ml	63438	__	HALDOL 5mg
61234	__	AMINOPHYLLINE 500mg/20ml	60848	__	VERAPAMIL 5mg/2ml	63669	__	INDERAL 10mg
61390	__	APRESOLINE 20mg/ml		__	OTHER	63768	__	ISORDIL 2.5mg
71639	__	ATROPINE 1mg/ml		__	OTHER	64006	__	LASIX 40mg
61614	__	BENADRYL 50mg/ml			**ANTIBIOTICS IM/IV**	64063	__	LIBRIUM 5mg
66530	__	BRETHINE 1mg/ml	61341	__	AMPICILLIN 500mg	69948	__	MOTRIN 600mg
61705	__	BRETYLLIUM 500mg/10ml	67793	__	ANCEF 500mg	60574	__	NIFEDEPINE 10mg
67538	__	BEROCCA-C 2cc	61796	__	MEFOXIN 1g	65110	__	PARAFON FORTE
61861	__	COGENTIN 2mg/2ml	65169	__	PENICILLIN 1mU	65813	__	QUINIDINE 200mg
72355	__	CALCIUM CHLORIDE 10cc	74146	__	SPECTINOMYCIN	69633	__	TAGAMET 300mg
61754	__	CALCIUM GLUCONATE 10cc	65532	__	WYCILLIN 2.4mU	66811	__	THORAZINE 50mg
62265	__	DECADRON 4mg/ml	61697	__	BICILLIN 2.4mU	60947	__	TYLENOL
62620	__	DIGOXIN 0.5mg/2ml		__	OTHER		__	OTHER
62638	__	DILANTIN 100mg/2ml		__	OTHER		__	OTHER
62703	__	DOBUTREX 250mg			**NARCOTICS IM/IV**			**P.O. LIQUID**
70490	__	DOPAMINE 400mg/10ml	46102	__	DEMEROL 50mg	61580	__	BENADRYL ELIXIR 25mg/5ml
62372	__	DEPOMEDROL 40mg/ml	46144	__	MORPHINE SULF.	71704	__	CHARCOAL POWDER 120cc
63321	__	GLUCAGON 10mg INJ.	46037	__	HYDROMORPHINONE 2mg	68163	__	DONNATOL ELIXIR
63388	__	HALDOL 5mg/ml	46011	__	CODEINE 30mg	68304	__	HALDOL CONC. 2mg
63487	__	HEPARIN 5,000U	46086	__	METHADONE 10mg	74062	__	IPECAC 30cc
63461	__	HEPARIN 100U/ml	46177	__	SECONAL 100mg	63867	__	KAPOECTATE
63354	__	HYDROCORTISONE 100mg	46219	__	VALIUM 10mg/2ml	64202	__	MAALOX 30ml
62539	__	HYPERSTAT 300mg/20ml		__	OTHER	64667	__	MYLANTA 30ml
63651	__	INDERAL 1mg/ml		__	OTHER	69930	__	MOM CONC.
63792	__	ISUPREL 1mg/5ml			**P.O. MEDICATIONS**	64501	__	MINERAL OIL
63164	__	LASIX 40mg/4ml			**ANTIBIOTICS - SULFA**	68825	__	PHENERGAN EXPT. 5ml
63974	__	LASIX 100mg/10ml	70243	__	AMPICILLIN 500mg	68924	__	POTASSIUM CHLORIDE 15cc
68528	__	LEVOPHED 4mg				68858	__	PHENOBARBITAL 50cc
64030	__	LIBRIUM 100mg				69104	__	TERPIN HYDRATE WITH CODEINE
						69161	__	THEOPHYLLINE ELIXIR 30cc

64097	LIDOCAINE 50mg/5ml
51664	LIDOCAINE 2g/500cc
68619	METHERGINE 0.2mg/ml
64295	MANNITOL
68635	MUCOMYST
70888	NARCAN 0.4mg/ml
64907	NIPRIDE 50mg INJ.
60475	NITROGLYCERIN 50mg/ml
70920	NORFLEX 60mg/2ml
70078	NUBAINE 10mg/ml
65102	PAPAVERINE 60mg/2ml
65300	PHENERGAN 25mg/ml
65318	PHENOBARBITAL 130mg/ml
65086	PITOCIN 10U/ml
68890	PITRESSIN 20U/ml
68957	PROGESTERONE 50mg/2ml
65649	PRONESTYL 100mg/10ml
65631	PRONESTYL 500mg/2ml
65714	PROTAMINE SUF. 50mg
65425	POTASSIUM CHLORIDE 20mg/10ml
61077	PLASMANATE 250cc
65805	QUINIDINE 80mg/10ml
66142	SODIUM BICARB
66167	SOLU MEDROL 40mg/ml
66183	SOLU MEDROL 125mg/2ml
66175	SOLU MEDROL 1g
60715	SUSPHRINE 0.5cc
66415	TAGAMET 300mg/2ml
72249	TENSILON 100mg/10ml
66928	TIGAN 200mg/2ml
69203	THIAMINE 100mg
66761	THORAZINE 50mg

63024	ERYTHROMYCIN 250mg
63198	GANTRISIN 500mg
65748	PYRIDIUM 100mg
66621	TETRACYCLINE 250mg
___	OTHER
___	OTHER

NARCOTICS

73189	COCAINE 4ml
46292	CODEINE 30mg
62364	DEMEROL 50mg
46441	PERCOCET
46458	PERCODAN
46490	SECONAL 100mg
46235	TYLENOL #3
46565	VALIUM 5mg
___	OTHER
___	OTHER

60988	ACTIFED
61119	ALDOMET 250mg
67447	ASA 650mg
71621	ASA 75mg
61606	BENADRYL 25mg
61630	BENEMID 500mg
66548	BRETHINE 2.5mg
67769	CATAPRESS 0.1mg
67876	CHLORASEPTIC LOZENGE
61879	COGENTIN 1mg
61960	COMPAZINE 5mg
62240	DARVON 65mg
62828	DYAZIDE 50mg

69278	TYLENOL
67298	XYLOCAINE VISCOUS 20ml
___	OTHER
___	OTHER

TOPICAL

70912	NTG OINTMENT 2%
66050	SILVADENE CREAM 400g
60665	SILVADENE CREAM 20g

SUPPOSITORIES

67421	ASA 600mg
61945	COMPAZINE 5mg
66902	TIGAN 200mg
71530	TYLENOL
62810	DULCOLAX

PEDIATRIC P.O. MEDS

73668	AMOXICILLIN 250mg/5ml
61473	ATARAX SYRUP 10MG
71647	BACTRIM SUSP. 5cc
65136	PARAGORIC 5cc
68767	PEN-V-K (SUSPENSION) 250mg
66858	PHENOBARB ELIXIR 20mg
71183	SLOPHYLLINE 15ml
66647	THEODUR 100mg
73817	SLOBID GYROCAPS 100mg
___	OTHER
___	OTHER

AFFIX PATIENT LABEL HERE

Source: Reprinted with permission of Albert Einstein Medical Center, Northern Division, Philadelphia.

Discharge Instructions

All patients discharged from the ED must have written discharge instructions. Although it is simpler to use one comprehensive check-off form for all patients, this type of form is not always appropriate. There is usually so much information that must be included on a single form of this type that the print size has to be reduced to fit all the necessary instructions. Elderly patients and patients with poor vision have difficulty reading the small print. Particular patients may require more information than what is on the discharge form. Using separate specific instruction forms allows for larger print size, more patient teaching, and instructions specific to patient illnesses and injuries. It is impossible to have separate discharge forms for every type of patient problem; however specific forms can be developed for the problems most often seen, such as hypertension, gastroenteritis, hypoglycemia, asthma, allergic reaction, fever, upper respiratory infection, urinary tract infection, seizure, pelvic inflammatory disease, wound care, head injury, cast care, sprains and strains, and back pain. A general form can be used for problems for which there is no specific instruction form and should have space provided for writing in specific instructions. Exhibits 10–7 to 10–9 are examples of ED discharge instructions.

Space on the instruction form or ED treatment record must be provided for the patient to sign that instructions were explained and received in writing. The ED treatment record must also document which instruction form(s) was given to the patient. This can be accomplished by numbering the forms and documenting the form number or by attaching a copy of the actual form(s) given to the patient to the ED treatment record.

Trauma Record

A standard ED nursing or critical care form does not always meet the special documentation needs of the multiple trauma patient. Therefore, a separate form specific to trauma care is needed. It should be comprehensive, yet easy to complete, because accuracy and completeness of documentation are needed quickly. Exhibits 10–10 and 10–11 are two different formats of trauma records.

Other ED Forms

A patient register, which must be maintained continuously, should include: all patients who arrive at the ED for treatment, date and time of arrival, means of arrival, sex, presenting problem, triage prioritization, discharge diagnosis, disposition, time of departure from the ED, and billing number.

Exhibit 10–7 Sample Discharge Form

ALBERT EINSTEIN MEDICAL CENTER – NORTHERN DIVISION
EMERGENCY DEPARTMENT DISCHARGE FORM

The examination and treatment which you have received has been on an emergency basis only, and not intended to be a substitute or replacement for complete care from your personal physician. If you do not have a private physician, we will refer you to a physician for appropriate follow-up care.

DISCHARGE INSTRUCTION SHEETS GIVEN:

—— Surgical   —— Pelvic Inflammatory Disease
—— Medical   —— Threatened Miscarriage   **Pediatric Discharge Instruction Sheet:**
—— Chest Pain   —— Venereal Disease
—— Diabetes   —— Work Related Injuries   —— Fever
—— Seizures   —— Specific   —— Colds
—— Asthma   —— Vomiting/Diarrhea
—— Nosebleeds   ——————————   ——————————

TREATMENT RECEIVED

—— Examination by M.D.   —— Other Culture
—— X-Rays   —— Sutures   —— Tetanus-Toxoid Booster
—— Lab Work   —— DPT   —— Tetanus & Diptheria Booster
—— Throat Culture   —— EKG   —— Tetanus Immune Globulin (250 units)

MEDICATIONS PRESCRIBED

Other Instructions ——————————————————————————

Precautions ——————————————————————————————

—— You have received or been prescribed a medication that may cause drowsiness – do not drive or operate machinery that requires you to be alert.
—— You have received or been prescribed a medication that may interact with alcohol – **no alcohol permitted.**
—— Your culture results are not available through the Emergency Department. You may obtain these results by making an appointment in clinic, or your private doctor may call the laboratory. The laboratory will not give you these results.
—— Call your family doctor for follow-up care.
—— Call as soon as possible to make an appointment for follow-up care.

PLEASE CALL THE SERVICE CHECKED BELOW TO SCHEDULE AN APPOINTMENT – MONDAY THROUGH FRIDAY – BETWEEN 9 A.M. AND 4 P.M.

—— Northern Medical Association 456-6500
—— Ear, Nose, Throat 456-7140
—— Eye 456-7140
—— Orthopedics —— Hand —— Urology —— Surgery 324-3755
—— Pediatrics 456-7160
—— OB/GYN Associates 456-7170
—— Neurology 456-7180
—— Rheumatology 456-7190
—— Dental 456-7380
—— G. I. Clinic 456-7130
—— Allergy 456-7163
—— Renal 456-7386
—— Pulmonary 456-6933
 456-6950

NOTE: Patients under 18 years of age must be accompanied by a parent or responsible adult to be treated.

—— If an EKG and/or X-Rays were taken, a review will be made. All EKG and X-Ray impressions made in the Emergency Center are subject to review by a Radiologist and/or Cardiologist. If the review indicates additional information, you or your physician will be contacted.
—— Fill prescriptions and take according to directions.

I understand that the treatment I have received was rendered on an emergency basis only and therefore, I may have been released before all of my medical problems were apparent, diagnosed, and/or treated. I have read and understand the above, received a copy of the form and applicable instruction sheets, and will arrange for follow-up care as indicated above.

Date ———————   Instructed by ——————————————————————

Patient Signature ——————————————————————

Source: Reprinted with permission of Albert Einstein Medical Center, Northern Division, Philadelphia.

Exhibit 10–8 Emergency Department Discharge Instructions

ALBERT EINSTEIN MEDICAL CENTER
NORTHERN DIVISION
EMERGENCY DEPARTMENT

Discharge Instruction Sheet #9

PELVIC INFLAMMATORY DISEASE

An infection in the reproductive organs—tubes, womb (uterus), internal lining of the pelvis, or the pelvic blood vessels.

General Information
Major causes:
  venereal disease
  infected abortions
  infections from IUD (coil, etc.)
  disease-producing organisms, such as Staphylococcus and Streptococcus
Symptoms:
  discharge with foul odor from the vagina
  lower abdominal pain or back pain
  nausea and vomiting
  fever

POINTS TO REMEMBER

1. Avoid use of tampons. Handle sanitary napkins with extreme care; deposit in a bag for disposal. Wash hands before and after handling the napkin.
2. No sexual contact for 2 weeks after medication is begun.
3. Wash underwear and bedclothes separately from those of other family members.
4. If venereal disease is suspected, encourage all sexual partners to receive treatment.
5. Avoid reinfection.
6. Follow-up care is important; return to our gynecology clinic or a public health center within 2 weeks.
7. Take medication as prescribed.

RETURN TO THE EMERGENCY DEPARTMENT IF THE FOLLOWING SYMPTOMS OCCUR:

1. Rash or hives
2. Difficulty breathing
3. Increase in symptoms

Source: Reprinted with permission of Albert Einstein Medical Center, Northern Division, Philadelphia.

Exhibit 10–9 Emergency Department Discharge Instructions

ALBERT EINSTEIN MEDICAL CENTER
NORTHERN DIVISION
EMERGENCY DEPARTMENT 456-6666

Discharge Instruction Sheet #11

SPRAIN CARE
1. Apply cold compresses or ice bag to sprained area for 24 hours.
2. After 24 hours, apply warm compresses or warm soaks.
3. Keep the affected area raised to reduce swelling.
4. Keep weight off the affected extremity.
5. An ace bandage may be used for support; reapply 2–3 times a day.
6. Take aspirin or other prescribed medication for discomfort.
7. Follow-up care is important by your private physician or in an orthopedic clinic.

NOTIFY YOUR PHYSICIAN OR RETURN TO THE EMERGENCY DEPARTMENT
    IF ANY OF THE FOLLOWING OCCUR:
1. Swelling increases or skin becomes bluish.
2. Extremities become cool or numb.

Note: A sprain may take 6 weeks to heal. The above instructions will aid in this process.

* These instructions are given to you to help explain what is necessary for your condition to improve. Please remember, however, that our main function is to serve you and others in time of emergency, so please consult your family physician whenever possible.

Source: Reprinted with permission of Albert Einstein Medical Center, Northern Division, Philadelphia.

A form is needed to list patients who are admitted to the hospital. Information that can be documented on this form can include patient name, date and time of arrival in the ED, admitting service, admission diagnosis, time that the admissions department was notified, time and location of bed assignment, time of bed availability, time of call to transport services, and time of departure from the ED.

This form aids in organization and awareness of ED patient flow and can be referred to later when trying to locate an ED patient who was admitted to the hospital. It can also be used to extract information for statistical purposes, such as the number of patients admitted through the ED on a daily basis, length of stay in the ED of admitted patients, numbers of patients admitted through the ED to particular units, and delays in obtaining bed assignments and transport.

Exhibit 10–10 Sample Nursing Assessment Form

ADMITTING AREA

NURSING ASSESSMENT

UNIVERSITY OF MARYLAND MEDICAL SYSTEM

MARYLAND INSTITUTE FOR EMERGENCY MEDICAL SERVICES SYSTEMS

DATE	MILITARY TIME	TEAM LEADER	

ARRIVAL MODE	AIR	LAND	SCENE	TRANSFER
TRANSFERRING FACILITY		PRIMARY ADMITTING NURSE'S SIGNATURE		

NEUROLOGICAL

R. PUPIL
1mm 2mm 3mm 4mm 5mm 6mm 7mm 8mm

L. PUPIL

LIGHT REACTION: RIGHT   YES   NO   LEFT   YES   NO

ORIENTED TO: PERSON   PLACE   TIME

UNRESPONSIVE CONFUSED INCOMPREHENSIBLE UNABLE TO TEST

MOTOR RESPONSE:

SENSORY RESPONSE:

ADM. WITH CERVICAL IMMOBILIZATION: YES   NO

CERVICAL TRACTION: YES   NO

TYPE-   WEIGHT-

CAROTID ARTERIOGRAM: YES   NO

ICP-

C/T SCAN: YES   NO

OTHER

RESPIRATORY

ADMISSION STATUS:

SPONTANEOUS AMBU BAG DEMAND VALVE EOA ETT TRACH MASK

INTUBATED ON HELI PAD   YES   NO   METHOD:

BREATH SOUNDS: PRESENT-   RIGHT   LEFT

CLEAR-   RIGHT   LEFT

DIMINISHED-   RIGHT   LEFT

ADVENTITIOUS SOUNDS:

CHEST TUBE(S) LOCATION

CLOSED DRAINAGE   AUTOTRANSFUSION

OTHER:

PROPERTY DISPOSITION

VALUABLES ENVELOPE NO.   NONE SAFE FAMILY

CLOTHING: CLOTHING ROOM   NONE   FAMILY   DISCARDED

POLICE DEPT.

CARDIOVASCULAR

INVASIVE LINES (IV, ARTERIAL, PULM ART)

TYPE/GAUGE	LOCATION

PULSES: INTACT   ABSENT

QUALITY: GOOD   THREADY   WEAK   BOUNDING

EKG RHYTHM   EBL

12 LEAD EKG: YES   NO

MASTROUSERS: FIELD   ADMITTING AREA

INFLATED: YES   NO   LEGS ONLY

ARREST: YES   NO | CPR IN PROGRESS   YES   NO

SKIN COLOR:

OTHER

GASTROINTESTINAL

NASOGASTRIC   OROGASTRIC

DRAINAGE: COLOR   AMOUNT

ABDOMEN:

FLAT   DISTENDED   OBESE   SOFT

FIRM   RIGID   TENDER   NON-TENDER

BOWEL SOUNDS: PRESENT   ABSENT

HYPOACTIVE   NORMOACTIVE   HYPERACTIVE

PERITONEAL LAVAGE: YES   NO

RBC	WBC	AMYLASE

AMOUNT INFUSED: AMOUNT DRAINED:

METABOLIC

CARBON MONOXIDE LEVEL: SCENE   ADMITTING AREA

MIEMSS LAB WORK	6/60 FLEX	TOX SCREEN	URINE	BLOOD
TYPE & CROSS-MATCH FOR •	UNITS	URINALYSIS	MIEMSS URINE	HAA
OTHER TESTS				

INFECTIOUS DISEASE

TEMP.-RECTAL   ORAL   AXILLARY   PROBE

CULTURES:

Exhibit 10–10 continued

PHARMACOLOGIC						GENITOURINARY					

ALLERGIES

CURRENT MEDS:

	DRUG	AMT	ROUTE	(MILITARY) TIME	INITIALS
1					
2					
3					
4					
5					
6					
7					
8					
9					
10					
11					
12					

INITIALS/SIGNATURE/TITLE

GENITOURINARY

FOLEY: YES   NO   PRIOR TO ADM.

OUTPUT:

DIURESIS   ADEQUATE

OLIGURIC   ANURIC

IVP: YES   NO   CYSTOGRAM: YES   NO

COLOR   CHARACTER:

DISCHARGE

X-RAYS

PAST MEDICAL HISTORY

DISPOSITION

OR	CCRU	41CU	4IMCU	NTC
OHP	LIVE-IN	UMH		MORGUE
OTHER FACILITY		HOME	MILITARY TIME	

FAMILY

FAMILY SPOKESPERSON: RELATION:

HOME PHONE: WORK PHONE:

ASSESSMENT:

RELIGION:

KEY

A - ABRASION	E - GSW'S	J - RASH
B - LACERATION	F - STAB WOUND	K - SCARS
C - CONTUSION	G - OPEN FRACTURE	L - CASTS
D - AMPUTATION	I - POOR CIRCULATION	

NURSES NOTES

Source: Reprinted with permission of Maryland Institute for Emergency Medical Services System, Baltimore.

Exhibit 10–11 Sample Trauma Record

ALBERT EINSTEIN MEDICAL CENTER

EMERGENCY DEPARTMENT
Trauma Record

PATIENT'S NAME: _____
E.D. NO.: _____
Date: _____

ADMISSION DATA	BODY INJURY CHART

ADMITTED VIA: Rescue _____ police _____ ambulance _____ self _____ Helicopter _____
stretcher _____ wheelchair _____ ambulatory _____ other _____

REPORT OR ARRIVAL FROM: _____

HISTORY OF TREATMENT PRIOR TO ARRIVAL: _____

TRUMA SCORE ON ADMISSION: _____
CODE CALLED: time _____

ASSESSMENT ON ARRIVAL

AIRWAY: open _____ obstructed _____ no respirations _____

CAROTID PULSE: present _____ faint _____ not palpable _____ absent _____

PERIPHERAL PULSE: present _____ faint _____ not palpable _____ absent _____

HEART SOUNDS: present _____ absent _____

LUNGS: breath sounds — clear L _____ R _____ absent L _____ R _____
other _____

ABDOMEN: distended — yes _____ no _____ bowel sounds — present _____ absent _____
rigid — yes _____ no _____ rebound tenderness — present _____ absent _____

EXTREMITIES: right arm — normal _____ other _____
right leg — normal _____ other _____
left arm — normal _____ other _____
left leg — normal _____ other _____

BURNS: total body % _____
PERTINENT MEDICAL HISTORY: _____

CURRENT MEDICATIONS: _____

ALLERGIES: _____

TRAUMA CODES
A – abraision
Amp. – amputation
B – burn
D – deformity
G – gunshot
L – laceration
OF – open fracture
P – puncture
S – stab
__ – _____

BURN %	adult	child
head	9	13
trunk		
front	13	18
back	16	13
ea. arm	9	9
ea. leg	13	14
genitalia	1	1

Exhibit 10–11 continued

COMA SCALE CODE

Response	1	2	3	4	5	6
EYES OPEN	Never	To Pain	To Sound	Spontaneously		
VERBAL	None	Incomprehensible Sounds	Inappropriate Words	Confused Conversation	Oriented	
MOTOR	None	Extension	Flexion-Abnormal	Flexion-Withdrawl	Localizes Pain	Obeys Commands

PATIENT'S NAME: _____

NO: _____

Date: _____

COLOR CODES
N = Normal
P = Pale
D = Dusky
F = Flushed
J = Jaundice
M = Mottled
C = Cyanotic

ACTIVITY CODES
1 = Spontaneously Active
2 = Active when stimulated
3 = Lethargic
4 = Limp, unresponsive
5 = Decerebrate
T = Twitchy, irritable
S = Seizures
R = Rigid
RR = Restless & Rammy

NEURO CODE
Extremities movement
+1, +2, +3, +4
Pupil Reaction
+ = Reactive
− = Nonreactive
D Dilated
C Constricted
< Less than
> Greater than
= Equal
± Sluggish
Responds to:
a. Name
b. Shaking
c. Light Pain
d. Deep Pain

VITAL SIGNS

Time	Heart Rate	Rhythm	Blood Pressure Cuff	Resp. Rate	Arterial Line	CVP	PA	PCW	LA	ICP		

NEURO WATCH

	GLASCOW COMA SCALE				Responds to	Activity	Right Arm	Left Arm	Right Leg	Left Leg	R. Pupil	L. Pupil	Pupil Reaction	Color
	Eyes Open	Best Verbal Response	Best Motor Response	Total										

Temp — PO — R   EKG Result

LAB DATA

Time		Result	Time		Result
	H&H			ELEC CO₂, Cl	
	WBC			Na, K	
	T&C			DRUG LEVEL	
	PT			ALCOHOL LEV.	
	PTT			URINALYSIS	
	BS			C&S	
	CREAT/BUN			OTHER	
	AMYLASE			PLATELETS	

X-RAY

Time		Result	Time		Result
	SKULL				
	CAT SCAN		ABDOMEN		
	FACIAL BONES		EXTREM. rt. leg		
	SPINE CERVICAL		rt. arm		
	SPINE THORACIC		lt. leg		
	LUMBO-SACRAL		lt. arm		
	HIP		N.M.R.		
	PELVIS		OTHER		

Exhibit 10–11 continued

PATIENT'S NAME: _____

E.D. NO: _____

Date: _____

MEDICATIONS

MEDICATION	DOSE	DIRECTIONS	TIME	INITIALS
TETANUS TOXOID	0.5cc	IM		
HYPERTET	250 Units	IM		

SPECIFIC INFUSIONS

Time	Volume	Rate	SOLUTION AND ADDITIVES	Amt Abs
			D5W MG. DOPEMINE	
			D5W MG. XYLOCAINE	
			D5W mg. ISUPREL	

INTAKE

IV SOLUTIONS | COLLOID

Time Started	Time Ended	Site:	Volume	SOLUTION	Rate	Amt. Abs.	Time Started	Time Ended	Site:	Volume	COLLOID	IV Meds	Specific Infusions	Intake Totals

Intake Total

OUTPUT

Time	Urine	Chest Tube	Nasal Gastric	Vomitus	Other	Output Totals

Output Total

ABG's

Time	pO2	pCO2	pH	Bicarb	O2 Sat.

VENTILATION DATA

Time	MA-1,MA-2	Airway	Assist Control Rate	Tidal Volume	Fi O2

Time

AIRWAY

O2 THERAPY VIA

AT _____ L/min.-

_____ % O2

BLOOD GIVEN WAS
_____ TYPED & CROSSMATCHED
_____ TYPE SPECIFIC
_____ UNCROSSMATCHED
_____ TYPE "O" NEG.
_____ TYPE "O" POS.

COLLOID CODE
WB = Whole Blood
PC = Packed Cells
SPA = Salt Poor Alb 25%
PLMT = Plasmonate 5%

"B"
PLACE "B" NO. HERE

Exhibit 10–11 continued

PROCEDURES					
Time					
AIRWAY:					
Intubation					
Tracheotomy					
Cricoid Airway					
CIRCULATION:					
Open Chest					
Closed Chest					
Defibrillation					
Cardioversion					
Mast Trousers					
PERFUSION SITES:					
Central					
Peripheral					
Venesection					
HEAD:					
Cervical Collar					
Crainiostomy					
Ventriculocentesis					
Burr Holes					
CHEST:					
Thoracotomy					
Chest Tubes					
Pericardiocentesis					
Pacemaker					
Transvenous					
Transthoracic					

ABDOMEN:	Pos.	Neg.
NG Tube		
Abdominal Tap		
Peritoneal Lavage		
Suprapubic Tap		
Foley Cath		

EXTREMITIES:
Splints
Immobilization
Amputated parts
OTHER:
Burn Care
Wound Care
Sutured

Note Trauma Res.:

PATIENT'S NAME: _____

E.D. NO.: _____

Date: _____

CONTINUING NURSING ASSESSMENT

Time

RN Signatures: 1.   2.

TIME: _____   **DISPOSITION**

PATIENT TRANSFERRED TO: OR _____ CC4 _____ CC5 _____ ROOM _____ TOH _____

EXPIRED: TIME _____

CLOTHING/VALUABLES: WITH PATIENT _____ GIVEN TO FAMILY _____ SECURITY_

POLICE _____ VALUABLES ENVELOPE NO. _____

FAMILY NOTIFICATION: TIME _____ BY _____

ANCILLARY SERVICES: HOSPICE _____ RELIGIOUS REPRESENTATIVE _____

LAST RITES BY _____

COMMUNITY RELATIONS NOTIFIED: YES _____ NO _____

Source: Reprinted with permission of Albert Einstein Medical Center, Northern Division, Philadelphia.

MANUALS, LISTS, AND BOOKS

Manuals that should be available to the ED nursing staff include:

- nursing service manuals
- infection control manual
- disaster plan manual
- laboratory manual
- pharmacy formulary
- ED policy and procedure manual
- poison control manual
- ED nursing orientation, standards, and protocol manual
- lists of resource services
- beeper list
- physician on-call and consultation lists
- anecdotals of patients who frequently return to the ED (names, dates of ED visits, problems, dispositions, special information)
- lists of referral agencies
- current *Physician's Desk Reference*
- medical dictionary
- emergency nursing reference books
- hospital telephone directory

JCAH and the Department of Health have specific requirements for ED policies, procedures, and guidelines. Be aware of the requirements for your particular ED. Review and update policies and procedures at least once a year.

Part III

Planning and Developing New Programs

Chapter 11

Development or Revision of a Nurse Triage System

The word "triage" originates from the French word "trier," which means to sort out or choose. Triage procedures were first used during World War I to sort out casualties on the battlefields for the primary purpose of providing quick treatment to the soldiers who could return to battle. Triage also determined who should be transferred to medical facilities and who were critically injured with little chance of survival. Since World War I, triage procedures have continued to be used on battlefields, in disaster situations, and, more recently, in hospital EDs. Triage classification of victims in all three situations is similar and has the same goal: to obtain maximal survival rates.

The military classifications are:

- *Minimal care*: little or no treatment is required; minor injuries
- *Immediate care*: immediate life- or limb-saving measures are required; these victims receive highest priority
- *Delayed care*: treatment is required, but the injury is not life- or limb-threatening; treatment can wait for a short period of time
- *Expectant care*: major injuries requiring extensive time and supplies; these victims would most likely expire even with immediate treatment; treatment is rendered only after immediate care victims are treated

In disaster situations, triage categories are often:

- *Emergent*: life- or limb-threatening injuries requiring immediate care
- *Urgent*: care can be delayed for a short period of time
- *Nonurgent*: minimal to no care is required; these victims are ambulatory
- *Dead*

Triage in the ED occurs in a more controlled setting than on a battlefield or during a disaster. The types of patients differ from the casualties of wars and disasters, yet the ED patients still need to be sorted out and prioritized to ensure that the most seriously ill or injured are treated first.

Without a triage system in the ED, patients generally are evaluated and treated in order of their arrival at the ED. This causes delays in care for patients who require immediate care. Unless patients are overtly sick or have an obvious major injury, often patients who are truly emergencies may wait for care in unobserved waiting rooms. Patients with chest pain, abdominal pain, and blunt trauma are most likely to be hurt by lack of a triage system. Nonprofessionals with no assessment training or skill take on the responsibility of deciding what the patient's problems are and who should be sent to treatment immediately and who should wait. The risk then exists that a patient with the complaint of jaw pain, as an example, may be sent to the ED waiting room inappropriately and there may develop cardiac arrest, or a patient who complains of vomiting is actually experiencing gastrointestinal bleeding and develops hypovolemic shock while waiting.

There is undue risk to the health of patients, as well as hospital liability, when there is no triage system in the ED.

TYPES OF TRIAGE SYSTEMS

The types of triage systems used in EDs in the United States include:

- *Nonprofessional determination of priority of care*: Assessment and prioritization are carried out by the registration clerk according to how sick the patient appears.
- *Basic triage*: A quick assessment is done by an RN, LPN, or physician to ensure that the most seriously ill or injured patients are treated first; a chief complaint is determined with little or no collection of other data; little to no documentation is done.
- *Comprehensive triage*: Assessment and prioritization are done by an educated, experienced ED RN; standards are developed and followed for assessment, prioritization, plan of care, immediate nursing action, and documentations; established triage categories are utilized.

The type of triage system used in individual EDs often depends on staffing levels, the number of patient visits, patient acuity levels, and physical space in the ED for the triage function. In an ED with low patient visits, triage may not be as necessary if all arriving patients are immediately brought into a treatment room, and no patient waiting occurs. However, in any ED where patients must wait for care or there are simultaneous patient arrivals, an effective triage system is necessary for appropriate emergency patient care.

COMPREHENSIVE TRIAGE

A triage system utilizing the knowledge and skills of an experienced RN facilitates timely care of those patients requiring immediate or urgent care through use of assessment, prioritization, clinical intervention, evaluation, and documentation skills. An experienced ED RN also develops the necessary intuition to recognize occult problems.

The advantages of a comprehensive triage system performed by an RN are:

- The patient is greeted by a professional, which helps establish immediate communication, rapport, and an appearance of sensitivity to the patient and family needs. It also enhances the public relations image of the hospital.
- When a nurse has immediate contact with the patient, patient stress is alleviated.
- Initial communication with hospital (or ED) does not concern insurance or ability to pay.
- Treatment of patients requiring immediate care is expedited by use of an acuity category system.
- Immediate assessment and documentation of patient problems are provided for.
- Certain diagnostic procedures and/or treatments can be initiated without delay.
- It provides for continuous reassessment of patients waiting in the waiting room.
- It provides for continued communication with family in the waiting room.

Priorities of Care/Triage Categories

Patients arriving at the ED should be prioritized into established categories to promote the triage concept and ensure timely care of the acutely ill or injured. Most triage programs use three levels of acuity. What the category standards are is more relevant than what they are named. Most common categories for hospital triage systems are emergent, urgent, and nonurgent or category I, II, or III. Patients classified as emergent require immediate attention and must be brought into the treatment area immediately. An urgent patient is one whose condition is evaluated as stable, but who requires treatment as soon as possible. If treatment is delayed for more than 1½ hours because no treatment room is available, the patient should be re-evaluated by the triage nurse. Nonurgent patients have problems that are minor or not acute. These patients are brought into a treatment room when one becomes available, when personnel are available, and after emergent and urgent patients are seen. Some EDs have separate areas for the nonurgent patient, which helps prevent extensive waiting times in busy facilities. Every attempt should be made in all EDs to examine and treat even the nonurgent patient as soon as possible. If the nonurgent patients have to wait for more than 2–3 hours, they also should be briefly re-evaluated for changes in condition while waiting.

Setting up the Triage Area

In some EDs, the triage function is performed in the waiting room. This prevents effective assessment and communication with the patient due to lack of privacy. However, if no other space is available for triage, using the waiting room is better than not triaging patients at all. When possible, a partitioned area or a room with a clear view of arriving patients should be used. I recommend the following equipment and supplies for the triage area:

- desk
- one chair for the triage nurse and one chair for the patient
- telephone
- intercom to the nurses station
- oral and rectal thermometers
- sphygmomanometer with three cuff sizes: adult, extra large, child
- ice packs
- splints
- bandages, dressings, tape
- basins
- irrigating water: a sink if possible
- specimen containers
- phlebotomy supplies
- supplies and fluids for emergency IV infusion
- airways, Ambu bag
- wheelchair
- bulletin board
- necessary forms and lists, such as:
  triage form
  ED nursing documentation form

referral forms
referral services and agencies
catchment area list
beeper list
hospital telephone directory
triage manual
- computer terminal in EDs with computerized registration

Triage Nurse Qualifications

The triage function requires special knowledge and skills, which include:

- experience in emergency nursing: minimum of 6 months
- emergency nursing clinical knowledge and assessment skills; demonstrated clinical competence
- ability to prioritize appropriately
- leadership skills
- assertiveness
- ability to solve problems
- ability to make quick decisions using good judgment
- good verbal communication skills
- common sense
- ability to empathize with patients, family, and colleagues
- ability to act as a patient advocate and public relations representative
- ability to document accurately and concisely
- organizational skills
- high tolerance for stress

Triage Standards and Priorities

Standards for levels of acuity and prioritization categories should be developed so that each nurse who performs in the triage role classifies patients according to the same established standards. A triage manual should be developed and kept in the triage area, so that it can be referred to by the triage nurses at any time. The triage manual should include the established triage procedure for the individual hospital, supplies and equipment to be maintained in the triage area, definitions of category terms, and an index of patient complaints or problems with specific levels of priority; the index makes up most of the manual. Exhibit 11–1 is an example of the index and Exhibit 11–2 displays priority standards. Separating each section by

Exhibit 11–1 Triage Priorities of Care Index

Section	Presenting Problem	Page
1.	Neurologic	
	Headache	
	Altered mental status	
	Fainting	
	Motor weakness	
	Sensory changes	
	Seizure	
	Unconsciousness	
	Shunt dysfunction	
	Head trauma	
2.	Eye	
	Visual changes	
	Drainage	
	Swelling	
	Foreign body	
	Trauma	
3.	Ear/nose/throat	
	Ear:	
	Drainage	
	Pain	
	Tinnitus	
	Foreign body	
	Trauma	
	Nose:	
	Epistaxis	
	Nasal congestion	
	Foreign body	
	Trauma	
	Throat:	
	Sore throat	
	Laryngitis	
	Tonsils	
	Foreign body	
	Stridor	
4.	Dental	
	Toothache	
	Bleeding gums	
	Bleeding from extraction	
	Abscess	
	Mouth lesions	
	Mouth trauma	
5.	Cardiovascular	
	Cardiac:	
	Chest pain	
	Indigestion	

Exhibit 11–1 continued

Exhibit 11–1 continued

Exhibit 11–1 continued

Section	*Presenting Problem*	*Page*
	Contusion	
	Hematoma	
	Infection	
	Wound check/suture removal	
	Dressing change	
	Bites/stings	
	Puncture	
	Laceration	
	Amputation	
	Gunshot	
	Stab	
15.	Toxic Substances	
	Inhalation	
	Ingestion	
	Skin contact	
	Alcohol	
	Drug	
16.	Thermal/cold	
	Heat	
	Burns	
	Hypothermia	
	Cold injury	
17.	Near Drowning	
18.	Psychological/psychiatric	
19.	Social	
	Abuse or neglect	
	Disposition problems	
	Rape	

Exhibit 11–2 Explanation of Priority Categories

E = EMERGENT

Patients who require imediate treatment. Life- or limb-threatening conditions that should be briefly evaluated and sent directly to the treatment area.

U = URGENT

Patients whose conditions are evaluated as stable but who should receive treatment as soon as possible. These patients must be re-evaluated within 1 hour if a treatment room is not immediately available.

N = NONURGENT

Patients whose conditions are not acute and are in no obvious distress. These patients will be seen when a treatment room and personnel are available.

dividers and tabs aids nurses in finding specific patient problems and priority levels quickly.

The staff, and the ED clinical specialist in those EDs that have a clinical specialist, can assist you in developing triage standards and a manual. The ED medical director should also have input or the opportunity to review the manual before it is used. A standard triage manual can also be used that can be modified to fit most EDs with only minimal additions or changes.

Triage Procedure

The manual should include specific guidelines for the triage nurse to follow.

Expectations of the Triage Nurse

The triage nurse is to ensure prompt evaluation of all patients within 2–3 minutes of their arrival at the ED. This may mean a brief interruption during a patient interview to evaluate if newly arriving patients can wait to be assessed by the triage nurse.

All patients are to be assessed within 15 minutes of arrival. When the number of patients waiting to be triaged at one time is more than one triage nurse can manage, an additional nurse to assist temporarily should be requested so that patients do not wait a long time for a triage nurse. (EDs with daily patient visits over 200 often have more than one nurse assigned to triage at all times.)

Referrals

There should be a list of established hospital or public health clinics and services that the triage nurse can refer patients to on the same day; the list should include their hours of operation.

Triage Procedure

The triage nurse introduces her- or himself to the patient and asks the patient for the following information: name, "what brought you here today" (to determine the presenting problem), a brief history of the presenting problem, and if the patient has a private physician who referred him or her or should be notified.

The triage nurse documents the following information:

- patient's name and sex: other required information may be race, birthdate, and age
- assessment: subjective and objective (with vital signs)
- allergies
- level of acuity: emergent, urgent, or nonurgent

- plan: if the patient is to be sent directly to the treatment area or waiting room; what medical service the patient is to be assigned to (medicine, surgery, GYN, pediatrics, psychiatry, etc.)
- nursing interventions: treatments, such as ice pack, splint, elevation, cleaning and dressing of a wound; neurocheck; patient teaching; referral
- re-evaluation of patients waiting

Other Responsibilities of the Triage Nurse

The triage nurse should:

- be aware of arriving patients: evaluate if a patient can wait to be triaged, if he or she needs to sit down while waiting, or if he or she should be brought into triage ahead of others or directly into the treatment area
- maintain contact with patients in the waiting room to evaluate any change in status
- have a warm and caring manner with all patients; act as a patient advocate; explain delays
- be in ongoing communication with the charge nurse
- assign patients to treatment rooms or notify the charge nurse of patients who need emergent or urgent treatment, so that those patients are called in for treatment as soon as possible
- demonstrate understanding of patient and family requests and concerns and deal with them appropriately; refer problems to management personnel.
- determine priorities of care and who should be brought directly in for treatment
- determine how nonemergent patients are brought in or called into the ED proper for treatment: either by the triage nurse, charge nurse, or individual staff nurses as treatment rooms become available; all patients should be called in by the order determined by the triage nurse, not by the order of arrival; to avoid problems with patients waiting, this procedure should be explained to patients as they are triaged.

In very busy EDs it is imperative that the triage process be completed as quickly as possible. Documentation should be concise. If extended periods of time are spent with each patient in the triage area, there may be a line of patients waiting to be seen by the triage nurse, which defeats the purpose of triage. In EDs with a small number of daily patient visits, more time can be spent with each patient in triage.

Triage Inservice Training

Before beginning a triage program, the nursing staff who will be assigned to the triage function should attend educational classes to prepare them for the role. The classes should cover the purpose of triage, rapid assessment and prioritization of presenting patient problems according to established standards and categories or levels of patient acuity, required documentation, policies, resources, and a specific triage procedure. The triage assignment can be rotated among the staff, so that most of the ED nurses maintain triage skills, as well as the skills required to perform in the treatment area. An ED nurse who only performs in the triage role loses confidence and some skill required in the treatment area where he or she may need to perform in certain circumstances.

The triage nurse should have the authority to decide what patients are to be brought directly in for treatment. This decision should not be challenged by peers, because the triage nurse is the initial assessor of the patient and is the only person aware of the patient's degree of illness. However, the triage nurse must empathize with co-workers and only bring those patients who require immediate attention directly into the treatment area during times of high activity and ED overload.

As new RNs are hired to work in the ED, the triage function must be an important part of the ED orientation process. A new ED RN should spend at least four shifts in triage with an experienced RN before being allowed to triage alone. Even after the triage orientation, the newer RN's triage assessments and prioritization should be reviewed and evaluated by you.

Patients Requiring Extra Caution

The following types of patients require extra caution during assessment and prioritization:

- injured alcoholic
- injured comatose
- head injury
- history of loss of consciousness
- change in mental status or behavior
- chest pain
- abdominal pain
- blunt trauma
- children

Staffing Requirements for Triage Hours of Operation

Most EDs do not need a triage nurse 24 hours a day. Generally, the number of patient visits greatly decreases between midnight and 7–8 A.M., allowing all patients arriving then to be brought into a treatment room as soon as they arrive. Therefore, the triage function may only be necessary during the day and evening shifts. To begin a triage program and staff it for triage 7 days a week with an RN, additional positions will be required, according to how many hours triage will be operational. A minimum of 3.2 RN FTEs will be required to staff two shifts, 7 days a week ($2 \times 1.6 = 3.2$). If two RNs are required, the FTEs must be doubled. The triage nurse cannot be counted as a direct patient care provider, because the function is not in the ED proper.

Chapter 12

Planning for a New Emergency Department

During the past decade many hospitals have undertaken new building programs. The new construction was undertaken to replace antiquated hospital buildings, to enhance a hospital's ability to compete with other health care facilities, and as a marketing strategy to attract patients. Yet, even when new buildings were added or old ones renovated, EDs were often overlooked until recently. Now that EDs are being seen more as a financial asset to hospitals, as is discussed in Chapter 13, more EDs are being included in new building programs or are at least being renovated.

Good planning is essential for the development of a functional, effective, safe, economical, and attractive ED. The ED nurse manager and ED medical director must be actively involved in the planning and design processes. Who else knows best what is needed for the ED?

Before actual planning begins, it is beneficial to look at the facilities of other EDS to develop ideas about what design and function could work best for you. Usually, when a new ED facility is planned, it is designed to be larger than the existing one. However, it is important to forecast future needs, so that by the time the building project is completed, the new facility is not already too small or outdated. Although building developers and architects have experience with designing new hospitals, each individual hospital and/or ED has its own specific needs.

DESIGN

The location of the ED should be easily accessible to the hospital, emergency vehicles, and pedestrians. Close proximity to the operating room, critical care units, and radiology is also important. The entrance should be easily identified, well lighted, and protected from wind and weather. A roof over the outside entrance area protects patients as they are transferred from vehicles into the ED. There should be enough temporary parking bays for vehicles, with wheelchair or stretcher ramps in appropriate locations. In busy EDs, two entrances may be necessary: one for the walk-in patient and the other for patients brought in by stretcher. If two entrances are designed, they must be clearly marked and be large enough to accommodate equipment, patients, and those accompanying them.

The size of the ED is determined by the need of the individual hospital. Obviously, an ED with a larger number of patient visits requires more area than the ED with fewer patient visits. When determining space requirements, forecast annual ED patient visits and average length of stay for the following 10 years. In addition, also determine whether the hospital is planning a marketing program to acquire trauma designation, or to develop walk-in clinics or a convenience care area, all which will affect the number of ED patient visits. Be aware, however, that an increase in physical space affects ED and nursing functions. It is unrealistic to assume that current nursing staffing patterns will be sufficient in a new facility that is two to three times larger than the original facility. It is easier to care for and observe patients in a smaller area than when they are spread over a larger space.

The waiting room should be large enough to provide seating for all visitors and waiting patients. It should have lavoratories, pay telephones, a water fountain, and comfortable, durable seating. There should be an entrance and emergency exit that are large enough for wheelchairs and stretchers to pass through. The waiting room should be well lit, clean, and attractive. A television that is secured and an area sectioned off for children to play or color make the waiting easier for patients. It is also a good idea to have vending machines in the waiting room so that those waiting do not have to travel through the hospital for coffee and soft drinks.

The triage area should be close to the entrance or, if two entrances are designed, close to the ambulatory entrance. The triage area is most effective if designed as an office that ensures privacy for conversations yet still allows the triage nurse to see all patients as they arrive. The doorway to the triage area must be large enough to accommodate stretchers and wheelchairs.

In many urban hospital EDs, safety of the staff and patients is a concern. Doors that can be locked and/or panic buttons can be installed, or a security guard office should be located by the entrance and waiting room.

The registration area should be adjacent to the triage office with enough space to provide for at least two registration clerks and room for additional registrars when needed. Because some patients are unable to stand to give information to the registrar, there should be enough space for a patient to be able to sit in a chair.

The nurses' station should have adequate space for nursing and clerical functions, with an area sectioned off for medications, or a separate medication room. Having a room for the physicians to write, use the phone, and discuss patients helps reduce the noise level and confusion in the nurses' station. There should be adequate writing space separate from the clerical area for the nurses to write and use telephones. The number of telephones in the nurses' station must be considered. If the ED has five main lines, there should be at least five extensions in the nurses' station. Having extra telephone lines, in addition to the main ED number, is useful for making outgoing calls and freeing up the main ED lines for incoming calls. There should also be direct lines to and from the police/EMSS. Table or desk space should be allocated for computer terminals. Even if computers are not yet used in your ED, they most likely will be in the near future. Terminal and printer space then must also be allocated in the registration area.

The number and design of the treatment areas are determined by the allocated space in the building, shape of the space (square, rectangular, round), and current or forecasted patient needs. Whichever design is chosen for placement of treatment rooms, it should minimize congestion and maximize their visibility. The most functional design for the nursing staff is placing the most acute care areas closest to the nurses' station. Necessary specialized treatment areas are:

- cast with special sink and storage area
- suture
- gynecologic/urologic
- eye/ear/nose/throat
- critical care
- shock/trauma
- pediatric
- observation

Generalized treatment areas should be planned based on the number of daily patient visits expected during the next several years. An area to treat patients sitting in chairs, such as the asthmatic patient who is more comfortable sitting up, can also be considered.

Patient treatment areas can be either designed as bays with curtains or as individual examination rooms, some of which can hold more than one patient, that are divided by a curtain. Using actual rooms, instead of open bays, allows for auditory and visual privacy for patients. It also lowers the noise level in the department and reduces stress levels of patients, because they cannot see or hear what is occurring with other patients. Each treatment area should be equipped with oxygen, suction, sink, work desks, which can be the fold-up type, mayo stand, stool, trash can, intercom, nurse call button, and shelving and/or cabinets and drawers for storage of supplies and linen. Having wall-mounted blood pressure and suction devices in each area is most effective and time saving. Wall-mounted oto-ophthalmoscopes can be placed in each treatment room or between bays. The doorways to treatment rooms must be large enough to allow passage of a stretcher with a patient, equipment, and personnel. Each treatment room should be large enough to hold equipment and personnel required for a resuscitation code.

The general medical rooms should be multipurpose and equally equipped and stocked. There should be wall-mounted cardiac monitors in the critical care and shock/trauma rooms with a central monitor in the nurses' station. Pressure modules should be considered in the shock/trauma room. Ceiling- or wall-mounted IV poles keep IVs immediately accessible when needed. Lighting in all the areas must be adequate, with special lighting for suturing, special procedures, and pelvic exams. These special lamps can be portable or ceiling- or wall-mounted. Each treatment area should have hooks for patient clothing.

There should be an adequate number of lavoratories for patients and separate lavoratories for staff. If there are 50 ED employees, one or two lavoratories is hardly sufficient. Lavoratories, especially for the staff, should be inconspicuously located. A decontamination shower must be located near the ED entrance. A patient tub or shower room in the ED is also very useful. Safety rails and nurse call buttons should be provided in the tub room and in all lavatories.

Other areas that may be included in the ED are a grieving room for families and friends of critically ill or injured patients or of patients who expired; a waiting area with chairs for patients to wait for test results; a police/EMT room with a writing space and a separate telephone; a seclusion room for patients who are acting out or are violent; an area for volunteers with a desk and phone; clean and dirty utility rooms; storage rooms for equipment, supplies, and linen; storage space for stretchers and wheelchairs; staff lounge, locker room, and conference room away from the mainstream of patient activity; a pantry with a refrigerator, ice machine, and patient nourishments; and storage space for housekeeping supplies.

Office space should be available for the ED clinical nurse specialist or instructor and social worker if these resource people are assigned specifically to the ED. However, though optimal, it is not necessary that their offices be located in the ED. Offices for the ED medical director, the ED nurse manager, the ED secretary(s), and other managerial staff should be located in the ED, but away from patient care areas.

An x-ray room and stat laboratory are other facilities that improve ED function.

An adequate number of paper towel and soap dispensers located by all sinks, bulletin boards, file cabinets, x-ray view boxes, resuscitation carts, portable carts for other purposes, and the number and location of electrical outlets and water fountains must also be part of the design. On-call and patient location boards are also helpful.

If new furniture is to be purchased, it should be comfortable, attractive, and durable. When purchasing large equipment, such as stretchers, evaluate several types. Many manufacturers allow a trial usage for evaluation, which can be arranged through their sales representative.

Signs clearly directing patients to the ED must be placed both inside and outside the hospital.

Use the planning and design phase of the project to plan carefully for everything that is necessary for effective functioning of the ED. If changes have to be made, it is much easier to make them before construction begins. Poor or after-the-fact planning produces defects and great expense. However, if a minor change is absolutely necessary once construction has already begun, bring it to the attention of the administration as soon as possible. Usually, once construction is completed, it is very difficult to have money approved to make changes.

REFERENCES

Joint Commission on the Accreditation of Hospitals. *Accreditation Manual for Hospitals, Emergency Services Section*. American Hospital Association, Chicago, 1986.

Peisert, Margaret. *The Hospital's Role in Emergency Medical Services System*. Chicago: AHA, American Publishing Co., 1984.

Chapter 13

Marketing the Emergency Department*

Because of the prospective payment system of DRGs and PPOs and the strict cost-containment regulations of HMOs and other third party payers, hospitals have recently experienced a decrease in admissions, decreased length of stay for admitted patients, and decreased reimbursement for expenses. However, as of 1986, DRGs do not apply to reimbursement for costs in the ED; they only become effective when the patient is admitted and becomes an inpatient. Therefore, with effective patient item charging and billing systems, reimbursement for actual cost is still possible for ED patients who are discharged. The ED should be recognized and utilized as a marketing tool to increase the inpatient census by increasing the ED census. The same patients who utilize the ED for urgent or nonurgent care begin to view the hospital as the facility for their total health care needs, including in-hospital care. At some point, a percentage of ED patients will require admission, many of them with financially favorable DRGs.

Emergency patient acuity levels are also increasing, which increases the number of admissions to the hospital. Therefore, the higher the ED census, the better the opportunity to increase the inpatient census.

WHAT IS MARKETING?

The function of marketing is to plan, create, price, promote, and render services. It requires an understanding and forecasting of social and psychological conditions that contribute to success, with the ability to project future needs and utilization of emergency services.

Marketing communicates services, benefits, and an image properly so they are appropriately perceived. The image or perception that the patient has of the

---

*Adapted with permission from "Marketing the Emergency Department" by Linda Buschiazzo in *Nursing Management*, Vol. 16, No. 9, pp. 30B–30D, © September 1985.

hospital is often formed by his or her experience in the ED. If the visit was positive, the image of the hospital will then be positive. Communicating a caring, capable image will increase demand for the hospital's services.

Before beginning a marketing program, internal changes may be needed if the hospital is to live up to the image that is being communicated to the public and to enable it to handle the increase in demands for services generated by the marketing efforts. The hospital board of directors and administration must be firmly committed to correcting and/or improving ED systems and staffing levels. If it is advertised that all patients in the ED will be seen within 10 minutes of arrival, but realistically there is a 1–2 hour wait for less urgent patients, the marketing effort will yield negative results.

WHY MARKET THE EMERGENCY DEPARTMENT?

The growth of convenience care centers or free-standing emergicenters (FECs) is creating competition for hospital EDs. In 1981, there were approximately 260 FECs in the United States. By the mid-1980s there were over 1500 FECs, and it is estimated that by 1990, there will be about 4500 FECs in this country. Some HMOs are joining with convenience care centers to provide emergency services for those enrolled in the HMO at a lower premium and lower reimbursement rate than at a hospital ED. FECs are attractive to patients because of their convenient location, no waiting time, and decreased costs. Although hospital EDs as of the mid-1980s still have the highest market share of emergency care, marketing efforts should be planned and implemented to compete with alternative emergency care facilities and to maintain this market share.

Hospitals are also competing with each other for patients. Patients shop for their care based on such conveniences as the hospital's proximity to their home, a pleasant atmosphere, short or no waiting times, decreased cost, past positive experiences, and image of the hospital as perceived by the public. The *quality* of care given by the hospital may not be a major determinant of patient choice. Industry has recognized and converted to a customer orientation; hospitals are now doing the same.

Hospital governing boards and administrators now must view the ED as a front door to the hospital, rather than as the back door, which was the common perception in the past. That view relegated the ED to a low priority status for budgetary approvals and expense. This low status must change if the ED is to meet the expected high standards of the consumer.

MARKETING STEPS

Market Research

A market research study should be conducted to determine who the competition is and what types of patients should be reached through advertisement and promotion.

First, establish research objectives, which include determining:

- what are the competing health care facilities, where they are located, what services they offer, their advantages and cost, and their image as perceived by the public
- what services your hospital offers, advantages and benefits for the patient and community, timeliness of service, cost, atmosphere and environment of the ED, current perceived image by patients and the community
- to whom and where to market; an urban hospital with a large self-pay patient population in the surrounding community will need to market outside the hospital's geographical area to attract patients with health care insurance to ensure reimbursement for services rendered

Decide which research methods to use. Patient questionnaires, patient histories of their experiences, personal interviews, such as exit interviews, or phone or mail interviews can all provide marketing data (Exhibit 13–1).

To identify what patients want or need, questionnaires can use the following formats:

- yes or no questions
- multiple choice responses
- ranking
- probing questions—"what" or "why"

Choose the type of format based on the general educational level of the patient population to be surveyed. Conduct the research in a set time frame with an established schedule. After the research is completed, the data must be collected and analyzed.

Marketing Plan

Developing a marketing plan is the next step. The plan has to be communicated to and be supported by top management, or it will fail.

First determine the purpose, objectives, and expected or desired results of the marketing effort. Develop strategies that are practical, flexible and workable. Then write a simple and clear plan, keeping in mind:

- competition—other hospitals, clinics, convenience care centers
- target—who and what type of patient, what communities
- communication and promotional requirements

Exhibit 13–1 Emergency Department Survey

This survey is to help us learn the preferences of our patients. Please mark an X on the line next to your answer for each question. Thank you.

1. Is this your first visit to this emergency department?
   _____ yes _____ no
2. Have you ever been treated in another emergency department?
   _____ yes _____ no
3. Why did you come to *this* emergency department today?
   _____ My doctor sent me
   _____ It is close to my home
   _____ It is close to where I work
   _____ The hospital has a good reputation
   _____ I had a good experience in this emergency department in the past
   _____ The police or paramedics brought me here by their choice
   _____ Other reason _____
4. Do you live in the community near the hospital?
   _____ yes _____ no
5. Please mark the line next to the answer that is most important to you in choosing an emergency department for your care.
   _____ to be seen quickly by the doctor
   _____ to be treated and discharged quickly
   _____ the appearance and comfort of the emergency department
   _____ caring staff
   _____ knowledge and skills of the physicians and nurses
   _____ modern equipment
   _____ cost
   _____ other _____
6. What is your age (or the age of patient if a child)
   _____ 1 week–1 year   _____ 19 years–45 years
   _____ 1 year–12 years   _____ 46 years–65 years
   _____ 13 years–18 years   _____ over 65 years
7. What is your race?
   _____ Asian _____ Black _____ Caucasian _____ Hispanic _____ other
8. What is your highest completed level of education?
   _____ elementary _____ high school _____ college _____ postgraduate
9. What is your family income?
   _____ below $10,000   _____ $10,000–15,000   _____ $16,000–25,000
   _____ $26,000–$45,000   _____ $46,000–65,000   _____ over $65,000
10. What time did you arrive at the emergency department?
    _____ midnight–6 A.M.
    _____ 6 A.M.–9 A.M.
    _____ 9 A.M.–12 noon
    _____ 12 noon–4 P.M.
    _____ 4 P.M.–7 P.M.
    _____ 7 P.M.–midnight

- budgetary costs—startup, promotional, and overhead expenses for a marketing program
- what your ED can offer and what are its advantages over competitors
- perceived image
- staffing requirements
- means of promotion and advertisement

Once the plan is written, it must be communicated to and approved by hospital administration. The next step is to implement the plan. Finally, ongoing evaluation and updating of the plan are needed based on research, data collection, and interpretation of the data once the plan has been in effect.

MARKETING STRATEGIES

Viewing the Patient as a Consumer

You should explain to the staff the effects of reimbursement systems on hospital revenues and the need to increase the ED and hospital census. Share the marketing program plan with the staff, encouraging their ideas and input and discussing their role in promoting the ED.

ED personnel often view nonurgent patients as inappropriate users of the ED and therefore discourage their visits. Hold staff meetings on all shifts to explain the fiscal effects of DRGs, HMOs, and PPOs; the decreased length of stay and decreased census of inpatients; and competition for emergency services. Help them understand that the ED can have a positive effect on increasing census in the hospital, which ultimately affects the financial well-being of the ED and individual staff members, especially relating to available money for equipment requests, salaries, and required additional FTEs. A guest relations program to educate staff about how to treat patients as guests, and how to treat consumers who have expectations of hospital service, is helpful, with mandatory attendance by all staff members, including physicians and clerks, to increase their understanding of the behaviors, wants, and needs of emergency patients and their families and to teach them how to deal with the public, especially the difficult patients, more effectively. Consistently displaying a warm and caring attitude and assuming the patient advocacy role have to become priorities and expectations of all staff members. Courtesy and promptness most often result in a satisfied ED patient. They need to understand that they are selling a product: themselves, the ED, and the hospital. If the consumers do not like what they see or receive, they can shop elsewhere. Use a patient questionnaire to ascertain current patient perceptions of the staff and their care in the ED (Exhibit 13–2). This type of patient survey should be done before and after a guest relations program.

The image that is perceived by patients is often more important than the reality. Many large companies and individuals achieve success because of their image. An example of the importance of a good image was the election of John F. Kennedy to the presidency. His image—young, attractive, enthusiastic, family oriented, energetic, and caring for the people—helped elect him to the office of president.

Improving Communication

Continually providing updated information about the patient's condition to the patient and family or significant other is an important factor in decreasing anxiety levels, humanizing patient care, and developing rapport with those who are waiting. Explaining procedures, describing the patient's progress, and providing reasons for waits in the ED are very important. Personalized care should be ensured.

A liaison person, or patient relations representative, could be very helpful in providing updated information to the family and meeting their needs in the waiting room. The ED staff members are often too busy treating the patient, because the priority of the physicians and nurses is the care provided to the patient. They may lose track of the time that they last communicated with the family. This liaison role can be performed by a mature volunteer, social worker, or an individual with experience in dealing with the public. This person could provide a welcoming atmosphere as patients and visitors arrive, assist with providing updated information to the family in the waiting room, answer questions of those in the waiting room, and report any obvious changes of patient status while waiting.

Decreasing Waiting Time

In the ED, patients wait for various reasons: They wait to be registered, to be put into a treatment room, for a nurse, for a doctor, for diagnostic studies to be completed, for test results, for communication about their progress or disposition, for an available bed once admitted, or for the aide to escort them to their hospital room. Decreasing waiting time is extremely important for patient satisfaction. Usually it takes intradepartmental efforts and change to decrease waiting times, because supportive services, such as labs and radiology departments, often cause delays in ED patient care. In addition, in teaching hospitals, participation of residents and medical students may increase the time needed for decision making for treatment and disposition.

The nursing staff becomes used to delays, and to them, it is the norm. Yet, these factors causing delays need to be recognized and changed. Often administrative involvement at the top level is required to direct the changes required of the other

Exhibit 13–2 Emergency Department Patient Survey

Please circle your response to the following questions. This survey will help us improve our service to you and the community.

1. When you arrived in the emergency department, how long did you have to wait to see the triage nurse?
   a. 0–5 minutes
   b. 6–10 minutes
   c. 11–15 minutes
   d. more than 15 minutes
2. Did the triage nurse understand your problem and have a caring manner?
   a. yes   b. no
3. Was the registration clerk courteous while obtaining information?
   a. yes   b. no
4. How long did you wait in the waiting room?
   a. no wait
   b. 10–20 minutes
   c. 21–45 minutes
   d. 45 minutes–1½ hours
   e. 1½ hours–2 hours
   f. more than 2 hours
5. If you waited more than 1 hour, was the reason explained to you?
   a. yes   b. no
6. When you were brought into the emergency department proper for treatment, were you greeted by a friendly atmosphere?
   a. yes   b. no
7. Was privacy maintained?
   a. yes   b. no
8. Did you wait long in the treatment room to see a doctor?
   a. yes   b. no
9. Did the nurses keep you informed of your progress?
   a. yes   b. no
10. How would you evaluate your overall visit to this emergency department?
    a. excellent
    b. good
    c. fair
    d. poor
11. Were you admitted to the hospital?
    a. yes   b. no
12. Were you ever a patient in our emergency department before this visit?
    a. yes   b. no
13. If you answered yes to #12—was today's experience
    a. better
    b. same
    c. worse
14. Additional comments: _____
    _____
    _____
    _____
    _____

THANK YOU

departments. Patient advocacy should be consistent, with the nursing staff, physicians, and medical clerks doing everything possible to prevent patient waiting. Staffing patterns may have to be adjusted to meet patient activity needs during the busiest hours. Adjusting nursing FTEs may be required to manage properly current or increasing census and/or acuity levels.

Improving the Facility

After many years in a too-small facility, the ED at the Albert Einstein Medical Center, Northern Division, was moved to a new building. The original facility was too small for appropriate patient care and flow. The environment was unappealing, with minimal provisions for comfort or privacy, and the equipment was antiquated. The new facility, which is three times the size of the original ED, is comfortable, clean, and appealing. It has additional treatment rooms and space, enabling privacy for patients and family members. All new equipment, furniture, and prints for the walls were purchased. Even though access to the ED is very inconvenient from the street—through a long curved driveway, far from the bus and subway—the patients have managed to find their way. In fact, during the first 6 months in the new facility, there was a 7% increase in census, and the census has continued to grow. Patients have come from other areas of the city, bypassing other hospitals. When we asked some of the patients why they came to our ED when other hospitals were closer to them, some of their responses were: "It is prettier here," "the staff is nicer here," "there is a color TV in the waiting room," and "there is more privacy." A new facility may not be planned for your ED, but a facelift can make a major difference.

Promoting and Advertising

As hospitals are viewed and managed more as businesses, advertising, which once was taboo, has become an accepted and required means of attracting patients. Radio, television, or newspaper ads or publicity generated by the hospital public relations department can promote the hospital's services. The telephone book is also an important advertising tool. The ED nursing staff can be involved in promoting the ED and the hospital by giving educational programs to the public, such as (1) free emergency/first aid programs, accident prevention, or other health care presentations or services at schools, community meetings, and shopping malls; and (2) by inviting the public to the ED for a tour or free service, such as free blood pressure taking. Publishing articles in community newspapers or magazines concerning emergency services or prevention of illness or injury also brings attention to the ED department. Follow-up phone calls to emergency patients after their discharge is also a positive promotional tool. If your staff cannot call all patients, it may be possible to make calls to selected groups of patients, such as the geriatric patient or to parents of children who were treated.

Advertisements should be placed frequently in the various media and should communicate the advantages and special services offered by your ED.

Developing a Convenience Care Center in the Emergency Department

The walk-in, nonurgent patient makes up a large percentage of the patients who come to the ED for service. To facilitate prompt care of the emergent and urgent patients and to decrease delays in service for nonurgent patients, a convenience care or primary care area can be set up in or adjacent to the ED. This area will also aid in increasing inpatient census by enabling patients who require admission to be admitted directly from the hospital's convenience care area to an inpatient bed.

To plan for this type of area, administrative commitment and financial support are required. An area segregated from the acute area but close enough to it so that supportive services are immediately available should be used. A slight increase in the number of staff is usually required to allow personnel to be assigned specifically to the convenience care area without adding responsibilities to the nurses assigned to work in the ED proper. Initially, the convenience care area should be open during the busier hours for the ED, which is usually between 11 A.M. and 9 P.M.; at a later point, hours can be expanded according to patient activity.

A convenience care center can be easily promoted by advertising the promptness of service offered and the benefits and advantages of its connection to the ED and hospital. The convenience care patient can be charged a lower fee than the patient treated in the ED. Having a separate area for the nonurgent patient may be more cost effective in regard to reimbursement approval. Many insurance plans reimburse for ED service only if the patient had a true emergency, whereas reimbursement for service of the nonurgent type of patient may be possible in a convenience care setting.

SUMMARY

Marketing the ED may provide little or no financial gain for the ED, but it will definitely enhance hospital gain derived from patients admitted through the ED. Each patient attracted to another ED, convenience care center, or free-standing emergicenter may be one less potential admission for your hospital. An investment in the ED department can only provide gains for the hospital. As the ED nurse manager, you can and should take an active part in the planning and implementation of such a marketing program.

REFERENCES

Bonoma, Thomas V. "Making Your Marketing Strategy Work." *Harvard Business Review* 84:2, 1984.

Buschiazzo, Linda. "Marketing the Emergency Department." *Nursing Management,* September, 1985, pp. 30B–30D.

Coddington, Dean; Palmquist, Lowell E.; and Trollinger, William V. "Strategies for Survival in the Hospital Industry." *Harvard Business Review* 63:3, 1985.

Eliopoulos, Charlotte. "Selling a Positive Image Builds Demand." *Nursing Management,* April, 1985, pp. 23–26.

Frank, Iris, and McGovern, Frank. "Marketing One Hospital's Emergency Department." *Journal of Emergency Nursing* 9(6):324–26, 1983.

Freko, Deborah, and Dolkert, David. "Costs Hike Causes Cuts in Stay, Beds, FTEs." *Hospitals,* November 1, 1984, pp. 45–46.

Klein, Rene. "Solving Marketing Problems." Presentation at ENA Scientific Assembly, New York, 1985.

Inguanzo, Joe M., and Harju, Mark. "What's the Market for Emergency Care?" *Hospitals,* June 1, 1985, pp. 53–54.

Inguanzo, Joe M., and Harju, Mark. "Hospitals Still Dominate Emergency Care Market." *Hospitals,* July 1, 1985, pp. 84–85.

Maister, David. "Quality Work Doesn't Mean Quality Service." *The American Lawyer,* April 1984.

Powills, Susan, and Matson, Ted. "Hospital Emergency Departments Learn How to Make Money." *Hospitals,* October 16, 1985, pp. 122–124.

Ranseen, Thomas. "Hospital E.D.s Face 'Sink or Swim' Time as Urgent Care Center Competition Rises." *Emergency Department News,* October, 1983, pp. 1, 6–7.

Ranseen, Thomas A. "Convenience Care Centers—Why Not One in Your Emergency Department." *Urgent Care Update,* November, 1984, pp. 3–7.

Ranseen, Thomas, and Thornton, Theresa. "The Emergency Department—A Financial Winner in the 1980s." *Healthcare Financial Management,* January, 1985.

Shaffer, Frank. "Nursing Power in the DRG World." *Nursing Management* 15:6, 1984, pp. 26–30.

Stahl, Dulcelina. "Developing and Marketing Ambulatory Care Programs." *Nursing Management* 15(5):20–24, 1984.

Chapter 14

Computer Information System in the Emergency Department

A computerized information system in the ED can save you a great deal of time. It can collect, store, analyze, and report information more quickly and with fewer errors than can be done manually. Using a computer is cost effective as it saves personnel time and labor costs and the expenses of extensive research studies. The information obtained helps you manage current operations and plan for the future.

At the Albert Einstein Medical Center, a multidisciplinary group met to determine goals and requirements for the computer system, which would be integrated with the already existing hospital system. This group was comprised of data processing personnel; administrators; the directors of admissions, labs, radiology, and finance; the ED medical director; and myself as the ED nurse manager. The primary goals and objectives for the ED computer system were to:

- release nursing, clerical, and physician time by automating forms, labels, logs, and statistical information
- recall information about prior visits
- provide for increased revenue collection through automation of registration and accounting functions
- provide for a direct link to the inpatient admission function
- provide for analysis of case mix
- provide for managerial control information
- reduce patient waiting times

Forms, work flow charts, reports, menus (computer directories), screens and personnel responsibilities were designed and determined. Before implementation of the system, a prototype was developed with visual displays, and modifications were made as necessary. All the ED staff attended training sessions to learn how to use the system.

IMPLEMENTATION

The process begins when the triage nurse probes "Triage" on the master menu (Exhibit 14–1) and enters the following required information: patient name, sex, race, complaint, and priority. Additional information obtained and entered by the triage nurse includes assessment, interventions, last menstrual period, last tetanus toxoid, allergies, current medications, probability of admission, and whether the patient was sent to the waiting room (WR) or to treatment (TR). Once the information is entered and the triage nurse sees the information on the video display, corrections can be made, and the information is then entered into the system. Exhibit 14–2 shows the triage screen.

A patient identification plate is generated upon completion of the triage function. Because some patients arrive via rescue units or ambulance, or their name is unknown, or they must be brought into a treatment room immediately, an "emergency arrival" screen (Exhibit 14–3) is used instead of the triage screen. When one of the three options is probed, a screen similar to the triage screen is displayed. The system automatically enters the priority as emergent, that the patient is a probable admission, and the location is TR.

After the triage or emergency arrival function is performed, the next function is registration. A registration clerk enters patient demographic and insurance data. If

Exhibit 14–1 Emergency Department Master Menu

```
                    A.E.M.C. PATIENT CARE SYSTEM              03/12/84   1315
                      EMERGENCY UNIT MASTER MENU

    TRIAGE PATIENT                              UPDATE TRIAGE DATA
    EMERGENCY ARRIVAL                           DISPLAY PATIENT DATA
    CALL PATIENT TO TREATMENT                   REPRINT EU TREATMENT RECORD
    REGISTER PATIENT                            EU CENSUS
    DISCHARGE PATIENT                           REACTIVATE/DISCHARGE IN ERROR
    UPDATE PROCESS                              DOWNTIME ARRIVAL
    VOID/REACTIVATE PATIENT NUMBER              DISPLAY EU LOG
    PHYSICIAN BILLING INFORMATION               INQUIRE ON INPATIENT NAME




                                                                      SIGN-OFF
```

Source: Reprinted with permission of Albert Einstein Medical Center, Philadelphia.

Exhibit 14–2 Triage Screen

```
X              TRIAGE PATIENT                                    05/03/83    1515

          NAME (L, F M): HORNICKLE, CAROLYN          SEX: F    RACE: W
         DATE OF BIRTH: 01/08/945   AGE: ...
     PATIENT COMPLAINT: SEVERE PAIN IN LOWER BACK


        BLOOD PRESSURE: 120 / 080
           PULSE RATE: 65
          RESPIRATION: 20
          TEMPERATURE: 37.2


             ALLERGIES: PENICILLIN, SULFA
   CURRENT MEDICATIONS: COMBID, ASPIRIN


    PROBABLE ADMIT (Y/N): N
              PRIORITY: S
              LOCATION: WR (IF A PATIENT IS SENT DIRECTLY TO TREATMENT AFTER TRIAGE
                        YOU MUST ENTER THE TIME SENT TO TREATMENT)
        TREATMENT TIME:


  . . . . . . . . . . . . . . . . . . . . . . . . . . . . . . . . . . . . . . . . . . . . . . .
  KEY THE APPROPRIATE DATA AND PRESS THE ENTER KEY
  EUTR02SN                                                                    MASTER
```

Source: Reprinted with permission of Albert Einstein Medical Center, Philadelphia.

Exhibit 14–3 Emergency Arrival Screen

```
                    A.E.M.C. PATIENT CARE SYSTEM              05/03/83    1520
                    EMERGENCY ARRIVAL FUNCTIONS

                    PROBE THE APPROPRIATE OPTION BELOW:




                    EMERGENCY ARRIVAL (WITH NAME)

                    EMERGENCY ARRIVAL (JOHN DOE)

                    EMERGENCY ARRIVAL (JANE DOE)








  . . . . . . . . . . . . . . . . . . . . . . . . . . . . . . . . . . . . . . . . . . . . . . .
  EUEA01SA                                                                    MASTER
```

Source: Reprinted with permission of Albert Einstein Medical Center, Philadelphia.

the patient had previously been a patient in the ED or the hospital, the computer already has this data, and only updating of information is necessary. Once the registrar completes this function, the ED treatment record is printed with all the data obtained up to this point. The "update" process allows data to be changed or added after triage or registration functions have been completed. The computer automatically assigns a billing number and time of each function.

The "Call Patient to Treatment" process displays the name and condition of all patients waiting in the waiting room. It also enables staff to determine how long patients have been waiting. As a patient is called in for treatment, the "Call Patient to Treatment" process is probed. The computer automatically changes the patient's location and calculates the time from arrival to treatment (Exhibit 14–4).

"Discharge Patient" displays all patients who have not been discharged from the ED. When a name is probed, a discharge screen appears with the time automatically recorded. Discharge information, including disposition, treating physician, and ICD-9 CM diagnosis code, is entered.

Additional information can be entered for statistical reports. For example, as part of the discharge function, the patient classification level is entered, which enables the development of computerized patient classification reports. Reports can be generated about the financial mix, patients' means of arrival, percentages of patients from specific areas of the city or suburbs, and all patients with a particular diagnosis.

The computer automatically maintains a patient log and current census report from the data that have been entered. Because the system is integrated with the hospital admissions system, it has the ability to obtain information on patient names, billing information, room number, and physicians of all current inpatients. This is particularly helpful in responding to telephone calls or visitors looking for someone who had been admitted through the admission office or through the ED earlier or on a previous day. The log is shown on Exhibit 14–5.

LOGS AND REPORTS

Once the computer system is implemented, management reports can be easily obtained, as shown in Tables 14–1 and 14–2. The printed trauma registry, daily ED patient log, patient classification, and quality assurance information can be obtained. Thirty-five hours of nursing management time required to generate monthly patient classification reports and daily nursing hours and staffing information was reduced to 3 minutes by using the computer.

SUMMARY

There are various benefits of and opportunities for a computer information system. It is important that the design of such a system meet the needs of the ED patients, staff, and managers. It is vital that the ED nurse manager have input into the design of the ED computer information system and into reports to be generated.

Exhibit 14–4 Call Patient for Treatment Screen

```
X    CALL PATIENT TO TREATMENT       CURRENT CENSUS FOR E.U.        05/03/83   1516
     ACC                                                     CUR     S T A T U S
     NUM  BILL NUM   PATIENT NAME     SEX SRV AGE ADM  LOC PR TR RG TM
18   0003 889000-6   JONES, JOHN       M             N    WR  S  N  N  N
          AUTO ACCIDENT
19   0001 000078-6   HORNICKLE, CAROLYN  F      038   N    WR  S  Y  N  N
          SEVERE PAIN IN LOWER BACK




............................................................................
                         PROBE THE DESIRED PATIENT
     EUCN02SA                   PAGE BWD                           MASTER
```

Source: Reprinted with permission of Albert Einstein Medical Center, Philadelphia.

Exhibit 14–5 Patient Log

```
X    DISPLAY LOG              LOG FOR 05/03/83                  05/03/83   1523
     ACSN                     S P ARVL TRMT DISCHARGE
     NO   BILL NO  PATIENT NAME      T R TIME TIME TIME DSP      COMPLAINT
     0001 000127-1 ENGLANDER, DAVID  D S 0939      1002 AD   CUT OF SCALP
     0002 000128-9 GREGOROWICZ, GENE A P 1342 1345           RESPIRATORY DISTRE.
     0003 000129-7 HATHAWAY, MARY    A E 1340 1415           BACKACHE
     0004 889005-5 REED, WILLIAM     A P 1335 1350           BROKEN LEFT LEG
     0005 000078-6 HORNICKLE, CAROLYN A S 1515               SEVERE PAIN IN LOW




............................................................................
                    PROBE THE DESIRED PATIENT OR FUNCTION
     EUDL02SA                          RESELECT DATE          MASTER
```

Source: Reprinted with permission of Albert Einstein Medical Center, Philadelphia.

Table 14–1 Computer Statistical Report

ALBERT EINSTEIN MEDICAL CENTER
NORTHERN DIVISION

MONTHLY E.D. STATISTICS
MARCH 1986

------CATEGORIES------	FIRST SHIFT (8–4)	SECOND SHIFT (4–12)	THIRD SHIFT (12–8)	OVERALL
TOTAL PATIENTS TREATED AND ADMITTED:	325.00	234.00	91.00	650.00
—AVERAGE NUMBER OF PATIENTS PER DAY:	10.48	7.55	2.94	20.97
—TOTAL NUMBER OF HOURS IN E.D.:	1440:18	953:11	396:10	2789:39
—AVERAGE HOURS PER PATIENT IN E.D.:	4:26	4:04	4:21	4:17
—AVERAGE HOURS WAITING FOR TREATMENT:	:14	:15	:37	:17
—AVERAGE HOURS WAITING FOR REGSTRATN:	:17	:05	:29	:14
TOTAL PATIENTS TREATED AND RELEASED:	908.00	1000.00	381.00	2289.00
—AVERAGE NUMBER OF PATIENTS PER DAY:	29.29	32.26	12.29	73.84
—TOTAL NUMBER OF HOURS IN E.D.:	2984:32	3382:56	1058:55	7426:23
—AVERAGE HOURS PER PATIENT IN E.D.:	3:17	3:23	2:47	3:14
—AVERAGE HOURS WAITING FOR TREATMENT:	1:03	:58	:41	:57
—AVERAGE HOURS WAITING FOR REGSTRATN:	:21	:01	:14	:11

TOTAL PATIENTS SEEN (EXCLD VOIDS/WALKS):	1233.00	1234.00	472.00	2939.00
—AVERAGE NUMBER OF PATIENTS PER DAY:	39.77	39.81	15.23	94.81
—TOTAL NUMBER OF HOURS IN E.D.:	4424:50	4336:07	1455:05	10216:02
—AVERAGE HOURS PER PATIENT IN E.D.:	3:35	3:31	3:05	3:28
—AVERAGE HOURS WAITING FOR TREATMENT:	:50	:50	:40	:49
—AVERAGE HOURS WAITING FOR REGSTRATN:	:20	:02	:17	:11
TOTAL PATIENTS MONITORED (CRIT. CARE):	126.00	78.00	52.00	256.00
—AVERAGE NUMBER OF PATIENTS PER DAY:	4.06	2.52	1.68	8.26
—TOTAL NUMBER OF HOURS IN E.D.:	469:14	286:34	208:56	964:44
—AVERAGE HOURS PER PATIENT IN E.D.:	3:43	3:40	4:01	3:46
TOTAL NONURGENT PATIENTS:	308.00	277.00	118.00	703.00
TOTAL URGENT PATIENTS:	564.00	660.00	271.00	1495.00
TOTAL EMERGENT PATIENTS:	361.00	297.00	83.00	741.00
TOTAL PATIENTS 0–17 YEARS OF AGE:	187.00	301.00	83.00	571.00
TOTAL PATIENTS 18 AND OVER:	1042.00	933.00	388.00	2363.00
TOTAL PATIENTS WITH UNKNOWN BIRTHDATE:	4.00		1.00	5.00
TOTAL VOID AND WALKED OUT W/O TREATMENT:	84.00	112.00	24.00	220.00
—AVERAGE NUMBER OF PATIENTS PER DAY:	2.71	3.61	.77	7.10
—TOTAL NUMBER OF HOURS IN E.D.:	196.08	291:53	61:22	549:23
—AVERAGE HOURS PER PATIENT IN E.D.:	2:20	2:37	2:34	2:30

Source: Albert Einstein Medical Center, Northern Division, Philadelphia.

Table 14–2 Monthly ED Arrival and Discharge Statistics

ALBERT EINSTEIN MEDICAL CENTER
NORTHERN DIVISION

MONTHLY E.D. ARRIVAL/DISCHARGE STATISTICS

JULY 1986

ARRIVAL-TYPE	THIS MONTH					FISCAL YTD					PRIOR YEAR				
	TOT SEEN	TOT VOID	TRTD RLSD	TRTD ADMD	PCT ADMD	TOT SEEN	TOT VOID	TRTD RLSD	TRTD ADMD	PCT ADMD	TOT SEEN	TOT VOID	TRTD RLSD	TRTD ADMD	PCT ADMD
WALK IN	2459	239	2124	335	13.62	2459	239	2124	335	13.62	2717	139	2419	298	10.96
POLICE	284	21	251	33	11.61	284	21	251	33	11.61	323	21	278	45	13.93
FIRE AND RESCUE	223	5	139	84	37.66	223	5	139	84	37.66	165	2	99	66	40.00
AMBULANCE	314	1	149	165	52.54	314	1	149	165	52.54	331	3	142	189	57.09
AEMC AMBULANCE	7	0	2	5	71.42	7	0	2	5	71.42	8	0	3	5	62.50
HELICOPTER	0	0	0	0	.00	0	0	0	0	.00	0	0	0	0	.00
OTHER	7	44	3	4	57.14	7	44	3	4	57.14	6	54	2	4	66.66
TOTAL	3294	310	2668	626	19.00	3294	310	2668	626	19.00	3550	219	2943	607	17.09

DISCHARGE-TYPE	TOTAL VISITS THIS MNTH	TOTAL VISITS FISC YTD	TOTAL VISITS PRIOR YR
TREATED/RELEASED	1778	1778	1117
TREATED/ADMITTED	626	626	607
REF TO AGENCY	16	16	30
REF TO PRIV PHYSN	216	216	375
REF TO O/P DEPT	597	597	1296
REF TO S.P.M.G.	0	0	0
REF TO OTHER HOSP	25	25	36
WALK-OUT WITH TRT	12	12	51
EXPIRED D.O.A.	2	2	5
EXPIRED E.D.	10	10	15
WALK W/O TRT VOID	265	265	152
VOID	45	45	67
OTHER	12	12	18
TOTAL	3604	3604	3769

REFERENCES

LoRusso, Paul M.; Alexander, Raymond S.; and Goldsmith, Martin H. "A Computer Based Emergency Unit Management System for a Multiinstitutional System." *Journal of Ambulatory Care Management,* February, 1985, pp. 30–45.

McCarthy, Laura J. "Taking Charge of Computerization." *Nursing Management,* July, 1985, pp. 35–39.

Walreth, Jo Marie. "Computer Assisted Management in an Emergency Department." *Journal of Emergency Nursing* 9(4):235–242, 1983.

Index

About the Author

Linda Buschiazzo has been involved with emergency nursing during the past 17 years. She is currently the Emergency Department Nurse Manager at Albert Einstein Medical Center in Philadelphia, where she has nursing personnel, operational, and financial management responsibility for the Emergency Department. She is an adjunct clinical instructor for Widener University's Burn/Emergency/ Trauma graduate nursing program. She is also the owner of, and management consultant for, Emercon Associates (Emergency and Critical Care Consultants).

She has several publications in professional journals relating to emergency nursing and management, and has extensively lectured on those topics. She has coordinated and taught continuing education programs and has been a consultant for various ED nursing managers, nursing and hospital administrators, public agencies, and professional publications. She is an active member of the Emergency Nurses Association and was chairperson for education for the Philadelphia Chapter in 1984–1986. She is certified in emergency nursing and nursing administration. She has been involved with ED management for 15 years and has been utilized as a resource for ED managers throughout the United States, Canada, and England.